AN INTRODUCTION TO THE ENGLISH LEGAL SYSTEM

AN INTRODUCTION TO THE ENGLISH LEGAL SYSTEM

MARTIN PARTINGTON

OXFORD

UNIVERSITY PRESS

OXFORD
UNIVERSITY PRESS

Great Clarendon Street, Oxford OX2 6DP

Oxford University Press is a department of the University of Oxford.
It furthers the University's objective of excellence in research, scholarship,
and education by publishing worldwide in

Oxford New York

Athens Auckland Bangkok Bogotá Buenos Aires Calcutta
Cape Town Chennai Dar es Salaam Delhi Florence Hong Kong Istanbul
Karachi Kuala Lumpur Madrid Melbourne Mexico City Mumbai
Nairobi Paris São Paulo Shanghai Singapore Taipei Tokyo Toronto Warsaw

with associated companies in Berlin Ibadan

Oxford is a registered trade mark of Oxford University Press
in the UK and in certain other countries

Published in the United States
by Oxford University Press Inc., New York

British Library Cataloguing in Publication Data

Data available

Library of Congress Cataloging in Publication Data

Data applied for

ISBN 0–19–876383–2

1 3 5 7 9 10 8 6 4 2

Typeset in Adobe Minion
by RefineCatch Limited, Bungay, Suffolk
Printed in Great Britain by
T. J. International Ltd., Padstow, Cornwall

OUTLINE CONTENTS

CONTENTS

PART II THE INSTITUTIONAL FRAMEWORK

PART III THE DELIVERY AND FUNDING OF LEGAL SERVICES

LIST OF BOXES

LIST OF DIAGRAMS

FOREWORD AND ACKNOWLEDGEMENTS

The original proposal that I should write this book came from Professor Peter Cane when he, with Professor Jane Stapleton, were editors of the Clarendon Law Series, published by Oxford University Press. Though it has now been decided that the book should not appear in that series, I have nonetheless adhered to my initial instructions. These were that the book should: be genuinely introductory; be around 200 pages long; be relatively uncluttered by footnotes; be accessible to the more general reader; but at the same time offer an approach to thinking about the English legal system and its place in society not found elsewhere. With these strictures in mind, this book has been written particularly for those coming to the study of law for the first time. I also hope that others, keen to look behind the magical veil that all too often shrouds the legal system and its actors in mystery, will find the book of interest. It is, in short, intended for all those interested in the phenomenon of law and the important role it plays in the ordering of our society but without any detailed knowledge of it.

Over the last thirty or so years, I have been associated with a wide range of bodies and institutions, from whom I have learned much and who have helped to inform my ideas about the English legal system and the forces that shape it. They include, at different stages, and for different lengths of time: the Hillfields Advice Centre in Coventry; the Legal Action Group; the Training Committee of the Institute of Housing; the Management Committees of Citizens' Advice Bureaux in Coventry, Paddington and Uxbridge; the Education Committee of the Law Society; the Lord Chancellor's Advisory Committee on Legal Aid; the Independent Tribunal Service for Social Security Appeal Tribunals; the Judicial Studies Board (both the main Board and its Tribunals Committee); the Council on Tribunals; the Civil Justice Council (and its sub-committee on Alternative Dispute Resolution); the Committee of Heads of University Law Schools; the Socio-Legal Studies Association; and the Socio-Legal Research Users' Forum. I am grateful to the numerous friends and colleagues from all these bodies – too numerous to list here – for their generosity of spirit, enthusiasm; and sheer hard work in the development of the practices and institutions of law in England.

I also thank my colleagues at Bristol for their support, in particular Rebecca Bailey-Harris, David Cowan, Gwynn Davies, Clare Lewis, Donald Nicolson, Stratos Konstadinidis, and Andrew Sanders. I am grateful to successive generations of students at Bristol, and before then Brunel, Universities to whom I offered instruction in English Legal System and English Legal Methods for their critical responses to what I have had to say. I have been particularly fortunate that, as part of the writing process, I was able to deliver early versions of this text as introductory lectures to first year students at the University of Bristol; and to discuss them in an informal 'reading group'. They helped me determine important questions of structure and content. I am most grateful to all those who offered their comments. However, I remain wholly responsible for what follows.

My editor at Oxford University Press, Michaela Coulthard, has been a model of tolerance as I have failed to meet a variety of deadlines.

I am not sure that my children Adam and Hannah have ever been particularly conscious of what I do in my professional life. Nonetheless I am grateful to both for allowing me to share some of my initial thoughts about this book with them. They were particularly encouraging at times when encouragement was needed. As always I am especially indebted to Daphne for her insistence that I retain a sense of balance in my life.

I have sought to bring the text up to date as at the date shown below.

Bristol

27 April 2000

INTRODUCTION

1

'KNOWLEDGE', THEMES, AND STRUCTURE

INTRODUCTORY

The purposes of this text are to consider a number of themes about how law and the legal system has developed over recent years, and how they might develop in future, to encourage the reader to think about law and the legal system and to question the extent to which that system is fit for its purpose.

The book is primarily about the *English* legal system, (though for most practical purposes that also includes the legal system operative in Wales). There is a quite different system in Scotland and a rather different system in Northern Ireland, not considered in this book. There will be times when it is not sensible to refer just to 'England'—for example the phrases 'Great Britain' or 'United Kingdom' will be used where they seem more appropriate, particularly considering the place of this country in the wider world. However, the particular focus of the book is on the English Legal System.

Many of those who study law in England come from other countries. Despite this focus, I nonetheless hope that overseas readers can not only learn from the issues discussed here, but also relate the questions raised to the situation in their own home countries. Are the legal systems with which they may be more familiar fitted to their purpose? Are there lessons to be learned from the English experience? What should the English be learning from experience elsewhere?

'KNOWLEDGE'

IMAGES AND PRE-CONCEPTIONS

Even the reader of an introductory work will come to it with a good deal of knowledge about law and the legal system, shaped by personal experience or what they have otherwise read or heard in the media. It is impossible to identify all those images and pre-conceptions, but there are at least five which it may be suggested many readers of this book may have.[1]

---

[1] For a rather more scientific survey of attitudes to the Civil Justice system, see, Genn, H., *Paths to Justice* (Oxford: Hart Publishing, 1999), ch. 7.

1. The scope of the legal system

Many would define the scope of law and the legal system in terms of what happens in criminal trial courts. After all, it is there that the major murder cases or other serious criminal cases (such as theft or fraud) are dealt with. This perception of the central place of the criminal justice system in the English legal system is quite understandable, being taken from endless television dramas and press reports.

But such a view is too narrow. First, as will be seen in Chapter 5, many of the key decisions in the criminal justice system are not taken in court, but elsewhere, e.g. the police station or the parole board. Second, focusing on the criminal trial process results in a failure to appreciate the existence of other parts of the English Legal system, the *Administrative Justice, Family Justice,* or *Civil Justice* systems, considered in Chapters 6–8.

2. Providers of legal services

If asked who provides legal services, many would respond: the lawyers. Again this is too narrow a view. As will be seen in Chapter 9 (and part of Chapter 7) many others apart from professionally qualified lawyers provide legal services to the public.

In addition, perceptions of lawyers may be very unflattering. Some regard them as cynical parasites, willing to undertake any task for which a client is willing to pay—the 'hired gun' or 'prostitute' model of the lawyer. Others note the salaries lawyers are paid (indeed this may have been an element in the thinking of those readers now contemplating the study of law!). There may be views about the sort of person who becomes a lawyer. Some will describe them as pompous; conservative in temperament (or even Conservative in political outlook); pedantic; even untrustworthy. Some argue that lawyers use their legal education and training and professional status to enhance their earning capacity by creating a 'mystique' around the law which prevents the ordinary lay person from being able to make effective use of the law. There may be perceptions about the education, class background, gender, or ethnicity of lawyers. While there may be *some* truth in some of these perceptions, a more detailed look provides a picture that is both more complex and more interesting.

3. The English legal system: resistance to change

Another perception people have of law and the legal system is that it is conservative and resistant to change. The Victorian architecture of law's landmark buildings, such as the Old Bailey or the Royal Courts of Justice in London, harks back to a bygone age, as do the robes and old-fashioned styles of dress that lawyers adopt, particularly when appearing in court. This may lead to a more general impression of conservatism and resistance to change. It is natural that many who practice law will resist change. It is disturbing and unsettling. Again, these perceptions, though perhaps correct in part, do not reflect the total position. For many, change is what prevents life becoming boring. The last thirty or so years have witnessed a large number of changes in law and legal process, many of which have been very dramatic.

Another of the themes to be explored in this book relates to the forces for change—

the *dynamism*—within the law and the legal system. In Chapter 4 we consider the contribution of Government to the pressure for change. And throughout the work, we note numerous examples of how practice and procedure have changed in recent years. Implicit in this discussion is the question whether those who work in the legal system should be more willing to embrace change and proclaim it as an important part of our legal culture than they have perhaps been willing to do in the past.

4. Inefficiency, expense, and delay

A further perception is that legal proceedings are too long-drawn out and that the whole system suffers from inordinate delay and expense. This is, perhaps, a perception that is closer to the truth than some of the others suggested above. It is certainly a perception that has driven much current debate about reform of the Civil Justice system, discussed in more detail in Chapter 8. It underlies many of the other changes made to the justice system. Before concluding that the whole of the system is dogged by inefficiency, delay, and expense, we once again need to consider the evidence carefully to see how far popular preconceptions reflect the whole truth about the English legal system. We also need to ask whether pressure for greater speed and efficiency can, in some circumstances, act against the interests of justice.

5. Miscarriages of justice

A final issue which tends to dominate media treatment of law relates to miscarriages of justice. This may suggest that there are serious, even structural, defects with the legal system that result in these miscarriages. There is no doubt that from time to time things do go seriously wrong. Cases are improperly investigated, or inadequately presented in court, or inexpertly handled by the trial judge, or insufficiently considered on appeal. It is right that the media draw attention to them.

But miscarriages of justice also demonstrate another side to the English legal system. Whatever the difficulties, there are those within the system willing to challenge decisions that have not been arrived at by 'due process of law'. Many of those arguing that miscarriages of justice have occurred are themselves lawyers. Miscarriages of justice may lead some to perceive the legal system as a system in crisis. Paradoxically, though, they may also be a source of reassurance, that the system and those who work within it are sufficiently independent and robust to challenge those who have made mistakes.

The primary purpose of this book is to provide a general overview of the framework within which the law of England (and Wales) is made and practised, which will illuminate and where necessary alter the initial images and preconceptions. Where there is truth in those images and preconceptions, particularly negative ones, I hope the reader will be able to learn from the fact that not everything is perfect and reflect on what may need to be changed. Where images of law and the legal system are unfair, I hope the reader will at least be better informed.

THEMES

Although an introductory book, it seeks to address themes inadequately considered in other books with the same or similar title.

- First, many current accounts of the English legal system are rather 'practitioner-driven'; they focus on those parts of the system in which professionally qualified lawyers practice their law. Here a more holistic approach is taken, designed to introduce the reader to a wider range of activities and functions often ignored elsewhere.

- Second, other introductory accounts are somewhat descriptive and 'static' in nature, providing a snapshot of the system at the moment of writing. As already suggested, the English legal system is considerably more complex, more dynamic, and more responsive to change than is often realized. A recurring theme will be on change and the forces that have shaped and are shaping the English legal system. At the same time, questions will be raised about the extent to which particular changes are desirable or should be resisted.

- Third, the English legal system is often portrayed as something distinct from the British system of government. Indeed one of the important claims made for law and its practice is that it is 'independent' of government. Yet the government of the country is based in law; the institutions of law derive their power and authority from the system of government. Understanding the constitutional function of the English legal system and the relationship of the legal system to other branches of government will therefore be another theme underpinning the discussion in this work.

- Finally, the assertion is often made that 'we have the best system of justice in the world'. It may be a good system, indeed a very good system. But this conclusion should be arrived at on the basis of evidence, not mere assertion. This book is intended to provide a basis for thinking critically about the institutions and practices of the law and contemplating change where inadequacy or inefficiency is demonstrated to exist.

STRUCTURE

Having considered the knowledge which those coming new to the study of law may have about the legal system, and the extent to which images and preconceptions held by such newcomers may, or may not, be well-founded; and having set out the themes that underlie the book, the rest of the book is structured as follows:

Part 1 consists of two chapters that discuss the social functions of law and the legitimacy of law. Chapter 2 considers the role law plays in the regulation of modern society. Chapter 3 considers how law is made, who makes it, where they get the authority for making it, whether the processes currently used for making law should be changed, and if so, how.

Part 2 considers the institutional framework within which law is developed and practised. The discussion opens, in Chapter 4, with an account of the role of government in shaping the institutions and practice of law. Chapters 5 to 8 look in turn at the four legal systems which, for the purpose of this account, comprise the English legal system:[2] the *Criminal Justice* system, the *Administrative Justice* system; the *Family Justice* system; and the *Civil and Commercial Justice* system. In each chapter there is consideration not only of formal legal institutions such as courts, but also informal or other processes that do not catch the public eye (or indeed which are not known about or properly understood by professional lawyers) but which form an essential part of the framework of the English legal system seen in the round.

Part 3 looks at the personnel of the law, and the tasks they perform in delivering legal services. Chapter 9 considers the role not only of those professionally qualified to practise law, but others who play a part in the workings of the legal system, including adjudicators and jurists. Chapter 10 reflects on how the provision of legal services is paid for.

Finally, a short concluding chapter asks whether the English legal system is in fact fit for the purposes it is required to perform. Is the English legal system 'the best in the world' in need of little or no change? Or is the system simply not delivering what is required of it, and thus in need of fundamental change? If changes are needed, what are they? What are the forces likely to render change difficult, if not impossible?

---

[2] Most other accounts draw a distinction between two systems only—criminal and civil. But I argue that the four-pronged approach adopted here offers the newcomer a clearer way of understanding the whole picture.

PART I

LAW, SOCIETY, AND AUTHORITY

PART I

LAW, SOCIETY, AND AUTHORITY

2
LAW AND SOCIETY: THE PURPOSES AND FUNCTIONS OF LAW

INTRODUCTION

One purpose of this book is to enable the reader to understand the *framework* within which rules of law are made and utilized, not to analyse specific rules of law, for example 'what is the legal definition of murder' or 'when is a contract legally binding'. Nonetheless, it will be hard to make any sense of that framework without at least some indication of what the rules of law are to which the framework of the English legal system applies and, in particular, what the *social purpose* or *social function* of those rules of law is. In considering this, a distinction will be drawn between what may be described as the macro and the micro functions of law. The macro functions of law may be defined as those which relate to general issues about the role law plays in the running and ordering of society. The micro functions—which derive from those macro functions—relate to the more specific uses to which law is put. The distinction should become clearer as the discussion proceeds.

THE MACRO FUNCTIONS OF LAW: LAW AND ORDERS

If the question is posed: 'what is the role of law in society?' a common response would be 'to maintain order'. Much public debate and political rhetoric makes the link between 'law' and 'order'. Such a response disguises considerable ambiguity about the concept of order. There is in fact a variety of orders in relation to which the law may be playing a role: for example

- 'public order';
- 'political order';
- 'social order';
- 'economic order';
- 'international order'; or

- 'moral order'.

In addition, the interactions of law with each of these orders are extremely complex. Only a brief and preliminary discussion of these issues is offered here.

To start, two general points may be made. First, the extent to which law is able to shape these different orders is not unconstrained, but is itself shaped by the political and other forces which shape the society in which law functions. Second, and related to the first point, law is not some 'neutral' force which contributes to the organization of society, but which is in some peculiar way detached from that society. The functions of law in any given society cannot be understood without an understanding of the political, social, and economic ideologies that underpin that society and which provide the framework within which law functions.

LAW AND PUBLIC ORDER

Many would argue that a—possibly the—primary function of law is to assist in the preservation of public order. The maintenance of public order is not exclusively a task for the law; many other factors such as pressure from family, friends, or work colleagues also play an important part. Nonetheless, the fact that law sets the boundaries of acceptable behaviour and prescribes sanctions for breaches of those boundaries (which is in essence the function of criminal law) does make a significant contribution to the preservation of public order.

The preservation of public order, however, immediately raises another and not necessarily consistent function of law: the *protection of civil liberties and human rights*. It is acknowledged that an important component in the ordering of a democratic society is the ability of people to argue freely about their beliefs and the freedom to dissent. Limits may be set to the freedom of individuals to advance unpopular views, for example those that are obscene, or defamatory, or which incite racial hatred. Nevertheless it is accepted that, within those limits, freedoms of speech and thought must be protected by law.

British constitutional arrangements have not, in the past, gone as far as, for example, the provisions relating to the freedoms which are formally enshrined in the constitution of the United States of America. Even so there are long-standing principles of English law which seek to allow people to indicate dissent, for example, by demonstrating peacefully, or engaging in other public activities such as taking part in political marches. The coming into force, in October 2000, of the Human Rights Act 1998 will lead to new interest in the development of human rights as a fundamental part of English law. Protection of human rights and civil liberties can therefore be identified as another function of the law, and a function not always consistent with the desire to preserve public order. There will be occasions when the preservation of public order may result in the imposition of restrictions on civil liberties. Conversely, the protection of civil liberty can on occasion result in some relaxation of controls over public order.

In highly repressive societies, the function of law in preserving public order may have the effect of destroying civil liberties and other fundamental freedoms. In more tolerant societies where dissent is permitted, there will always be a sharp debate about the extent to which law's function is to preserve public order, as opposed to protect other rights and freedoms. *Liberty*[1] and other pressure groups may not always persuade governments to change their minds on proposals relating to the development of law. But their ability to challenge and criticize Ministers is fundamental to ensuring that governments do not step too far over the boundary of what is politically acceptable. The law's function in relation to the maintenance of public order is, thus, highly contingent upon the nature of the society in which law operates.

LAW AND THE POLITICAL ORDER: THE CONSTITUTIONAL FUNCTIONS OF LAW

Another of the underlying functions of law is to underpin the political order of the country—the constitutional function of law. In this respect, the United Kingdom is something of an oddity in the world community, as it is one of the very few countries that does not operate under a written constitution. There are indeed many important practices within the British Constitution that arise from the operation of practice and 'convention', rather than from identifiable rules of law. (*See below Box 3.1*). Some of the most important aspects about the way the system of government is organized in England fall outside the scope of law altogether. Their basis is found more in political than in legal theory. In view of this, it might be thought that support for constitutional arrangements should not be regarded as one of the macro functions of law.

However, despite the lack of a written constitution in the UK, it is appropriate to include this topic under the macro head. It emphasizes the point that, although there is no written constitution in the United Kingdom, there is still a great deal of fundamental law which regulates the way in which our political system operates. Indeed as a result of many of the changes being introduced to our constitutional arrangements by the present Labour Government, it is arguable that, whatever may have been the correct analysis in the past, we are currently witnessing the birth of a legally based constitutional settlement. There are so many aspects of our constitutional arrangements that are now either enshrined in law or shortly will be. To give some examples.

- British membership of the European Union, recognized in such fundamental statutes as the European Communities Act 1972 and later amendment acts passed to take account of changes to the European Treaties has, among other things, set limits to the legislative power, or sovereignty, of the British Parliament.

- The Scotland Act 1998 and the Wales Act 1998 have both provided for

---

[1] The current name for the National Council for Civil Liberties.

devolution of powers from the government in London to, respectively, the Scottish Parliament and the Welsh Assembly. This provides a new legal framework for the regulation of the relationship between central and regional governments.

- The enactment of the Human Rights Act 1998 will profoundly affect the practice of government, as legislation will have to be compliant with the provisions of the Act, and thus the European Convention on Human Rights which is incorporated in that Act.

- Reform of the House of Lords—in progress as this book is being written—is also being achieved by very important legislation which will form another part of the new British Constitutional arrangements.

- Laws relating to official secrecy on the one hand and freedom of information on the other determine the extent to which governments can operate openly or in secret. Again there is the prospect of major new legislation in this area which will have a profound effect on the way government works. This is another example of the use of law to support our constitutional arrangements.

- Many other examples might be given: the detailed law relating to the running of elections; or the law regulating the relationship between central and local government.[2]

In the light of this rapidly growing body of law, the argument is now being heard that the British should take the last step and adopt a written constitution, which would codify into a single legislative measure all these constitutional provisions.[3] It is ironic that one of the legacies left by the British in the vast majority of its former colonies was a written constitution, when no such document exists in the United Kingdom itself.

LAW AND SOCIAL ORDER

Law also contributes to the preservation of the country's social order. Defining the nature of social order is extremely complex and an issue on which there are wide differences of opinion. However, it is clear that in the United Kingdom, as in many other countries in the Western democratic tradition, there are substantial differences between individuals that may depend on differences of ability, or differences of income or wealth, or differences of birth or class. These differences are reflected in many rules of law, in particular those that define concepts of property and contract. The present social order and the law that supports that social order has the effect of protecting the rights of those with property and the economic power to enter and enforce contractual arrangements. Much of the criminal law also seeks to protect rights of property. On this analysis, the relationship between law and social order may

---

[2] These are both topics on which there are currently proposals before Parliament: the Political Parties, Elections and Referendums Bill 2000; and the Local Government Bill 2000.

[3] The Constitutional Unit at University College London is taking a lead in this debate.

be seen as very conservative, in the sense that it seeks to conserve current social arrangements.

However, as with the role of law in relation to public order, there are other ways of thinking about the relationships between law and social order. Many would assert that a fundamental purpose of law today is to promote a more dynamic social order, designed to ensure that society is not locked into structures which sustain inequality, but rather promotes a society based on principles of equality and the prevention of social exclusion.

The bases for attacking inequality are the subject of fierce debate. Some argue that 'equality' can only be achieved if there is a complete levelling of the differences between people—so that, for example, everyone in employment receives more or less equal pay, that there should be equality in the amounts of wealth capable of being held by individuals, and so on. Others take the view that equality in this sense is neither the right nor sensible way to promote a new social order. They argue that the focus should be on *equality of opportunity*, for example in the provision of education, or health care, or work opportunities.

Many rules of law now exist which have as their specific objective the promotion of equality of opportunity. Both within the United Kingdom and more broadly in the European Union, there is law designed to combat the impacts of discrimination based on grounds of gender, ethnicity and race, or disability. This is driven not by simplistic notions of 'political correctness' but by the very practical belief that the collective good of nations will be enhanced by ensuring that all citizens are in a position to play a full part in the economic and social life of those nations. To give a simple example, if women are excluded from the workforce, 50 per cent of the available talent is thereby excluded.

In addition to specific measures of anti-discrimination legislation, a great deal of political debate and public policy making is directed to devising social, welfare, and educational policies which seek to assist in the creation of a new social order. Law gives legitimacy to those policies. There is nothing new about this. Since the development of the concept of the Welfare State in the middle of the nineteenth century, the argument has been heard that it is right that governments should seek, to varying degrees, to promote equality. The law has clearly had and will continue to have a part to play in these developments.

The mere fact that policies are developed and enshrined in legal Acts of Parliament does not mean that a new social order is thereby automatically created. The evidence is that in modern Britain, there remain very marked inequalities—whether based on class, education, employment, health, or other life opportunities. While there may be aspirations towards equality, the social reality is that equality—however defined—has not yet been fully realized.

The claim that law has a role in the promotion of equality is one that is frequently made, and can thus be included as one of the macro functions of law. However the part played by law in maintaining the existing social order may be said to be in conflict with that function. This leads some to argue that law has another, more political function, of supporting the status quo against any other way of organizing the social order. As with the tension between public order and human rights, there are tensions between the role of law in the preservation of the social order and its role in the promotion of equality.

Similarly, claims are made that a function of law is to promote social justice. The extent to which law and the legal system, by itself, can deliver social justice is limited. Social justice is more a political concept than a legal one. Law may be able to support steps taken to achieve social justice and thus promote a new social order; but it would be unrealistic to claim that law can achieve this in isolation from other non-legal factors which go to the foundations of modern society.

Even if the ability of law directly to foster social justice or equality is limited, there is nevertheless an important claim for law that it does have a role to play in protecting the weak against the powerful. This has become a very important function for law in the twentieth century as notions of the welfare state have developed, not just in England but across the developed world.[4]

LAW AND THE PROTECTION OF THE ECONOMIC ORDER

The relationship between law and the economic order raises similar matters to those considered in the relationship of law and the social order. The dominant economic philosophy in the United Kingdom, indeed throughout the Western World, is market capitalism.[5] Here, a very important function of law has been and is the recognition of rights in private property, whether in land or other forms of security. It is in law that definitions of the ownership rights in property are to be found. The law provides procedures for the transfer of property from one person to another. The law enables different property rights to coexist in the same piece of property. And the law provides mechanisms for the enforcement of those rights. There is little doubt that the notions of property developed in the law have, historically, assisted in the development of this economic framework and continue to sustain it.

Similar arguments can be made in relation to the law of contract. The recognition of the principle of the enforceable bargain (contract), breaches of which can be pursued and enforced through the courts, has been an essential tool in the development of the modern market capitalist economy. As with the function of law in the maintenance of the social order, law can also be seen as instrumental in the creation and underpinning of the economic order.

Nevertheless, there are other ways in which law is now used to regulate the economic order. It has long been recognized that there are activities which market

---

[4] Indeed there is a more historical claim that there have been situations in the past in which the law would seek to intervene to offer at least some protection to the weak: see Thompson, E. P., *Whigs and Hunters* (London: Penguin, 1990).

[5] Differences between different models of capitalism—e.g. the North American model, the European model, or the Japanese model—are not considered here. But it should not be assumed that the principles of capitalism are applied in exactly the same way in all countries.

economies are very bad at undertaking, or which do not make sense in crude market terms. Operating factories or machinery with proper regard for health and safety is one example. Certainly a great deal of modern law-making activity has been focused on the creation of regulatory frameworks within which business activity is required to be undertaken, which are justified on the basis that they fill the gaps left by market failure.

Similarly, it has long been recognized that untrammelled capitalist activity contains its own contradictions. There is an inexorable tendency for capitalists to wish to accumulate market position, and if possible dominate that position by the exercise of monopoly power. However, the shift from competition to monopoly poses a funda-mental threat to the operation of the market. Thus legal mechanisms have been put in place to promote competition and to limit the development of monopolistic positions.

There is also an inevitable tendency for those with greater bargaining power to seek to impose their wishes in contracts on parties with weaker bargaining positions. A great deal of modern law is designed to 'level the playing field'. There is a vast body of consumer law which has the effect of softening the binding nature of contractual relationships by giving added rights to consumers in situations where the bargaining power between the supplier of goods or services and the consumer of those goods or services is regarded as unequal. Thus there are legal requirements that those who sell insurance policies or other expensive financial products should allow the purchaser a cooling-off period within which he may change his mind. Housing law regulates the relationship between landlords and tenants. Employment law seeks to regulate the relationship between employer and employee. More generally there are measures which enable the consumer to challenge terms in contracts thought to be unfair.

Here again, as with law and public order or law and social order, in relation to the economic order, the law may be said to perform functions that are to some degree in conflict. Law has helped to legitimate the tools essential to the commercial context within which market capitalism is able to flourish. At the same time law is used to limit the excesses of market behaviour that might otherwise logically result from the operation of market capitalism.

LAW AND INTERNATIONAL ORDER

Another function for law is, arguably, the provision of support for international order. This is a complex and controversial subject not considered in any detail here. There are those who argue that there is really no such thing as international law; rather that maintenance of the international order is sustained by international rela-tions and diplomatic pressure. But in very many respects, international bodies and politicians like to assert that what they are trying to achieve has legal backing. For example:

- Recent incursions by the United Nations into particular world trouble spots have been justified at least in part by reference to the legal framework of the United

Nations Charter and its executive bodies, in particular the role of the Security Council.

- Attempts to deal with 'crimes against humanity'—a particular curse of the modern age—are being made through a special War Crimes Tribunal which has been established by the UN and which sits in the Hague.

- In other areas, such as the regulation of world trade, or the protection of the environment, the regulation of the use of the sea, or even space, there is an increasing tendency not only to enter treaties—which historically was common practice—but also to create special institutions and mechanisms for enforcement like courts or tribunals, which are independent of particular national governments.

- The conduct of war has long been subject to international legal constraints, for example the Geneva Convention on the treatment of prisoners of war. Similarly other constraints on behaviour in war and other situations of conflict, such as the prevention of torture, have been prescribed in instruments of international law.

- One of the most pressing of current social issues, protection of those seeking asylum in one country because of fears of persecution in another country, is essentially shaped by principles of international law.

These are important and controversial issues. Even though the focus of this work may be said to be on the rather more parochial subject of the 'English legal system', we cannot ignore the global context in which countries now operate. It has been argued that, following the collapse of communism, a 'new world order' has emerged. Legal instruments and institutions play a significant part in the development of that new order. Though the focus here is on what happens in England (and Wales), this significantly wider dimension should not be forgotten.

LAW AND MORAL ORDER

Another broad function of law may be said to be the provision of support for the moral ordering of society. This is extremely controversial. Some theorists argue that there should be little if any distinction between law and morality; that the law should clearly and deliberately mirror those issues of morality which people think ought to inform the way we should behave. Others, however, seek to draw a clear distinction between law and morality. They argue that the mere fact that many people *believe* that certain forms of behaviour or activity are morally wrong (for example engaging in homosexual activity) should not mean that such activity should be defined as being unlawful.

While there are clear dangers and considerable difficulties in seeking to equate law and morality, not least because of the problems of determining what the common morality on any given issue might be, nevertheless many rules of law are founded on a moral view of society. Perhaps the clearest example is that the moral imperative not to kill people is reflected in rules of the criminal law which outlaw such activity.

In general it may be suggested that rules of criminal law which reflect some common morality, however that may be defined, may be more acceptable and effective in regulating behaviour than those rules which do not so reflect a common morality. For example, there may well be behaviours which many would regard as repugnant— dressing shabbily, or drinking cheap alcohol in the streets—but which should not of themselves be defined as criminal. Conversely, there may be rules of criminal law, for example about not exceeding 30 m.p.h. in a built up area, which many would not regard as particularly morally repugnant, but which should nevertheless be defined as criminal.[6]

In a quite different context, much of the law which seeks to regulate relationships between individuals is also based in concepts of morality, for example relating to the institution of marriage. To an extent, therefore, it can be said that another function of law is to provide at least some support for the moral order, a function reinforced by the protection of family life under the provisions of the European Convention on Human Rights (Art. 8).

Related to a consideration of the relationship between law and the moral order is a consideration of the relationship between *law and religious order*. Despite an apparent decline in religious belief in England, there are still many who argue that religion— both formal and informal—remains an important component in the make-up of society at large. However, and by contrast with discussion about the relationship between law and morality, the argument is not in present circumstances often made that law should be supportive of religion. Indeed there would be many who would make a powerful argument, whether in general principle or because of their own religious (or anti-religious) beliefs, that law should *not* be used to support the religious order. Questions of spirituality and religious belief would be argued by many as falling within that private sphere of activity in which the law should not intervene.

Nevertheless, the historical role played by religion in the development of modern England cannot be wholly ignored. At its most basic, our calendar and major festivals are firmly based in the Christian tradition, not that of other religious groupings. There are a number of legal privileges that attach to the Church of England; there are others that apply to religious groups more generally. There remains a specific law against blasphemy which effectively applies only to the Christian religion. Thus it is arguable, though not often seen in this light, that present-day law still plays a residual part in the support of religious order, in particular the Christian religious order.

This is controversial, not least because of the rise in a number of countries of various forms of religious fundamentalism. These are often accompanied by degrees of intolerance towards others that many regard as quite unacceptable in a modern pluralistic society. Indeed it may be the case that, in order to protect social pluralism,

---

[6] Current campaigns to change people's perceptions about the non-desirability of driving above the speed limit are being directed as much to the moral issues as the legal issues involved.

the law should be used more to protect the ability of those of different religious beliefs to hold and practise their religion, another issue embraced in the European Convention on Human Rights (Art. 9).

OTHER MACRO FUNCTIONS

In addition to the ways in which law may interact with the maintenance of and challenges to different types of order, law also has a number of other macro functions.

THE RESOLUTION OF SOCIAL PROBLEMS

The response of politicians and their officials to many of the issues that are perceived as social problems is to create more law seeking to regulate the behaviour complained against. This is regarded as the appropriate or expected political response. Only rarely do politicians concede that there may be enough law and that what is needed is better understanding or enforcement of that law. Even more rarely are politicians willing to accept that a possible solution to a problem might be to repeal existing rules of law or to develop the law in such a way as to decriminalize the activity in question.[7] Their mindset assumes that a function of law is to solve social problems. Indeed whole careers are devoted to the promotion of legislation allegedly designed to address particular social issues—even if, as often happens, there is already perfectly satisfactory law already available, or where changing the law is not really a solution to the problem. (Perhaps civil servants and politicians who are responsible for *preventing* legislation from reaching the statute book should be rewarded more generously than those who seek to drive legislation forward.)

In addition, one obvious consequence of creating legal provisions to solve social problems is that people—ever mindful of their own self-interest—respond to new legal frameworks in ways not predicted by the law-makers. A hidden but often inevitable consequence of using law to solve social problems is, therefore, that the very process of creating new law results not in the solution of an existing social problem but rather in the creation of new social problems. The process of dealing with one issue leads to the creation of another issue which in its turn has to be solved at a later date.

---

[7] Historically this has often happened. For example many of the criminal offences that two or three hundred years ago might have led to Draconian punishments such as transportation or even the death penalty now seem very trivial and are either not criminal at all, or dealt with much less severely. Today many argue that a less criminal approach to the use of 'soft drugs' might not only lead to more equitable treatment, as compared with those who use alcohol or nicotine, but also lead to reductions in other forms of criminality resulting from the need for drug users to obtain the money to buy their drugs. On the other hand, there are powerful political arguments that any relaxation in the government's approach to drug use would send 'the wrong signal' to the community at large.

THE REGULATION OF HUMAN RELATIONSHIPS

Another very important function of the law is the regulation of the nature and extent of human relationships. The nature of and formalities relating to the creation of marriage is determined by legal rules, often supplementing different religious rules. Law provides a framework for the distribution of assets on the breakdown of marriage. The law is also currently being developed in relation to the regulation and underpinning of long-term relationships where persons have not gone though the formalities of marriage. These developments are being considered not only in the context of heterosexual relationships, but also homosexual relationships. Law sets boundaries to the scope of sexual relationships, whether heterosexual or homosexual, prescribing for example the minimum age of sexual consent, and making certain sexual relationships within the 'prohibited degrees of consanguinity' (incest and other close relationships) are unlawful. The law also sets down a framework for the treatment of children and other family members.

THE EDUCATIVE OR IDEOLOGICAL FUNCTION OF LAW

A further function of law is that, almost irrespective of its impact in particular cases, it has an educative function; it contributes to shaping part of the ideology of a nation. To give a simple if significant example: there is no doubt that attitudes to drinking and driving have changed dramatically over the last twenty years. In part this is the result of powerful advertising, demonstrating the devastating impact that drink-drive accidents can have on victims and their families. But the change in attitude has also been the result of changes in the law contributing to a climate of opinion in which drinking and driving is just no longer regarded as socially acceptable behaviour.

Another example, already mentioned above, is law dealing with various forms of discrimination. When such laws are brought into effect, those who argue for their introduction often accept that the law will not, on its own, alter the attitudes of mind that led to the patterns of discriminatory behaviour which have led to the creation of those laws. However, those who have sponsored such laws see them as not only creating certain legal rights which may be enforceable by individuals, but also sending a more general educative signal to members of society at large that discriminatory behaviour is not acceptable.

More generally, countries that embrace the principle of the rule of law are, in effect, asserting that powers of officials of the state must be limited and that the individual citizen should have both the right and the opportunity to challenge decisions, where they are thought to be wrong or in some respect unfair.

The recent decision by the British government to introduce the Human Rights Act, incorporating the European Convention on Human Rights directly into English law, is another example of legislation that will not only create legal rights which individuals may seek to pursue through the courts, but which also sends an important educative signal about the limits within which people, particularly those who work within government, must behave. In this sense, therefore, another function of law relates to the education of attitudes amongst members of the population.

MICRO FUNCTIONS OF LAW

Turning from the macro to the micro level involves consideration of rather more specific functions for law, many of which derive from the macro functions identified above. A number of examples are offered; this does not purport to be a comprehensive list. The reader is invited to think of other functions not identified here. In addition, the reader may be able to think of other examples to illustrate the particular functions which have been identified.

DEFINING THE LIMITS OF ACCEPTABLE BEHAVIOUR

The area of law with which most people have at least some familiarity is the *criminal law*. A major objective of this branch of the law is to prescribe the limits of behaviour which are socially acceptable. The criminal law seeks to prohibit many kinds of activity about which there would be widespread agreement, such as murder and violent crime. It also outlaws a wide range of other activities about which there may be more debate, such as the use of particular types of drug. The following points may be made in this context:

- Not all behaviour which may be regarded by many as undesirable is thereby characterized in legal terms as criminal. Thus there is no law preventing a person over the age of 18 from drinking alcohol. However, where the consequences of that conduct may impinge on others, the law often steps in. There is a strict law which makes it unlawful for persons who have been drinking alcohol to drive their car.

- There are more ways in which human conduct is regulated than simply by the use of law. Codes of morality, religious principles, the pressures of friends are all other factors which restrain the ways in which people behave.

- Different countries set the boundaries of their criminal law in different places; what is criminal in one country is not necessarily criminal in another.[8] Although there is a great deal of commonality between different bodies of criminal law, in important respects the boundaries of criminal law are *culturally determined*, set by the demands of the specific society. There are particularly important

---

[8] This can have an important practical consequence in that if a person commits a criminal act in one country and flees to another country where that act is not criminal, this is often the basis for successfully resisting extradition proceedings—official proceedings to bring the alleged miscreant back to the country where the original act took place for trial.

distinctions in societies with different religious traditions or moral backgrounds: laws operating in Islamic countries are often quite different from those in countries founded on the Judaeo-Christian tradition.

* The boundaries of the criminal law are *dynamic.* Activity which has been regarded as criminal at one point in time will not necessarily be regarded as criminal at another point in time. The prohibition of alcohol in the US during the 1920s is a good example.

The attempt by law to regulate human behaviour is not exclusively through use of the criminal law. Areas of *civil law* also seek to do this. For example, if parties to a contract break that contract, rules of law allow the party affected to claim compensation or other remedies from those in breach of contract. The law of negligence prescribes situations in which a person who has injured another has to compensate that other for the injury. In short, law seeks to define the scope of the obligations that exist between individuals. Although the objectives of rules of civil law are not to punish an offender, in the sense used in the context of the criminal law, it is nevertheless the case that rules of civil law indicate that a contract cannot be breached with impunity, nor can one person act negligently in relation to another. In this sense, therefore, the rules of the civil law also send the message that certain types of behaviour are not acceptable or are undesirable.

DEFINING THE CONSEQUENCES OF CERTAIN FORMS OF BEHAVIOUR

Law does not of course simply define those forms of behaviour which are unacceptable. It also prescribes consequences. In the case of criminal law, these are the punishments that attach to a finding of guilt. Similarly in the area of the civil law, the law prescribes the remedies that the person affected by a breach of contract or a negligent act may be able to obtain from the perpetrator.

In some situations the same facts may generate quite different legal consequences. For example, a road accident may be caused by a person driving a car carelessly or recklessly. This may result in the police seeking to get that person prosecuted through the criminal courts; if found guilty this may result in the imposition of a fine or even imprisonment. If the accident causes damage to another, that other person may seek compensation by bringing an action for damages in negligence. The driver may argue that the accident occurred because his car was improperly serviced, and may therefore bring an action for breach of contract against his garage. Three different legal consequences have thus arisen from the same incident.

DEFINING PROCESSES FOR THE TRANSACTION OF BUSINESS AND OTHER ACTIVITIES

A rather different function of law is to define procedures by which certain transactions must be carried out. Some of these are quite simple, such as those relating to the making of simple contracts. However, in many cases, particularly in situations where there is a concern to prevent fraud, considerable formality may be required. Many of these relate to transactions dealing with the transfer of entitlement to property rights. For example, the process of buying and selling houses is subject to a number of formal legal requirements, known collectively as the rules of conveyancing. There are detailed rules which relate to the creation of leases. There are special rules which relate to the creation of wills. Similarly, there are detailed requirements for the creation of trusts or settlements of property.

One of the problems with prescribing formal requirements is that, whatever the law states, people in practice attempt to carry out these transactions in ignorance of the rules. The law then has to develop supplementary principles which seek to prevent injustice occurring, notwithstanding the existence of procedural irregularity. Many of the principles of the law of Equity have developed in response to this problem.

CREATING REGULATORY FRAMEWORKS

Related to the last category a great deal of law seeks to regulate those who provide services to the public. For example, substantial bodies of law regulate the activities of solicitors, doctors, architects, nurses, or estate agents. There is a vast regulatory framework designed to control the activities of those who provide financial services to the public, to prevent fraud and other breaches of trust. A consequence of the privatization of the bulk of the former nationalized industries has been to create a vast body of law designed to regulate the activities of companies now in the private sector (such as telecommunications, utilities, and transport) including the promotion of competition and the regulation of prices. And specific areas of economic activity are subject to the most detailed legal regulation designed to promote standards and give the consumer value for money. The regulation of the housing market through housing law is a prime example.

A different form of regulatory law, but one that has been in existence for many years, is planning law regulating the use to which land can be put in this country. Law which seeks to regulate industry in order to protect the environment is another example. In this context, the law operates at an international as well as a national level.

Regulatory law also serves another purpose. It defines the categories of person able to make representations to government about a particular policy or decision. For example, again in the context of planning law, the relevant law determines who may challenge decisions of the planning authorities, and who may appear to make their case at any public inquiry resulting from a planning decision.

GIVING AUTHORITY TO AGENTS OF THE STATE TO TAKE ACTIONS AGAINST CITIZENS

Another function of law is to give power to state officials to take action against members of the public. There are numerous examples: the powers of the police to stop, search, question, arrest, and caution members of the public is one; the power of doctors to detain in mental hospitals those diagnosed as suffering from acute mental illness is another; the power of social workers to remove children from families where they are thought to be at risk and to place them in the care of the local authorities is a third. Similarly, agents of both central and local government are given power to take money away from members of the public through the taxation system.

A rather different example is the power given to government and other agencies of the state to acquire land compulsorily in the public interest.

PREVENTING THE ABUSE OF POWER BY OFFICIALS

Set against the last heading, much law is designed to prevent abuses of power by public servants. For example, the police are required to operate within a framework of powers prescribed by the Police and Criminal Evidence Act 1984, designed to set boundaries to their powers of arrest, search, and questioning.

The heart of the principles of administrative law, considered further in Chapter 6, relates to the importance of officials acting within the framework of the law which prescribes their power; not allowing officials to make use of discretionary powers in an abusive way; and giving people the opportunity to take advantage of certain procedural safeguards—for example a right to a hearing—before adverse decisions about them are taken. These are further examples of rules of law setting boundaries to the power of state officials.

GIVING POWER/AUTHORITY TO OFFICIALS TO ASSIST THE PUBLIC

In contrast to the preceding category, the law also sets down a vast range of requirements whereby agencies of the state must provide services or other goods to the public. At the most general level, all public expenditure has to be legitimated by special Acts of Parliament known as the Appropriation Acts. These give general authority for the expenditure of public money on the range of social and other policy programmes run by government.

More specific bodies of law deal with the details. Social security law is one example, setting out as it does the entitlements to social security benefits which have been created by government. Many other examples could be given: entitlement to free education is one, free treatment within the National Health Service another. All these activities of the social security, education, and health authorities, are underpinned by detailed legal frameworks.

PRESCRIBING PROCEDURES FOR THE USE OF LAW

In addition to prescribing procedures for conducting different types of transaction, there is another important body of law—procedural law—which seeks to control the ways in which courts and other adjudicative bodies are to operate. This body of law may set limits to the evidence that can be brought in different types of case. It also prescribes the way in which different types of proceeding, whether in the courts, or other fora, are to be conducted.

CONCLUSION: LAW AND SOCIETY

It is not claimed here that these examples of the macro and micro functions of law in society are exhaustive. Readers should think about whether there other functions for law and whether they should be regarded as macro or micro in character. There is indeed a huge literature on the relationship of law and society of which the foregoing is only a very limited summary. However a number of points need to be made here.

(1) All the functions of law, whether defined as macro or micro, are *contingent* upon the stage of development of that society. While many of these functions of law will be common to very many societies, other will certainly not be.

(2) The laws that exist and the ways in which they are used are dependent on the ideology and politics of the particular country. For example, current notions of social justice and equality in the United Kingdom have developed in the light of particular socio-political and economic theories. They will change again in the future. The list of functions proposed here should not therefore be regarded as set in concrete; it will reflect other broader changes in the social and political ideas and ideals of that society.

(3) The functions of law are by no means always consistent with each other: preservation of social order may on occasion be in sharp conflict with the function of protecting civil liberties; the role of law in advancing equality or social justice may be in conflict with its role in supporting current social and economic orders.

(4) It should be remembered that there are still activities which are not currently the subject of legal regulation. Governments frequently claim that they are seeking to limit the encroachment of law. Interestingly, however, when a new technology arrives which actually enables activities to occur outside the normally accepted regulatory frameworks—the internet is a good current example—politicians and others quickly become agitated.

(5) There are also significant techniques, apart from recourse to law, used to regulate and alter the ways in which people behave. For example, much of the practice of economics is based on the assumption that if financial incentives are right, then behaviour patterns will change. An interesting example is the current proposal that problems of global pollution and global warming must be tackled not just by laws saying what should or should not be done, but also by getting financial incentives right—higher taxes paid by those who pollute, for example.

(6) More fundamentally, there are significant issues about the way in which we order our society which are either not touched on at all by law, or only in relatively insignificant ways. For example, one of the major social issues of our time relates to the extent to which groups in the community are excluded from the mainstream of social life, whether through lack of monetary resources, or other material resources such as housing. To be sure, there are legislative provisions relating to the provision of social security benefits, or to the provision of accommodation to the homeless. But the entitlements contained in these bodies of law are highly contingent—those claiming benefits or access to housing have a substantial list of conditions that they must satisfy before they will be helped. The fact that the rhetoric of law employs concepts such as 'liberty' or 'justice' does not mean that the body of substantive law is actually able to deliver social justice to all the citizens of the United Kingdom.

With these examples of the use (and non-use) of law in mind, together with others that may well come to the attention of the reader, the rest of this book will consider the ability of the English legal system to enable the functions of law to be performed.

3

LAW-MAKING: AUTHORITY AND PROCESS

INTRODUCTION

In the last chapter, we considered a number of functions that law plays in the working of society. In this chapter we examine the principal law-making institutions. First though we ask: whence do these institutions derive their power or authority? What gives the work of the law-makers legitimacy?

POWER, LEGITIMACY, AND AUTHORITY IN THE LAW-MAKING PROCESS

One of the functions of law identified in Chapter 2 was support for the political order. Law provides much if not all of the legal framework within which power is exercised. But simply stating that constitutional principles provide governments or other executive agencies with the power to make law still begs the question: whence do these constitutional legal principles derive their authority?

The answer to this question is far from easy. Different countries base their claims for the legitimacy of their law-makers on different theoretical foundations. In broad terms, however, it may be said that law-makers derive their authority from two principal sources:

(a) the fundamental constitutional framework or constitutional settlement which operates within that country;

(b) the underlying political ideology of that country.

The reasons why people in general are more or less willing to accept these bases for the exercise of power are complex. One is that, once they have established a claim to exercise power, states invariably create the machinery—police, security services, and the like—whose function is to ensure that the law is obeyed. Another is that, on the whole, the majority of people do not want to run the country themselves and are happy to let the politicians and bureaucrats get on with the job.

But it should always be remembered that even the most fundamental of constitutional arrangements will fail if significant groups within a particular society find that constitutional basis unworkable. The fact that in some countries in the world there have been or indeed are civil wars, that in others there have been *coups d'etat*, demonstrates the point. The destruction of the Berlin Wall and the collapse of apartheid in South Africa may be cited as two particularly dramatic instances. But many countries, which now have the most stable and secure of constitutional arrangements, trace their current situation to resistance or even rebellion against earlier unacceptable constitutional arrangements. The United Kingdom and the USA stand as examples. Constitutional arrangements depend on the consent of the governed.

In the United Kingdom, and in many other developed countries, that consent is more taken for granted than actively sought (save on particular issues which are the subject of referenda). Free and regular elections are usually seen as the primary institution from which continuing consent is implied.

CONSTITUTIONS AND CONSTITUTIONALISM

One basis for the authority given to the law-makers can therefore be found in a country's constitution and its related principles of constitutionalism. What are these?

In most countries, there exists a *written constitution* or other form of 'basic law' which defines the powers of the law-making institutions of the country. In the United Kingdom, the constitutional arrangements are unusual in that there is no formal written constitution. Many of the most important constitutional principles are to be found not in any written document but embraced in unwritten practice, known as *constitutional conventions*. (See Box 3.1.)

These unwritten principles are now accompanied by an increasing number of fundamental statutory provisions.[1] Devolution, reform of the House of Lords, the Human Rights Act 1998, the proposed Freedom of Information Act all involve the use of legislative measures which have transformed the constitutional landscape. In addition British membership of the European Union and other international bodies such as the Council of Europe and the United Nations have also had significant constitutional implications. These all help to set the framework within which power in the United Kingdom is exercised.

British *constitutionalism*—the principles which underpin the constitution—rests on three essential features: the *sovereignty of Parliament*, the *rule of law*, and the *separation of powers*.[2]

- The *sovereignty of Parliament* asserts that the ultimate legal authority for law-making in the United Kingdom is Parliament.

---

[1] See the examples given in Chapter 2 at pp. 13–14.

[2] The definitions of these concepts have, over the years, been the subject of fierce intellectual and political debate—see below, Suggestions for Further Reading.

Box 3.1 CONSTITUTIONAL CONVENTIONS

A detailed account of the nature and extent of constitutional conventions is beyond the scope of this work; there is a substantial literature on what they are and the extent to which they have changed over the years and are still effective. But some examples of constitutional conventions may be noted:

Constitutional monarchy. Although the theoretical Head of State remains the monarch, the principle of constitutional monarchy means that the Queen takes no active part in the running of the country. Though the Parliamentary year starts with the Queen's Speech and though bills are given royal assent, the Queen does not intervene in the politics of the law-making programme. The Queen is still kept informed about what is happening in Parliament, and through audiences with the prime minister of the day, is briefed about significant developments. It would be surprising if, on occasion, she did not offer her views on particular issues. But the monarch is no longer the source of political decision-taking or law-making.

Prerogative powers. Nevertheless, there are still certain functions of government which are based not in legislative authority, but on the historic exercise of power by the monarch. These are known as Prerogative Powers. The most dramatic example of this is the power to go to war, which is exercised by ministers not under the authority of any Act of Parliament, but by exercise of prerogative powers. The Home Secretary's Prerogative of Mercy to reduce a sentence imposed by the courts in a criminal trial may be seen as another example.

Cabinet government and collective responsibility. The very existence of a Cabinet—the central committee of ministers chaired by the prime minister and responsible for determining the government's programme—is another aspect of the British Constitution founded in convention, rather than legislation. The related doctrine of collective responsibility, whereby ministers who do not agree with the policy of the government as determined in Cabinet are supposed to resign from the government, is also based in constitutional convention, rather than constitutional law.

Individual ministerial responsibility. Another constitutional doctrine is that ministers should take ultimate responsibility for what goes on in their departments. This certainly means that they must answer questions in Parliament or select committees about the work of their departments. On occasion, this may also lead ministers to resign, where something has gone very seriously wrong, though in practice these days this is a rare occurrence.

- The *rule of law* insists that power should not be exercised by persons acting by or on behalf of the state, without their being able to point to some form of legal *authority* for their actions.

- The *separation of powers* suggests that to prevent any particular arm of government from becoming too powerful, there should be a separation between the legislative (law-making), executive, and judicial functions of government. Thereby each branch of government is subject to *checks and balances*. This in turn leads to the proposition that the judges in particular, and lawyers in general, must have the power to act independently of government.

These principles relate to the central issues of power, namely who may exercise it, how it can be controlled, and how those who exercise power can be called to account.

POLITICAL IDEOLOGY

Stating these principles still leaves unanswered the question: what is the theoretical basis on which power to make law may be asserted by political institutions? To answer this question it is necessary to consider the underlying political ideology of the country.

In the United Kingdom, and indeed many other countries, the currently dominant political ideology is *representative democracy*, expressed principally through the holding of regular general elections. Democratic theory suggests that society is unable to function as effectively as it might if each individual retains his/her unique power to control their own lives or the lives of others. Instead, by electing Members of Parliament to *represent* the views of electors, individuals pass to those elected to Parliament some of that control or *sovereignty* which gives them power and authority to govern on behalf of the people.

Those in power are also subject to the principle of *accountability*. For example politicians are regularly called to account for themselves or their political parties when general elections are held. From the electoral process those elected to political office derive their authority to make laws on behalf of the citizens of the country, knowing that if their actions are not approved of by the electorate, they will be defeated at the next general election. They are also subject to accountability from the range of *checks and balances* that exist, both within the Parliamentary system (such as Parliamentary debates or questions to ministers) and outside. These comprise a wide variety of bodies and activities, including the essential part played by the Press and other mass media in exposing things that go wrong within government.

Principles in practice

The application of these theoretical principles is not as clear in practice as theory might imply.

- First, in the British system, the fact is that the Parliamentary process is strictly controlled by the political party which forms the government of the day. There are very few issues on which MPs will vote independently of what the party wants. There is the occasional backbench revolt; and the occasional free vote on a matter of conscience where the party whip is not applied. But these are the exception, not the rule.

- Second, all legislation in the United Kingdom passes not only through the elected House of Commons, but also the non-elected House of Lords. Although the House of Lords rarely exercises the power it theoretically has to delay bills becoming law, the fact is that on many occasions the House of Lords does amend legislation coming to it from the House of Commons. The threat of delay may result in substantial amendment or even the dropping of legislative proposals. While there is in the Commons some link between the democratic process of election and the outcomes of the law-making process, in the Lords this is not so, and even after reform will not be the case.[3]

- Third, knowing the extent to which the electoral process does in fact represent the will of the people is also very difficult. In the United Kingdom, the voting system of first past the post has meant that nearly all recently elected governments have attained power on the basis of a minority of the popular vote. Even in the election of 1997, which resulted in a Labour government with a huge Parliamentary majority, the Labour party attracted less than 50 per cent of votes cast. This leads many, particularly those in the smaller parties who struggle to get elected under the present system, to argue that a 'fairer' voting system would incorporate proportional representation, whereby seats in the Parliament would be distributed in proportion to votes cast. The primary argument against this apparently attractive proposition is that this tends to lead to coalition governments, in which the small minority parties thereby acquire a disproportionately powerful position. However, experiments with proportional representation have recently occurred in the United Kingdom in the elections of members to the European Parliament.

- Fourth, there are important sources of law other than Parliament. Under the British system of separation of powers, judges in the Higher Courts have in effect power to make new rules of law. This they may do through the development of rules of 'common law'—long-standing principles of law developed over the years, in some cases centuries, by the judges. Many examples of judicial law-making can be given:
  - the fundamental principles of the law of contract on which much economic activity is based;
  - the principles of the law of negligence, which relate among other matters to dealing with the aftermath of accidents and other forms of misfortune;
  - the development of procedures for dealing with disputes between the citizen and the state, especially the development of the principles of *judicial review*,

---

[3] Precise details of the membership of the reformed House of Lords were not decided at the time of writing.

which is the basis on which judicial control of the administrative arm of government is achieved.

Yet judges are not elected; they do not get their authority from any democratic theory. The legitimacy for their activity has to be found in other constitutional principles, in particular the separation of powers. The judges are recognized both to be a part of the machinery of government and, paradoxically, at the same time to be independent of it.

MEMBERSHIP OF THE EUROPEAN UNION

One respect in which the law-making process in the United Kingdom has been significantly altered in recent years has arisen from membership by the United Kingdom of the European Union. The fundamental constitutional documents of the Union, starting with the Treaty of Rome and developed by, for example, the Treaties of Maastricht and Amsterdam, provide not only that Member States must abide by those principles of European law that are made by the institutions established by the Treaty of Rome, but also that failure to do this will result in sanctions being imposed by the institutions of the European Union. As a result of these principles, the British government is *required* to incorporate certain rules of European law into British law, whether or not it likes them. Furthermore, the House of Lords has decided[4] that if the provisions of a British Act of Parliament are actually in conflict with European law, then the British Act is to be regarded as of no effect. Until this point was reached, the British courts had never claimed the power to overrule an Act of Parliament, which was always regarded as the sovereign law-making authority.

One criticism of the institutional arrangements of the European Union is said to be 'democratic deficit'. It is argued that too many of the institutions established to run the European Union operate without the authority/legitimacy bestowed by some process of democratic accountability. For example, the exclusive right to initiate legislation is held by the European Commission, whose twenty Commissioners are not directly elected by the people of the European Union. In practice, the powers of the Commissioners were constrained by the Council of Ministers, comprising elected ministers from each of the Member States, and whose approval of legislative proposals was always required.[5] But the argument was often made that the European Parliament— the only body with directly elected members—had no part to play in the law-making process, certainly not compared with the part played by the British Parliament.

These criticisms have been acknowledged, at least to a degree. Since the Maastricht Treaty was concluded in 1992, and more particularly since the 1997 Treaty of

---

[4] *Factortame v. Secretary of State for Transport (No. 2)* [1991] 1 AC 603; the jurisprudence of the European Court of Justice had long been clear on the point: *Costa v. ENEL* [1964] ECR 585.

[5] Initially, the Council of Ministers had to be unanimous; a single vote against a proposal would result in its not being adopted. In many circumstances the principle of unanimity has been replaced by the principle of the qualified majority, to enable some measures to be introduced despite the opposition of some ministers.

Amsterdam came into effect (on 1 July 1999), the European Parliament has acquired significantly more legislative power. It still cannot initiate legislative measures. But it now has significant power to control the content of measures. Around 75 per cent of all European law-making must now be approved by a majority of the European Parliament, as well as the Council of Ministers. The poor participation by the British electorate in European elections may be the result of the widespread lack of knowledge about the role of the Parliament and how it has changed.

EUROPEAN CONVENTION ON HUMAN RIGHTS AND THE HUMAN RIGHTS ACT 1998

The incorporation of the European Convention on Human Rights into British law, through the Human Rights Act 1998, will raise similar issues. It is not inconceivable that particular rules of statute law will be held by the English courts (as they have from time to time been held by the European Court of Human Rights in Strasbourg) to be contrary to the Convention. The Human Rights Act specifically prohibits the English courts from declaring principles of legislation invalid,[6] thus preserving the notion of the sovereignty of Parliament. However the Act does give the courts power to issue a 'declaration of incompatibility' which, in effect, is a direction to the government of the day that a particular statutory provision must be amended in order to comply with the provisions of the European Convention.

THE LAW-MAKING INSTITUTIONS

With these points in mind, we take a closer look at the functions of a number of the law-making institutions that exist in the United Kingdom:

- The British Parliament and central government
- European institutions
- The courts
- Other agencies.

THE BRITISH PARLIAMENT AND CENTRAL GOVERNMENT

The principal law-making body in the United Kingdom is the British Parliament. Its legislative programme is at the heart of the law-making process. By no means all legislative measures are the subject of detailed Parliamentary scrutiny (see Box 3.2),

---

[6] Section 4.

but the vast bulk of legislative measures derive their authority from the Parliamentary process. The nature of that process has undergone significant though inadequately publicized change in recent years—an example of the often understated dynamism that characterizes many developments in the English legal system.[7] The discussion here focuses on the process of enacting an Act of Parliament. Apart from the inherent importance of the subject there is a good practical reason why lawyers need to know about this aspect of the English legal system. There are now circumstances—albeit limited—in which what was said about a Bill as it passed through Parliament may be used by a court, when dealing with a question of statutory interpretation.[8]

Box 3.2 STATUTE LAW: THE CLASSIFICATION OF LEGISLATIVE MEASURES

The vast bulk of the new law that is brought into effect in England is statute law, that is law which has been passed through Parliament following analysis and debate in both the House of Commons and the House of Lords. Statute law comes in a variety of forms:

- primary legislation
- secondary legislation
- tertiary legislation, and
- (not strictly statute law) 'quasi-legislation' or 'soft law'.

Primary legislation comprises the eighty or so *Acts of Parliament* that are passed through Parliament each year. The process consumes a great deal of Parliamentary time, and lack of time is a significant constraint on the law-making process. Indeed, it is often said that an idea for legislation—particularly if it is not high on the government's political agenda—will only be brought forward when 'time is available'. This can also be used as an excuse for a government delaying bringing a new measure forward; but the non-availability of Parliamentary time is also a real constraint on the opportunities for introducing and then amending legislation.[9] Most Acts of Parliament are Public and General Acts, applying throughout the land; some are Local or Private Acts applying only in particular localities or to specific people. (See Box 3.3.)

---

[7] One of the most recent innovations—introduced in November 1999—is that of *backbench debates*. Because of the amount of time the legislative process takes in the House of Commons, backbenchers have only limited opportunity to raise matters of more general concern. Three days each week are now available for backbench debates on matters not related to the legislative programme. These take place not in the chamber of the House of Commons, but in Westminster Hall, which for these purposes has been arranged in a horse-shoe formation—thought to be less confrontational than the familiar 'head-on' arrangements in the House of Commons.

[8] *Pepper v. Hart* [1993] AC 593 (HL); as to statutory interpretation see below p. 53.

[9] There are occasions when measures can be introduced and passed with extreme rapidity; the enactment of the Northern Ireland (Emergency Provisions) Act in the aftermath of the Omagh bombing in August 1998 is an example.

Primary legislation is supplemented by a vast body of *secondary legislation*—regulations and orders made under the authority of an Act of Parliament. There are typically in excess of 3,000 such items, known generically as *statutory instruments*, made each year. These run to many thousands of pages of text. They are not subject to detailed Parliamentary scrutiny, though in many cases statutory instruments cannot be made by the government without a process of consultation with a specialist Advisory Committee. (See Box 3.4.)

In addition to primary and secondary legislation, there is also a vast array of *tertiary legislation*—legislative instruments which are made under the authority of an Act of Parliament, but which are subject to no Parliamentary scrutiny at all. For example, in Housing Law, numerous powers are given to Ministers to issue 'directions' or other instruments, which are drafted in the form of legislation and which effectively have the force of law, but which are simply issued by the government department in question. Similar examples are found in many other areas of government.

A great deal of rule-making authority is also held by those whose task it is to regulate industries of various kinds: for example the Civil Aviation Authority or the regulators of the privatized utilities.[10] Major new rule-making powers are being conferred on the new Financial Services Authority.[11] These legislative instruments are therefore made outside the conventional institutional framework of the government. However, following the process of privatization and other initiatives to transfer governmental activity to agencies, this has become an increasingly common practice.

There is, finally, a fourth category of instrument, sometimes referred to as *quasi-legislation* or *soft law*, which comprises statements of good practice or guidance. These may be made under the authority of an Act of Parliament and may in some cases be subject to Parliamentary approval. But, as with tertiary legislation, they are subject to no detailed Parliamentary discussion. Examples include codes of practice such as the Highway Code, or the Codes of Practice relating to police behaviour made under the Police and Criminal Evidence Act 1984. (See Chapter 5.) Many other examples could be given.

One practical problem with tertiary and 'quasi'-legislation is that it is not published in the normal way by the Stationery Office—the official outlet for government publications. For example Ministerial Directions will usually be made available to those who need to know about them; the ordinary member of the public who might wish to know about the existence of these documents may find them hard to track down.

An important issue of principle flows from this. There is a simplistic assumption that because legislation is published by a single authoritative source, 'everyone is deemed to know the law'. Such a claim is simply not sustainable in the case of such instruments.

---

[10] Baldwin, Robert, *Rules and Government* (Oxford: Oxford University Press, 1995).
[11] Financial Services and Markets Act 2000.

PRIMARY LEGISLATION

Acts of Parliament all start as bills. In addition, from the beginning of 1999, nearly all bills are accompanied by an Explanatory Note, a detailed note drafted by the bill's sponsoring department, which sets out the background to the bill and explains what it is trying to achieve in policy terms.[12] Four distinct types of bill may be identified:

(1) 'Political' bills, the result, usually, of the political programme of the party in government. Here the initial idea for a bill will be found in the political manifesto of the party in power. (Indeed, Acts of Parliament have been referred to as the 'corpses' of political debate: the remains left over from the sound and fury of political struggle.) The majority of the bills presented to Parliament are designed to further the political objectives of the government in power. These are often referred to collectively as Government bills. These bills are sponsored by individual ministers.

(2) 'Law Reform' bills which arise from time to time as the result of recommendations made by law reform agencies, such as the Law Commission. These tend to be less politically controversial.[13] Measures proposed by the Law Commission are all preceded by a detailed analysis of the issue to be addressed, and will have been the subject of considerable consultation with the public before recommendations are made. Many Law Commission reports contain a draft bill ready for use in the Parliament. There is no officially recognized label for these measures, though they are often referred to as technical measures of law reform.

(3) 'Consolidation' bills, which bring together into a single place a wide range of legislative provisions scattered through many Acts of Parliament and thus difficult to find.[14] These measures do not themselves introduce new law but tidy up and re-present what is already on the statute book. There is a special procedure to enable such measures to reach the statute book without going through the full parliamentary process discussed below.

(4) 'Private Member's bills' are a special type of bill introduced by backbench MPs.

(For further consideration of these different types of Act of Parliament, see Box 3.3.)

---

[12] This is one of the most important, though again inadequately publicized, procedural innovations of recent years. These notes set bills in both their policy and legal context.

[13] Recent attempts at divorce law reform, which derived from work of the Law Commission, but which generated a storm of controversy, were a notable exception to this general proposition.

[14] Failure to consolidate adds to the complexity of carrying out legal research; printed versions of Acts of Parliament may be quite misleading, having been substantially amended. New computer technology creates the opportunity to keep texts of statutes up to date. In some countries, e.g. Canada, the statute book is automatically consolidated every ten years.

Box 3.3 ACTS OF PARLIAMENT: PUBLIC AND GENERAL ACTS, LOCAL
AND PRIVATE ACTS, AND PRIVATE MEMBER'S ACTS

Most Acts of Parliament are known as *Public and General Acts*, that is to say that
they apply throughout the United Kingdom. Because of their different legal
systems, acts which apply only in Scotland may now be made by the Scottish
Parliament; and there are special rules relating to legislation which is effective in
Northern Ireland. All Public and General Acts contain a section which defines in
which parts of the United Kingdom that act will apply. All such acts are of
general application in all those parts of the countries to which they are stated to
apply.

By contrast, *Private and Local Acts* are of limited scope only. They may apply
only to a local area (say a town) or to a specific institution (say a body such as a
university, or a particular individual). The procedure by which Private and
Local Acts become law is quite different from the procedures by which Public
and General Acts become law. The detail is not considered here, but in essence
such acts are passed through a procedure involving Committees of the House,
not the full House of Commons.

Private Acts must be sharply distinguished from *Private Member's Acts*, which
are Public and General Acts, but sponsored—as their name implies—not by
government ministers, but by ordinary backbench Members of Parliament.
These bills are the subject of special rules relating to their content. Most important of these is that these bills cannot contain any provision that would result in
the expenditure of public money. These bills are also subject to special procedural rules, which have the effect of ensuring that only a very few such
measures reach the statute book in any given year.

The backbenchers who bring these bills forward are selected following a
ballot—a process which takes place early in each Parliamentary session. Private
Member's bills are only debated on Fridays—a day when the pressure of government business is usually less. Twenty private members are able to introduce
their measures following the ballot, but those near the top of the list have a
greater chance of seeing their bill introduced into law. For a bill to have any
chance of success it must either be supported by the government, or at least not
actively resisted by the government.

The Housing (Homeless Persons) Bill 1976 is a good example: as originally
drafted it would have given a range of legal rights to the homeless which the
government regarded as wholly unacceptable. In that case, the government
offered the bill's sponsor an alternative, which was the bill he then actually took
forward. With this government support the bill did eventually pass into law.

Private Member's bills can be used to introduce measures on which there are
fierce divisions of opinion, but where those divisions are not the subject of party
political debate. An excellent example of this is the Abortion Act 1967, which
was a very important, but obviously controversial measure, introduced by Mr
David Steel, to which none of the main political parties wished to tie their
political reputations. The willingness of a private member to take such an issue

forward can mean that the political parties, in particular the government party, can distance themselves to some extent from such an issue. Over the last fifteen years, or so, the average success rate for Private Member's bills has been about eight out of twenty reaching the Statute Book each year.

In addition to the ballot process, there are three other means by which back-benchers may attempt to introduce legislation: 'presentation bills', Ten Minute Rule bills, and bills from individual members of the House of Lords. The numbers of such bills passing into law are tiny and are not considered further here.

Preparatory stages

Before getting to Parliament at all, many bills start the process of becoming law with a process of consultation with persons or other agencies outside government. There are various ways in which this is carried out. A common process is for ideas for new policies and related changes in the law to be floated in a *Green Paper*,[15] this will often set out a number of proposals for change and ask for comments on them. The government may attempt to steer response by indicating its preliminary view on what should happen.

Following this initial consultative process, a further statement of the government's policy objectives may be set out in a *White Paper*[16] that summarizes the consultation and sets out the government's view on what it plans to do.

Procedural changes

The process of enacting bills has recently undergone three important changes.

Consultation. First, until very recently, Parliamentary practice required all bills to be presented first to Parliament. Indeed it was felt that to fail to do so would be an insult to Parliament. However, the wisdom of this principle has been increasingly challenged, and as the result of very important procedural changes,[17] some bills are now publicly circulated for comment and criticism by those most likely to be affected, prior to their formal introduction in Parliament.[18]

Hearings. In addition there are now cases where the draft of a bill is subject to special hearings—a practice common in the USA and other countries but not hitherto used here.[19] Thus, in the case of the Financial Services and Markets Bill 1999, a consultation paper was issued in July 1998, with a draft bill attached to it. This was the

---

[15] So called because years ago they were published with green covers. For some years, however, image-conscious governments have used designers and printers to produce Green Papers with covers containing all the colours of the rainbow!

[16] They too are no longer distinguished by the colour of their covers.

[17] See Select Committee on the Modernization of the House of Commons, *The Legislative Process* (July 1997) (HC 190, 1997–98).

[18] The Employment Rights (Dispute Resolution) Act 1998 is an example.

[19] An early example was the pre-legislative scrutiny by the Social Security Select Committee of the government's draft Bill on Pension Sharing on Divorce, published in June 1998.

subject of consultation with those likely to be affected by it. In addition it was the subject of hearings before two Parliamentary Committees: one the Treasury Commit-tee of the House of Commons,[20] the other a Joint Committee of the House of Com-mons and House of Lords, both of which issued reports on the draft bill. All these consultations led to further changes to the bill being made before it was formally introduced into the House of Commons in June 1999.

Carry forward. A further significant procedural amendment means that a bill can be considered over two Parliamentary sessions. If the passage of a bill through Par-liament is not completed before a session of Parliament is prorogued (formally brought to an end) in late October/early November, it can be taken forward into the following Parliamentary session. This procedure will be applied to a small number of complex government bills. The Financial Services and Markets Bill is an example.

The advantage of these developments is clear. Those affected are given the opportunity to comment on the adequacy of the legislation from a practical point of view before it reaches its final form. The ability to carry bills from one Parliamentary session to another means that there can be greater flexibility over the dates on which bills can be introduced into Parliament. The practice of front-loading the presenta-tion of new bills to the beginning of each Parliamentary session will, to an extent at least, be mitigated. It also represents a sensible attempt to prevent the detail of com-plex legislation being rushed through Parliament, at the end of a Parliamentary ses-sion, often with undesirable drafting consequences.[21]

Parliamentary stages

The formal procedure[22] for passing an act starts with the presentation of a bill in one of the Houses of Parliament. Most measures designed to advance the political object-ives of the government are presented first in the House of Commons; less contro-versial measures (including Consolidation bills) may start in the House of Lords. The analysis here assumes that the bill started in the House of Commons.

The bill's objectives will have been determined by the political imperatives of the government or other person presenting the bill. Those principles are transformed into legislative form by teams of specially qualified and trained civil servants known as Parliamentary draftsmen, or more properly Parliamentary counsel.

The parliamentary process starts with a *first reading*, a formal stage when the House orders the bill to be printed.[23] No progress can be made on a bill until it has been printed.

---

[20] Their report *Financial Services Regulation* was published in February 1999, with a response from government in March 1999.

[21] It is hard to say how often this procedure will be used. It was not used in relation to measures such as the Welfare Reform and Pensions Bill 1999, which proved to be extremely politically contentious.

[22] Lawyers do need to be aware of the different stages that a bill goes through in Parliament, not just for the sake of it, but because it may in some specific circumstances, where the meaning of a section in an act is not clear, be possible to refer to the debates in Parliament: *Pepper v. Hart* [1993] AC 591.

[23] All bills are printed on a light-blue coloured paper, to distinguish them from the subsequent act, which is printed on white paper.

The first opportunity for debate on the bill arises at the *second reading*. Here the minister responsible for the bill sets out the main policy objectives for the measure; the opposition parties set out their objections to the measure. This is followed by comments from other Members of Parliament—the back benchers. At the end of the debate, there is another summing up by a government minister. It is rare for a government bill to be defeated at this stage.[24] If a bill implies either the raising of taxation or the expenditure of public money, Parliament also has to pass (respectively) either a Ways and Means Resolution or a Money Resolution.

The bill then moves to the *committee stage*.[25] Detailed scrutiny of the text is carried out by a small group of MPs—usually about eighteen in number, known as a Standing Committee. They consider the clauses[26] of the bill, as drafted, consider amendments proposed to those clauses, and determine whether or not such amendments should or should not be accepted. This is a highly 'political' stage in the legislative process. Not only do the opposition members put down such amendments as they have thought of, but members of the Standing Committee are also subject to intense lobbying from groups outside Parliament, with a view to their putting down amendments which reflect the interests of those lobbying groups. (These groups will also, of course, exert pressure in other ways—press releases, airing their views on television, radio, and so on.)

Given that the government party always has a majority on the committee, and those MPs from the government side are instructed to vote as the whip tells them, it is usually the case that the government side either gets its way, or only makes those concessions which it is prepared to accept.[27] Despite the degree of control that government has, bills are actually frequently amended and often emerge from the overall process significantly changed from the form in which they were first advanced. On occasion, where a bill is being rushed though Parliament, or on a very significant constitutional change, the committee stage may take place in the whole House, but this is a rare occurrence.

Next comes the *report stage* in which things that have happened to the bill in committee are reported to the main House. This may provide the government with the chance to undo things that the committee may have done to the bill which the government does not like. It is often the point at which amendments which the government wish to introduce into the bill (perhaps following debate in committee) are introduced.

[24] This was a fate suffered by the Shops Bill 1986, designed to deregulate Sunday Trading.

[25] The Committees of the House of Commons which look at bills are known collectively as 'Standing Committees'. Rarely, on a very controversial measure, the Committee stage may be taken 'on the floor of the House', in other words before the House of Commons as a whole. In the House of Lords, the Committee stage is always taken before the whole House. Standing Committees should be carefully distinguished from Select Committees which have the task of examining the activities of government carried out in the various government departments.

[26] Each of the separate provisions in a bill is called a 'clause'; after the bill has passed through Parliament and become an act, the clauses are transformed into 'sections'.

[27] A detailed, if now dated, analysis of the work of Standing Committees scrutinizing legislation is by Griffith, J. A. G., *Parliamentary Scrutiny of Government Bills* (London: Allen and Unwin, 1974).

The final stage is the *third reading*, a more formal stage in which the bill in its then form is brought together but no more amendments are made. The bill then goes to the House of Lords, where it begins a similar process.

Usually the progress of a bill is the subject of an informal timetable agreed between the government and the opposition whips. However, where a bill is extremely politic-ally controversial, and the opposition parties are taking every opportunity to slow progress of the bill through committee, the government may decide that a strict time table for the discussion of the measure is to be imposed. A timetable order, commonly known as a *guillotine motion*, is passed which prescribes the date by which each stage of the bill's progress must be completed. If it is not, the bill nevertheless proceeds to the next stage of the Parliamentary process, without any further debate or analysis of the draft provisions. Decisions to impose the guillotine are not taken lightly, but are not uncommon. In most recent years there have been a small number of examples; the record was in 1988–89 when ten such motions were passed.

Another important procedural innovation of the last two years has been the cre-ation of the *Programme Motion*. Here government and opposition agree a timetable, which can be amended, that sets out publicly the dates by which each stage of the bill will be complete. This provides more transparency than arrangements reached through the usual channels.

The House of Lords

Procedure in the House of Lords is broadly similar to that in the Commons. The major differences are:

(1) the Committee stage is taken on the floor of the House, i.e. there are no specially designated committees of Peers whose task it is to report back to the House as a whole;

(2) there is no guillotine and thus debate on amendments is not restricted; and

(3) amendments can be made at the Third Reading stage.

These potentially can be, and on occasion are, a source of delay. But although the Lords are in theory able to wreck or at least seriously delay legislation, they are aware that, given their current status as a non-elected legislative body, the ultimate decision on legislation must lie with the elected House of Commons. While they do not in practice destroy bills, there have been a number of occasions in recent years where they have secured significant amendments or even caused a bill to be withdrawn.[28]

Once the Lords stages are complete, there has to be a process for the Commons and the Lords to agree a single version of the text. Particularly at the end of the Parlia-mentary year (usually in early November) this can lead to dramatic horse-trading between Lords and Commons, especially where measures are very controversial. In

---

[28] A recent example was the Criminal Justice (Mode of Trial) Bill 1999; this had been introduced in the House of Lords, but was withdrawn following an adverse vote there. The government decided to introduce a new bill, revised in content but with the same title, in the House of Commons; see Chapter 5.

the last resort, the House of Lords does have power, under the Parliament Act 1911 to delay a Commons bill for up to one year (though not a Money bill). If there is an ultimate impasse, then the view of the elected legislature, the House of Commons, will prevail. Reform of the House of Lords will bring some detailed changes to these procedures.

Royal assent and commencement

The final stage is the granting of the *royal assent*. This has not been withheld since 1707, but, reflecting the nature of the British constitutional monarchy, is still a formal step that has to be completed.

The mere fact that an act has completed the legislative process does not mean it at once becomes effective. Commonly, new administrative arrangements have to be put in place before an act can become operational. In such cases, the legislation will only be effective when a *Commencement Order*—a special type of Statutory Instrument (see below)—is made. (The Easter Act 1928 has still not been brought into force.) It is clearly essential that those who may seek to take advantage of new rules of law discover whether or not statutory provisions are in force.

Reports of debates

The debates on all the Parliamentary stages are the subject of verbatim reporting in the Official Reports of the Houses of Parliament (known collectively as *Hansard*). Thus it is possible to research what was said and by whom at each stage of the Parliamentary process. These reports also detail how MPs voted. These reports are now also available on the Internet.

SECONDARY LEGISLATION

Because of the length of time which has to be taken to ensure the passage of legislation through Parliament, modern practice is for Acts of Parliament to contain the essential principles of legislation only. Much of the detail is left to be filled in by *secondary legislation* which is made under the authority of the act but which is not subject to the full Parliamentary scrutiny that a bill undergoes. Secondary legislation is technically collectively known as *statutory instruments*, which come in two forms, *Regulations* (the most common) and *Orders*.

Underpinning the creation of secondary legislation is a number of controls designed to ensure that governments only introduce measures which they have authority to introduce:

(1) regulations are subject to formal vetting by the Statutory Instruments Committee of the House of Commons;

(2) many categories of statutory instruments also have to be shown in draft to particular bodies or organizations detailed in the 'parent' act. Many governmental advisory committees are given the specific task of commenting on and

vetting proposed regulations (see Box 3.4). Some parent Acts require the government not just to consult with a specific nominated body, but with 'such bodies as appear to have an interest in the legislation'. This is code for requiring the government to discuss with a range of interested groups the content of proposed delegated legislation;

(3) there is the potential for some Parliamentary input though this rarely happens. All regulations are subject either to a *negative resolution procedure* or to an *affirmative resolution procedure*. (Two particular types of SI, Commencement Orders—which bring Acts of Parliament, or parts of Acts of Parliament into effect—and Orders in Council, are not subject to any Parliamentary procedure.) The *negative resolution* procedure is the more common. It means that, once laid before Parliament, a new regulation will become effective on the date stated in the regulation, *unless* Parliament passes a resolution stating that the regulations should be nullified. Given that regulations are introduced by government and that (usually) the government has a majority in the House of Commons, it will be realized that this will happen very infrequently indeed. By contrast, the *affirmative resolution* procedure means that a regulation laid before the Parliament cannot become effective unless Parliament adopts a resolution which *affirms* that the regulation should become effective. It cannot be said that this process actually gives the House of Commons much control over the detail, since debate is only permitted on the underlying issues, not the specific details. But positive resolution debates do give some opportunity for opposition parties to make broad political points about the regulation in question;[29]

(4) in an extreme case, the validity of a statutory instrument may be challenged in the courts, and if found to be *ultra vires* (outside the legal framework provided by the parent act) will be declared by the courts to be a nullity.[30]

COMMENT ON THE LEGISLATIVE PROCESS

Given the dominance of the Parliamentary timetable by the government machine, the question is sometimes asked whether the amount of time spent debating proposals in relation to which the outcome is totally or largely predictable is actually worthwhile. It has to be recognized that the elected Members of Parliament do not, in general, have any detailed control over the content of Acts of Parliament. Indeed, there is no guarantee that all provisions of bills are subject to considered debate; and the vast

---

[29] An example is found in the Annual Up-Rating of Social Security Benefits. The relevant regulations are subject to the positive resolution procedure. Debate on whether the new amounts should be 50p more or less is not permitted; but general debate about social security provision and social welfare policy is allowed.

[30] Although a relatively rare occurrence, there have been two recent examples: *R. v. Secretary of State for Trade and Industry, ex parte Thomson Holidays, The Times,* 12 January 2000; and *R. v. Secretary of State for the Environment, Transport and the Regions and Another, ex parte Spath Holme Ltd,* [2000] 1 All ER 125.

Box 3.4 CONSULTATION ON REGULATIONS: THE CASE OF SOCIAL SECURITY

An interesting example is the work of the Social Security Advisory Committee which looks at draft regulations relating to social security policy. They not only consider the proposals themselves, but also consult on those proposals with a wide range of bodies and pressure groups outside government. They reflect on these comments before making their own report to the government. The government then decides whether or not to accept the advice of its committee.

When it brings forward the final version of the regulations, the government is required to publish a special report which not only reproduces the report from the Advisory Committee, but also details the reasons why the government has (or more often has not) followed the advice of the committee.

This represents a particular form of accountability which to some extent replaces normal parliamentary debate; arguably it is more relevant since most of the commentators will have a specialist interest in and knowledge of the area. This is a model which, it has been forcefully argued, should apply in other regulation-making contexts.[31]

bulk of legislation—the Secondary Legislation—reaches the statute book with no consideration by Members of Parliament at all.

Nevertheless it should be remembered that much of the detail of the Parliamentary process was developed in an era where the party machine and the discipline over the Parliamentary party provided by the whips was not as it is today. Indeed the very power of the modern party machine in government to dominate the legislative process in terms of outcomes is perhaps the best reason for retaining the detailed process that currently exists. This arises from the very political theories, noted above, which underpin the British Constitution and its system of government. Although ministers may be able to achieve their desired goals in the end, the process ensures that they will have been subject to challenge by elected Members of Parliament, who will have called the relevant ministers to account. Without these procedures it will be far harder for ministers seeking to defend a particular measure to claim legitimacy for their legislative acts.

EUROPEAN LAW-MAKING INSTITUTIONS

There has been much debate about the impact that the involvement of the United Kingdom 'in Europe' has had on British law and the English legal system. Two quite separate institutional frameworks are often muddled. They are:

[31] Harden, Ian and Lewis, Norman, *The Noble Lie: The British Constitution and the Rule of Law* (London: Hutchinson, 1986).

- the Council of Europe; and
- the European Union.

THE COUNCIL OF EUROPE

The Council of Europe was established after the end of World War II. Its task was to prevent a repetition of the human rights outrages of the second world war period. More recently it has engaged in a process of assisting those countries of the former eastern bloc to create the institutional arrangements that will permit democratic principles to develop. Its most significant act in terms of its impact on English law was the creation in 1950 of the European Convention on Human Rights. This was a charter of fundamental rights and freedoms agreed by all the member states of the Council of Europe. As is common with all treaties, the Convention did not come into effect until it had been ratified by a number of governments. It came into force in 1953. The Convention has been amended on a number of occasions. The current version of the convention, amended by Protocol No. 11, came into effect in November 1998.

Normally treaties attempt to regulate relationships between nation states. They may provide that one country may take action against another where there is an alleged breach of an international treaty obligation. The European Convention on Human Rights is quite distinct. In it, provision was made for *individuals* to be able to take proceedings where it was alleged that a government was in breach of its obligations under the treaty. Individuals could not start proceedings unless the government in question permitted this to take place. In the case of the United Kingdom, the right of an individual to take proceedings against the British government for alleged breaches of the convention was conceded in 1966.

The impact of the Council of Europe on the law-making process in the United Kingdom has been indirect. Where cases are taken before the European Court of Human Rights in Strasbourg which result in a decision that a rule of British law or some practice of the British government is contrary to the provisions of the Convention, this will lead to the British government changing the law to bring it into line with the Convention, as interpreted by the Court.[32] The Interception of Communications Act 1985, which regulates phone-tapping, was the result of an adverse decision by the Court of Human Rights.

With the terms of the European Convention being directly introduced into British law following enactment of the Human Rights Act 1998, most of the principles of the European Convention will become directly enforceable in the English Courts. It is specifically stated in the Human Rights Act that, in interpreting its provisions, English judges must take account of the jurisprudence developed by the European Court of Human Rights in Strasbourg.

Once in force, the Act will have two effects on the law-making process in the United Kingdom. First, in presenting bills to Parliament, ministers will have to issue a

---

[32] There have been over thirty adverse decisions of the Court affecting the United Kingdom.

declaration that in their opinion the proposed legislation complies with the Convention provisions; indeed this has already started.

In addition, as noted,[33] British courts will have power to declare a legislative provision incompatible with the provisions of the Convention. Although not declaring unlawful an Act of Parliament, or a provision in an Act, this will bring overwhelming pressure on ministers to introduce changes so that the incompatibility is removed. In this important sense, the freedom of ministers to make law through Parliament will be reduced.

There is much debate about the impact that the Human Rights Act will have on British law. The British government has already introduced a number of measures to amend legislative provisions which it is thought might not be Convention-compliant; the Regulation of Investigatory Powers Bill 2000 is an example. Many lawyers are contemplating arguments about whether some aspect of British law does or does not offend against the principles of the European Convention. A number of the judiciary have, in lectures and other contexts, indicated that they look forward to hearing arguments about the impact of the Convention on English law.[34] The fact that such matters will be able to be raised directly in the British courts will certainly mean that in the short run there is likely to be a great deal of attention paid to the provisions of the Convention and the jurisprudence of the Court. What the long-term impact will be is harder to gauge.

THE EUROPEAN UNION

Although being a signatory to the European Convention on Human Rights has had an indirect impact on United Kingdom law-making, the accession of the United Kingdom to the European Economic Community in 1973 has had a direct impact on the English legal system. Ever since it became a member of the European Union, there has been an obligation on the United Kingdom to incorporate within its legal framework the rules of law prescribed by the institutions of the European Union: the European Commission, the European Council of Ministers,[35] and the European Parliament.

The essential purpose of the European Union is to create a huge free market for the provision of goods and services throughout the area of the EU. In order to achieve this, European law seeks to provide a framework within which trade between the countries of the EU can fairly take place. Thus, for example, the EU provides a framework for the promotion of competition and the regulation of anti-competitive

---

[33] Above p. 34.

[34] See Sedley, Sir Stephen, *Freedom, Law and Justice* (London: Sweet & Maxwell, 1999).

[35] Although in the formal descriptions of the EU there is only one Council of Ministers, there is in fact a substantial number of Councils of Ministers reflecting the different portfolios of those ministers, for example, agriculture, foreign policy, economic matters, trade matters, and the like. The supreme Council of Ministers is that which comprises the leaders of the governments of the Union, brought together to determine the most fundamental issues affecting the EU.

practices.[36] It aims to liberalize industries, such as telecommunications or the airline industries, to allow greater freedom of consumer choice. It seeks to prescribe EU-wide standards for the manufacture of goods, in order to protect consumers, and to try to ensure that industry overheads are broadly in line. Examples include European standards on the manufacturing of automobiles or the quality of food labelling.

In addition to trade policy, the EU also seeks to promote human rights, and tries to support measures for social cohesion. Thus certain common standards of social security provision for workers are set down, as well as entitlements for citizens of one country in the EU to work in other countries of the Union. There are specific rules relating to measures of employment protection, including safety at work, and the prohibition of discriminatory employment practices, particularly those based on gender, race, or ethnic origin.

The existence of law-making powers in the institutions of the EU means that, at least in those areas covered by the treaties that established the EU, British law-making institutions no longer have exclusive power. In the language of common political debate, the 'sovereignty of Parliament' has been diminished. This fact of modern political life causes much heated argument.

In recent years there has developed within the EU an emphasis on a different principle—that of 'subsidiarity'—designed to ensure that the European institutions exercise their law-making powers only in relation to those matters which are truly essential to the working of the aims and objectives of the Common Market. Other, subsidiary, matters are to be left to the national law-making bodies in each of the Member States. It is beyond the scope of this work to assess the extent to which adoption of the principle of subsidiarity has in fact reduced the amount of law-making activity undertaken in the institutions of the EU. But the tension between law-making bodies in the United Kingdom and those outside should be noted at this stage.

The law-making processes of the EU are extremely complex. They are not at all like the Parliamentary processes familiar in the United Kingdom Parliament. Under the European treaties, the European Commission has the exclusive right to initiate proposals for legislation. Whether or not those proposals then become law, and if so in what terms, depends on the outcome of a complex process of negotiation and consensus building between the Commission, the Council of Ministers, and the European Parliament. The nature of the exercise is more like the legislative system in the USA, where the President proposes legislation, and the Congress decides whether or not it passes into law.

A number of technical points need to be made about the different types of law that emerge from the EU institutions.

First, all the institutions of the EU draw their ultimate authority from the treaties that underpin the establishment of the EU.[37] These may be regarded as the *primary*

---

[36] The content of the Competition Act 1998 has been greatly influenced by the demands of EU law and policy.

[37] In particular, the Treaty of Rome, the Single European Act, the Treaty of Maastricht, and the Treaty of Amsterdam.

legislation of the EU. While many of these fundamental provisions of Community law are designed to deal with obligations between States, some have been held by the European Court of Justice to have 'direct effect' in the determination of individual rights and duties. For treaty provisions to have this effect, the content of the provision must be clear; the provision must be self-executing, in the sense that it imposes a specific duty; and the provision must not contain any conditions or qualifications.[38] There are many European Court of Justice decisions which have held particular treaty articles to be of direct effect; for example Article 81 (formerly Article 85),[39] which outlaws anti-competitive agreements, or Article 141 (formerly Article 119), establishing the principle of equal pay between men and women.

Secondly, where a treaty provision is found to be of direct effect it may be both vertically and horizontally effective. 'Vertical' effectiveness arises when an individual uses a treaty provision to challenge an act of the government or some other public body; 'horizontal' effectiveness arises where one individual or other body wishes to use EU law to challenge the behaviour of another individual body of similar status.

Thirdly, more detailed legislative measures which seek to implement the detailed policies of the EU can collectively be described as the *secondary legislation* of the EU. This emerges in three different guises: regulations, directives, and decisions.

Under Article 249 (formerly Article 189) of the treaty establishing the European Community, *regulations* are—like the treaty provisions considered above—of direct effect, that is to say they automatically become part of the internal law of each of the Member States of the EU. An example is Regulation 1408/71, which deals with aspects of social security law and the need to insure workers under a scheme of national insurance. As with treaty provisions, regulations may have both vertical and horizontal effectiveness.

Directives are somewhat more general in tone. They set down standards towards which Member States are required to aim, but some discretion as to the detail of how that is to be done is left to the Member States. Current debate about the implementation of the Working-Time Directive provides a good example. The principle of direct effect may, however, arise if there is a complaint that a government has failed so to incorporate the provision into national law. In the United Kingdom, directives are usually brought into effect in Statutory Instruments.

Decisions are rulings on particular matters addressed to either governments of Member States, corporations, or individuals. For example, an argument about whether a particular takeover bid was or was not anti-competitive would be the subject ultimately of a decision. Decisions are binding on those to whom they are addressed, (Article 249 (formerly Article 189)).

In addition to these forms of secondary legislation, the EU may also make *recommendations* and *opinions*, but these do not have any direct effect.

---

[38] O'Neill, A. and Coppel, J., *EC Law for United Kingdom Lawyers* (London: Butterworths, 1994).

[39] Following the adoption of the Treaty of Amsterdam, the treaties have been officially consolidated; the former number is however given for the benefit of those used to the old numbering.

THE COURTS

There are three main ways in which the courts—more particularly the higher courts—contribute to the development of English law:[40]

- *The development of common law.* England is a common law country. This means that many of the principal doctrines of law were first established, not by Parliament, but through cases determined in the courts.

- *Statutory interpretation.* The courts also play a very important role in the interpretation of the statutes that Parliament has enacted.

- *Procedural law.* The courts also make important contributions to the development of procedures which the courts follow.

THE DEVELOPMENT OF COMMON LAW

It may seem odd today, but the power of the judiciary to make law was for many years denied by them to exist. Judges were said merely to 'discover' the basic principles of the common law. No one seriously believes that now. It is recognized that judges do make law. However there is often unease as to the theoretical basis for this power. Certainly it cannot derive from any theory of democracy or electoral representativeness. Rather the power of the judiciary depends on the doctrine of the *separation of powers*, that to prevent dictatorial powers from being asserted, there must be checks and balances in the Constitution. The independence of the judiciary is at the heart of this separation, for it is the judges who have the primary task of ensuring adherence by ministers and other agents of the state to the principles of the *rule of law*. No specific legislative provisions gave the judiciary that power. Rather it is the assertion of this power by the leading judges over the years, and the place that they occupy in the structure of the government, that has resulted in the development of this fundamental judicial function.

The law-making powers of the judiciary are themselves supported by two other fundamental principles: the hierachical structure of the courts and the doctrine of precedent.

The hierarchical structure

The idea of the courts being arranged within a hierarchical framework is quite straightforward. The courts are organized on the basis of seniority (see Diagram 3.1); the higher the level of seniority, the greater the authority of the court. Thus the

---

[40] It should be stressed that not all courts are seen as having the authority to make law; only the higher courts have this function.

Diagram 3.1 An outline of the court structure in England and Wales

decisions of the House of Lords[41] are the most authoritative; the Court of Appeal comes next in line; the High Court level third. Decisions of courts at lower levels than these are not regarded as having any value as precedents, though very occasionally the judgment of a county court judge on a novel point of law may get reported. (On the importance of law reporting, see Box 3.6.)

There have been occasions on which this hierarchical structure has been challenged, most notably by the late Lord Denning when, as Master of the Rolls, he was the senior judge in the Court of Appeal. He was of the view that since most appeals ended in his court and did not proceed to the House of Lords, therefore his court

---

[41] Although the name is the same, the House of Lords sitting as a court is quite distinct from the House of Lords acting in its legislative capacity. The judges in the House of Lords can take part in debates in the House of Lords, but they sit 'on the cross benches'—outside the control of any political party—and by convention usually intervene in debates on law reform or the administration of justice.

should have similar law-making power to the House of Lords. His arguments did not prevail, though they do provoke a broader question: do we need all the levels of court, in particular all the levels of appeal, that currently exist?

The doctrine of precedent

This is also a simple idea, though not always an easy one to apply in practice. The essence of a precedent is that a principle of law, established in one case, must be applied in a similar situation in a later case. Indeed, such a rule of law will continue to be applied either until another court decides that, for some reason, the case was incorrectly decided, or for some other reason cannot be allowed to stand; or until a court higher in the hierarchy overturns the decision; or until Parliament decides to change the law by passing a new Act of Parliament which has the effect of overruling or otherwise altering the rule that has been laid down by the court.

There have long been arguments for and against the use of precedent. Against, it is argued that precedent introduces unnecessary rigidity into the law thereby preventing legal doctrine from developing as society develops. In its favour, the use of precedent is said to bring certainty to the law by enabling people to know how any issue in the future might be resolved. The principle of law in one case which forms the precedent is known by the Latin phrase, the *ratio decidendi*. Any part of a judgment that does not form part of the *ratio* is not part of the precedent, and thus not relevant in later cases. These are referred to as *obiter dicta*.

There are many reasons why this apparently straightforward principle can be exceptionally hard to apply in practice.

(1) The facts on which the ratio of one case is based never replicate themselves exactly in a later case. Thus lawyers wishing to argue that a particular precedent does not apply to the later case will seek to *distinguish* the two fact situations, thereby, they hope, rendering the earlier decision irrelevant.

(2) Given the large number of reported decisions, there may be cases where a decision reached in one case was so reached in ignorance of other relevant decisions. The argument will thus be made that the precedent in question was made incorrectly or, again to use the Latin, *per incuriam*.

(3) Again resulting from the very large number of cases that are now reported, there may simply be two inconsistent decisions in the law reports so that a straightforward application of a particular decision to a new situation is just not possible.

(4) Since 1966 the House of Lords has taken to itself the authority, in very exceptional circumstances, to change its mind and alter a precedent. It may therefore, on occasion and notwithstanding the existence of clear precedents, decide that earlier cases were wrongly decided and that the doctrine should now be changed.

There are also more technical reasons why the doctrine of precedent is not always simple to apply in practice. It may actually be very hard to decide what the precedent is. When the House of Lords found[42] that a manufacturer of ginger beer was negligent after it allowed a decomposed snail to enter the ginger beer bottle, was this a case about not allowing snails into ginger beer bottles? Or about not allowing foreign bodies in general into manufacturing processes? Or was it about the care which any person—including a professional person giving advice to a client—should demonstrate in preparing that advice? In short, what was the 'level of generality' at which the particular instance of snails in ginger beer bottles was to be treated in future cases?

Even if a principle of law which can be derived from the cases is clear—such as the principle of negligence, that one person owes a 'duty of care' to his 'neighbour'—who will be categorized for these purposes as a neighbour? And what will be the standard of behaviour that will result in a conclusion that the duty of care has been broken? If teachers take a party of teenage pupils to the seaside, and one of the pupils is washed out to sea by a freak wave, were the teachers in breach of a duty of care to the pupil who drowned in those circumstances? Or did that fault lie with the pupil who ignored advice and went clambering onto the rocks from which he was swept?

Much of the litigation that arises out of the principles of the law of negligence is not seeking to redefine the principles of the law, but rather exploring the extent to which those principles will be applied in new situations of risk. This is not the place for a detailed analysis of the law of negligence. The point to be stressed here is that, even though at one level the law may be quite clear, the situations to which the law may be applied in future can be far from clear.

STATUTORY INTERPRETATION

Statutory interpretation is another way in which it may be said that those courts that have authority within the hierarchical structure of the courts are able to develop the law. The work of the courts when interpreting statutes may not be as dramatic as when they develop principles of common law, as they clearly have to work within a framework that has been prescribed by Parliament through the legislative process. Nevertheless the interpretative process can lead to clear development in the meaning of words in statutes, and thus in the implementation of those statutory rules. (For a particular example, see Box 3.5.)

The scope for the development of the power of the court to interpret statutes will inevitably increase once the Human Rights Act 1998 is brought into force in October 2000. This will have the effect of giving the power to the British courts, not just to interpret legislative provisions but also to test the substance of legislative provisions against the standards laid down in the Human Rights Act, which derive from the articles of the European Convention on Human Rights. In cases where the courts find that they must declare a statute or provision within a statute to be incompatible with

---

[42] In *Donahue v. Stevenson* [1942] AC 562.

Box 3.5   STATUTORY INTERPRETATION: THE CASE OF MR FITZPATRICK[43]

In English housing law, a tenant is entitled on death to pass on his right to occupy premises to a 'member of his family'. The question has arisen in a number of cases over the last fifty years: who is a member of the family? Initially, in the 1940s, it was held that the phrase was limited to blood relatives only; thus the former mistress of a deceased tenant could not take over the tenancy, despite having lived together for many years. Later, in the 1960s, it was held that, with changes in the nature of relationships and society's attitudes, the mistress of a deceased male tenant could in such a circumstance be regarded as a member of the family and thus take over the tenancy.

Most recently, in 1999, the House of Lords decided that the long-standing homosexual partner of a deceased tenant could similarly take over the tenancy. The judges found that, in terms of love and affection and thus the attributes of family, a distinction could no longer sensibly be drawn between a couple of the same sex living together and a couple of the different sex. Reference was made to the provisions of the European Convention on Human Rights which creates a right to respect for a person's private and family life (Art. 8).

This case illustrates that, even within a single statutory framework, there can be scope for the development of the law to reflect changes in social practices and attitudes.

the Convention—thus in effect requiring ministers to change the law—the courts will have acquired a significant new power to develop English law.

One question that may be asked is: why—if Parliament has passed legislation—should there be any need for the courts to intervene at all? There are two basic reasons why this needs to happen: the unpredictability of fact situations and the ambiguities of language.

The unpredictability of fact situations

However detailed the provisions of statutes or statutory instruments may be, they can only set down legal principles at a certain level of generality. There will always be those whose particular situation is not captured *precisely* by the legislative provisions. In such cases the facts will need to be determined by the courts—in itself not always a straightforward task—and once this has been done, a judgment reached as to whether or not the relevant legislative provision covers that situation. Particularly where legislative provisions seek to impose some burden or penalty on the citizen, there is a general judicial policy that this should not happen unless those provisions quite clearly 'bite' on the individual circumstances concerned. To give one example: the 'tax avoidance industry' is dedicated to the careful and detailed analysis of the provisions

---

[43] *Fitzpatrick v. Sterling Housing Association* [1999] 3WLR 1113.

of tax legislation to see whether there are arrangements which can be reached whereby those who might otherwise have to pay tax may—quite legitimately—be able to avoid paying it.[44]

Many of the apparently pedantic points that may be taken in some criminal trials are, similarly, the result of the principle that a person should not be able to be convicted of a crime unless the factual situation that has been established in the court is quite clearly caught by the relevant statutory provisions.

The ambiguities of language

The other justification for the role of the courts is that the meaning of language is not itself precise. There may be ambiguities arising from the way particular rules have been drafted. There may be differences in the meaning of words chosen. Some statutory provisions are often deliberately drafted using words such as 'reasonable' or 'fair' which do not have a precise meaning and which therefore give scope to officials and others for the exercise of discretion or judgment. There may be changes in the meaning of a word (see Box 3.5) resulting from broader developments in society.

There is, in the literature on statutory interpretation, a set of principles—rather inaccurately described as 'rules'—designed to be of assistance. These include:

- the literal rule;
- the golden rule;
- the mischief rule; and
- the 'unified common approach'.

The *literal rule* is what it implies. The words of a statute should be given their literal meaning. This does not avoid the problem of linguistic ambiguity.

The *golden rule* suggests that the courts should use the literal rule unless this would lead to manifest absurdity.

The *mischief rule* asks the judge to consider what was the legislative purpose of the act—what was the 'mischief' the act was trying to deal with. Any question of interpretation should be resolved in such a way as not to thwart that purpose. The problem with this view is: how does it relate to the concept of the independence of the judiciary? If the mischief rule is rigidly adhered to, does this not result in the judges losing their independence and doing the government's job for it? On the other hand, if the legislative intention is wilfully ignored by the judge, how does that square with the constitutional principle that the primary law-making authority should rest with the democratically elected Parliament, not the unelected judiciary?

It will be quickly appreciated that these principles are not consistent with each other; indeed they offer great scope for reaching different conclusions. The reality is

---

[44] The distinction between tax avoidance, which if successful is lawful, and tax evasion, which is clearly unlawful, should be noted. In recent years governments have become increasingly adept in their attempts to thwart the tax avoiders. Tax incentives—schemes which attract tax advantages and are part of the government's fiscal policy, e.g. tax relief on pension premiums—are quite different.

Box 3.6 LAW REPORTING

An essential part of the ability of the courts to develop principles of common law or to give authoritative interpretations of statutory principles rests on the publication of law reports—which contain the reasoned judgments prepared by judges in particular cases, from which general principles may then be drawn.

Decisions as to which cases get reported are not, in general, taken by members of the judiciary themselves, but by editorial teams responsible for the publication of law reports. Very many sets of law reports are now published. Maintaining a complete library of all sets of reports is a very expensive business, only possible for the best endowed university libraries, the libraries of the Law Society and the Inns of Court, and the most prosperous law firms.

It should be stressed that the production of law reports is not seen as a function of government (though some government departments do in fact publish the text of decisions in specialist areas, such as taxation cases, and immigration appeal reports).

The most authoritative of the generalist sets of law reports are those published by the Incorporated Council of Law Reporting, who publish a range of reports, including: Appeal Cases (decisions of the House of Lords), the Queen's Bench Reports; and the Chancery Division Reports. The Council also publishes the Weekly Law Reports. Other sets of law reports available are published by commercial publishers. The most widely available generalist set is the *All England Law Reports*, published by Butterworths.

In addition there is a wide range of specialist reports available in areas ranging from local government to housing, from education to family law, from criminal appeals to judicial review. Indeed it is now hard to think of sub-specialisms in legal practice that do not have their own sets of law reports.

Legal electronic data bases

In addition to reports in paper format, there is now an increasing tendency for law reports to be published in electronic format. For many years a vast electronic data base, *Lexis*, has been available providing full-text versions of decisions from a range of the most senior courts. The use of these reported cases as precedents has, however, been limited by the refusal of the judiciary to take into account judgments that only appear in the *Lexis* format. If they have not been reported elsewhere, in printed form, they have not been usable.

The internet

A more recent development has been the appearance of a range of decisions on the internet. Reports from the House of Lords and the Court of Appeal are now so available. One change is that, for those who have access to the internet, the costs of obtaining the report of a particular case are limited to the costs of going on-line and printing the text. The provision of the report itself is at the present time free.

> *The future*
> There seems little doubt that the balance between the use of reports in paper format and electronic format will change in the years ahead, particularly as the judges themselves are both provided with and become more adept at using computers. The fundamental principles of hierarchy and precedent are however unlikely to change.

that different judges favour different approaches; and indeed individual judges are themselves not consistent.

The *unified common approach* is a label that seeks to provide a broader, less specific label to the process. It implies that a judge should start by considering the literal meaning of the words; but if they are really not clear, or would lead to absurd results, then the judge should consider what the purpose of the act was and interpret the act so as to advance that purpose.

The inference should not be drawn from this discussion that the bases on which the judiciary interpret legislation are so varied that there is no principle at all. Reading the reported judgments in decided cases reveals that those judges in the higher courts whose decisions get reported go to great lengths to try to ensure that their decisions are founded in rationality and principle. But that there are different approaches cannot be denied, and the inevitable consequence is that different judges will, as a consequence, reach different decisions in individual cases.

PROCEDURAL LAW

A third way in which the judges may be said to make law is by the development of new procedures. A number of examples may be briefly mentioned:

- The day-to-day practice of litigation is regulated by rules of practice which are drafted by the judiciary—the Rule Committee—acting under legislative author-ity. Many of these rules of court are supplemented by Practice Directions, also made by the judiciary. (See Chapter 8.)

- The rules of evidence—what evidence is or is not admissible in a court of law—has to an important degree been developed by the judiciary, though it is sup-plemented by very important statutory provisions, for example the Police and Criminal Evidence Act 1984 or the Civil Evidence Act 1991. (See Chapter 5.)

- A number of powers of the court are asserted on the basis of what it claims as its 'inherent jurisdiction'—the High Court's powers of wardship over children may be given as an example. (See Chapter 7.)

- Perhaps the most important judicial development of the last generation has been the shaping of the rules and practice relating to judicial review, which goes to the heart of the powers of the judiciary to render government departments and other public bodies legally accountable for their actions. (See Chapter 6.)

THE EUROPEAN COURTS

The European Union has, as one of its constituent bodies, the European Court of Justice, which sits in Luxembourg. The Council of Europe has the European Court of Human Rights, which sits in Strasbourg. Both courts have played a significant role in the development of the jurisprudence of, respectively, the European Union and the European Convention on Human Rights.

It is hard to summarize the 'European' approach of the judges in these courts, though it is the case that the legal instruments of both the European Union and the Council of Europe are drafted more in the relatively broad-brush European continental tradition, than the British very linguistically precise tradition. As a consequence the approach of judges in the European Courts has been to decide cases, very much bearing the purposes of the relevant treaty provisions in mind. The British legal mind often regards this as a rather distinct approach. Perhaps more accurately it may be said to represent something of a hybrid between the common law and statutory interpretation. Decisions of the European Court reflect features of the development of legal principle found in the case-by-case common law tradition. At the same time, these developments are set within a legal framework of treaty and other provisions which have emanated from the institutions of the European Union and the Council of Europe.

OTHER SOURCES OF LAW-MAKING

At the end of a lengthy account, the existence of other sources of law-making will be mentioned only briefly.

LOCAL AND REGIONAL GOVERNMENT

Local government has long had power to make by-laws—in effect a form of tertiary legislation (see above Box 3.2)—since by-laws are made under the authority of Acts of Parliament, but apply only in the area of the local authority in question. Present discussion about regionalization and the creation in England of bodies of regional government may eventually lead to additional forms of regional legislation. In addition under the terms of the Scotland Act, the Scottish Parliament has been given authority to pass legislation in areas within its competence, a privilege currently denied to Wales. There are also potentially powers of independent law-making available in Northern Ireland, though at the time of writing their continuance was in doubt.

OTHER INTERNATIONAL INSTITUTIONS AND BODIES OF INTERNATIONAL LAW

We have considered the Council of Europe and the EU in context above. Many other international institutions also have an impact on detailed rules of English law. There are many industries, for example, aviation or telecommunications, where at least some of the legislative framework results from the provisions of international treaties. Increasing globalization of economic activity combined with increasing pressure to deal with some of the major issues of the day—the environment, genetic engineering, global warming—is likely to result in this trend developing.

It is also relevant to note the existence of a separate body of private international law—these are essentially rules of English law, but designed to assist in the international regulation of private law rights and entitlements.

CONCLUSION

Law-making is a key aspect of modern government. It is theoretically based in demo-cratic principle though by no means all the sources of law can be said to derive their authority from those principles. Law-making and other normative statements also occur in a variety of formats. This all makes for considerable complexity, which has increased enormously in recent years. It is unlikely that the ordinary person in the street is aware of more than a fraction of the legal regulation which in theory might affect her. It is fanciful to claim that ordinary people can be assumed to know the law. One of the challenges that faces the modern world is to explore ways in which new technologies may be used to transform the vast mass of legal information into legal knowledge that can actually be utilized by the ordinary citizen.

PART II

THE INSTITUTIONAL FRAMEWORK

4

SHAPING THE INSTITUTIONAL FRAMEWORK: THE ROLE OF GOVERNMENT

INTRODUCTION

One obvious respect in which the English legal system has changed over the years has been the increased assertion by government of its power to the shape the legal system. Central government provides funds not only for running the court services and publicly funded legal services, including paying the salaries and fees of the judiciary, but also for a huge array of other services which are part of or impact upon the legal system. The police, prison service, and administrative tribunals are just three examples. All governments are concerned with keeping levels of public expenditure under control and securing value for money. Inevitably, therefore, the involvement of government in the planning of the legal system and the delivery of legal services has grown. Any understanding of the forces of change within the legal system must today include an analysis of the role of government. The principal actors to be considered here are:

- The Lord Chancellor's Department;
- The Home Office;
- The Legal Services Commission (replacing the Legal Aid Board); and
- Other central government departments.

Lurking behind them is, of course, the Treasury, determined to control levels of public expenditure and ensure value for money in the provision of public services.

THE ROLE OF THE LORD CHANCELLOR'S DEPARTMENT

The Lord Chancellor's Department (LCD) plays the central role in the development of policy relating to the legal system. Uniquely in government, the chief minister—the Lord Chancellor—is not a member of the House of Commons but of the House of Lords. (This often leads to the criticism that his performance is less open to scrutiny by the elected Members of Parliament sitting in the House of Commons.) The LCD is a department that has grown very markedly in both size and importance in the structure of government. The days (in the 1920s) when its Permanent Secretary—the Head Civil Servant—was able to record that not one item of post had been delivered to the department are now long gone.

For many years the department was in some ways seen as a bit 'odd' in the overall government structure. in most government departments, lawyers are used as legal specialists advising on questions of law, drafting bills and regulations, and the like, rather than being closely involved in the development of policy. In the LCD the Permanent Secretary was required by law to be qualified as a practising lawyer. As a consequence he used to be perceived as slightly different from his counterparts in other departments. Recently this rule was abolished. The most recent appointment, Sir Hayden Phillips, is the first non-lawyer to be appointed to the post.

PRINCIPAL RESPONSIBILITIES

The principal responsibilities of the LCD fall into two broad categories.[1] First they are responsible for the development of substantive rules of law, particularly in those areas of law and social policy that do not obviously fall under the remit of any other government department. For example, the LCD is the lead department in the development of the law relating to the family, and also property law. Since this book is not dealing with substantive rules of law we shall not consider this function further, save to the extent it is relevant in Chapter 7.

Secondly, and of central importance to this book, the LCD is responsible for shaping the institutional framework within which the law is practised. It shapes policy relating to:

- procedures in the courts, in both criminal, civil, and family justice systems;
- the work and development of tribunals and the administrative justice system;
- the appointment and training of the judiciary, including lay magistrates and other judicial office holders (such as chairs of tribunals);
- legal aid and the delivery of legal services.

[1] For more detail, see the LCD Home Page: www.open.gov.uk.lcd/lcdhome.htm

Developments in the delivery of civil justice, following Lord Woolf's report on *Access to Justice*, is perhaps the most significant recent example (see Chapter 8). Plans for further developments were set out in the White Paper *Modernising Justice*.[2] The recent announcement of the review of the Criminal Justice system,[3] and the even more recent announcement of a major review of the Tribunals system are the next major steps in the modernization programme. Reflecting modern trends in government, much of the detailed implementation of these policies is now in the hands of specialist agencies, such as the Court Service, the Legal Services Commission (formerly the Legal Aid Board), and the Judicial Studies Board (see below). But it is the LCD that shapes the policy.

Although this is not a new development, the pace of change is much faster. The range of issues for which the LCD is now responsible is much wider than was the case even twenty or thirty years ago. It injects into the English legal system a dynamism that is often not fully appreciated—both in the sense of its not being understood by those outside the system, nor welcomed by those inside. The fact is, however, that many of the images of and preconceptions about law and the legal system referred to, if only by implication, in Chapter 1, have been swept away or radically altered by new policy initiatives from the LCD.

THE COURT SERVICE

One of the most important ways in which the LCD has been changed in recent years has been through the creation in 1995 of the Court Service—a governmental agency charged with responsibility for the efficient running of the courts. This development was part of an overall government strategy designed to give greater freedom to those who were running services to do so in a business-like fashion, leaving officials in the departments with responsibility for the evaluation of existing policy and the development of new policy. Its primary task—according to its official literature—is to provide appropriate administrative support to the judiciary. The Court Service is also responsible for delivering significant policy changes, such as the reforms to the Civil Justice system considered in more detail in Chapter 8. It may also take responsibility for promoting change. The publication by the Court Service of the consultation paper *Transforming the Crown Court: The Emerging Proposals*[4] is an example.

In common with other areas of government, the Court Service is now committed to the delivery of defined standards of service to those who come through the doors of the courts—whether as claimants, those defending claims, those appearing as witnesses, jurors, other friends and relatives, or general members of the public—standards unheard of only a few years ago. Many of the key tasks required of the

---

[2] *Modernising Justice: The Government's Plans for Reforming Legal Services and the Courts* (Cm 4155) (The Lord Chancellor's Department, December 1998).

[3] Being conducted by Lord Justice Auld.

[4] September 1999. This consultation exercise has been largely subsumed in the Auld review of the Criminal Justice system, mentioned above.

Court Service are those of administrative efficiency: dealing with people courteously; dealing with issues expeditiously but fairly; handling matters as economically as possible and seeking to reduce costs; and—in the civil courts—recovering from parties to proceedings the costs associated with the provision of court services.

The Court Service has also been engaged is a programme of administrative reform, including investment in computerization and new information technologies. This is not complete and indeed will take some time yet. But the implications, not only for the more efficient running of the existing system, but also for introducing fundamental change into the operation of the system are enormous. Computerization should help with very practical issues such as the listing of cases for hearing, and, more broadly, tracking the progress of cases through the system to ensure that they are not subject to unnecessary delay.

Increasingly sophisticated telecommunications and information technologies should also allow for routine proceedings to take place without the need for personal attendance at court. Professional lawyers could thereby be relieved from the need to waste time attending court on purely procedural matters. Parties to proceedings could similarly be allowed to 'attend' court from a distance. No doubt the presence of parties will still be required during trials; but a great deal of routine work does not require personal attendance in court. To impose such requirements merely wastes resources. Similarly there are experiments currently underway to enable more evidence to be presented through video links, thus making it easier for witnesses, who may be unable or reluctant to attend a particular court, to appear.

New forms of electronic data collection have great potential for reducing the amounts of paper that physically have to be brought to court for major trials. They also have the potential for considerably improving the library facilities available in courts to the judiciary—outside the principal courts these are often woefully inadequate.

As a result of these and other developments, the Court Service is also taking a strategic look at the location of its court buildings and their configuration. New modes of court working will entail new forms of court design, in particular to take advantage of the opportunities created by the increased use of technology.

MAGISTRATES' COURTS AND THE MAGISTRATES' COURTS SERVICE INSPECTORATE

The relationship between policy development and policy implementation in the magistrates' courts is more complex. The LCD provides the policy framework.[5] Implementation of the Magistrates' Courts Service takes place at the level of the local magistrates' courts and is the responsibility of Magistrates' Courts Committees (MCCs). Here, as with the rest of the court system, there has been a great deal of rapid change. (For the different types of magistrates' courts, see below Box 5.6.)

---

[5] The law on magistrates was recently consolidated into the Justices of the Peace Act 1997.

First, there is currently a programme of alignment of magistrates' courts boundaries so that they match those of the Crown Prosecution Service and the police. As a result, the number of MCCs is being significantly reduced (from 105 to 42), so that these committees become responsible for the management of magistrates' courts on the basis of larger geographical areas.[6] In addition, the government is creating a new magistrates' courts authority to cover the entire London area.[7]

Day-to-day management of the courts is now entrusted to Justices' Chief Executives,[8] a new statutory appointment. They have taken over many administrative responsibilities from justices' clerks, whose principal responsibility is to advise lay JPs on matters of law and procedure.[9]

The government is also planning to change the basis on which magistrates are empowered to deal with cases. At present they are appointed to 'commission areas' and may only deal with cases arising in their commission areas. An MCC that covers more than one commission area cannot at present transfer cases from one commission area to another. The government intends to ensure that the boundaries of commission areas should in general match those of the MCC areas. This should secure greater efficiency with better use of court personnel, magistrates, and premises. There may also be powers to transfer cases between commission areas in exceptional circumstances.[10]

In addition to these structural changes, the government has set common performance standards covering a variety of practical things such as reducing delays, ensuring that there are separate waiting areas for victims, witnesses, and defendants, and improving access for those with physical disabilities. The government is anxious that MCCs should where possible and practicable use the same systems and common services.

Monitoring of the outcomes of service delivery by MCCs is achieved by the Magistrates' Court Service Inspectorate (MCSI), a statutory body established in 1994.[11] It has now completed a first review of all MCCs. As might be expected, it found many examples of good practice in the delivery of service, but also worrying variations in performance—for example, fine enforcement. In some cases the MCSI found a disappointingly negative response to proposals for greater efficiency. In part this is the result of a lack of adequate infrastructure, in particular information technology. The coordinated computer system, Libra, will not be available throughout England and Wales until 2004. In part there is still a lack of understanding of how MCCs are currently expected to function—more like the management board of a company— which involves monitoring of the performance of their courts against defined targets and other performance indicators.

---

[6] Access to Justice Act 1999, s. 74.

[7] Ibid. s. 83.

[8] Justices of the Peace Act 1997 s. 40.

[9] Ibid. s. 45.

[10] Access to Justice Act 1999, s. 80.

[11] The Police and Magistrates' Courts Act 1994; the empowering provision is now found in the Justices of the Peace Act 1997, 62(3).

Recruitment

Recruitment of lay magistrates is undertaken, not by the MCCs, but by another set of committees which operate at the local level, the Lord Chancellor's Advisory Committees. They undertake a continuous programme of identifying possible candidates (in some areas through the placing of advertisements in the local press); shortlisting; interviewing; and making recommendations to the Lord Chancellor, who makes the final decision. Considerable efforts are made to ensure that there is a reasonable age spread, a good gender balance, representation of ethnic minority groups, and a representation of people with different political beliefs. Indeed, potential candidates are specifically asked about their political affiliations, not to screen out those who might be in opposition to the government of the day, but in order to try to ensure that a good spread of opinion—reflecting the wider society—is recruited to the Bench. Following the publication of a Consultation Paper in October 1998, the present Lord Chancellor has accepted that this may not be the best way to achieve the right mix of personnel and is looking for an alternative mechanism, possibly based on occupational groupings. The difficulty of devising such an alternative means, however, has led him to the conclusion that, for the time being at least, the use of political affiliation will continue.[12] The process of recruitment is far more open and founded on the principles of equality of opportunity than was the case some years ago.

Notwithstanding these changes, there can be difficulty in recruiting people in the younger age ranges, as employers may be resistant to their staff taking off the not inconsiderable amounts of time required to be a magistrate. The self-employed may find it hard to devote the required amounts of time to this work, particularly when their businesses are still developing. In some areas of the country, there have been difficulties in attracting sufficient numbers of volunteers of the right quality, able to take on the commitments of the role, both as regards requirements to be trained for the task and actually to perform the task by sitting in court. This has led to worries that the part-time lay justices are not as valued by government as they once were to deliver a localized system of criminal justice, and that there may be moves towards appointing more full-time salaried judges. This view, if widespread, would seem highly exaggerated. There are currently over 30,000 lay justices (1999 figure) as against just over 100 stipendiary magistrates (1998 figure); it seems unlikely that the lay magistracy will suddenly disappear.

Many of the changes noted above are very controversial, certainly at the local level. There is considerable *esprit de corps* in magistrates' courts. Many lay magistrates do not welcome changes in organization that they feel lead to reduced identification with a particular court or location. Nevertheless, the programme of change currently being implemented seems to strike a balance between the delivery of justice at the local level and the need for as much administrative efficiency as possible. It cannot be ignored, however, that at least one reason why the government likes the system is that the lay justices are all unpaid. Whether and for how long this tradition of public service will

---

[12] LCD Press Announcement, 329/99, 25 October 1999.

survive into the twenty-first century is at present a matter for speculation. Should recruitment difficulties get worse and demands for payment become more regularly heard, then the case for the retention of the lay bench may well weaken.

JUDICIAL STUDIES BOARD

The Judicial Studies Board (JSB) is another part of the English legal system that has been rapidly developed in recent years by the Lord Chancellor's Department, with the support of the judiciary. For many years, there was an assumption amongst many judges that they knew all that there was to know about law and legal process, and that therefore judicial training was unnecessary; some regarded it as impertinence to suggest otherwise. Notwithstanding this complacent view, there has long been an acceptance that some judicial training was needed. As early as the 1960s, judicial conferences were convened to try to tackle the particular issue of inconsistency in sentencing practices by the judiciary.

The scope of training for the judiciary was put on a more formal footing in 1979 with the creation of the Judicial Studies Board. Over the last twenty years the board has grown in size and stature and now delivers a very considerable programme of judicial training, not only to judges sitting in criminal trials, but also those handling civil trials, and to the chairs of a wide range of tribunals. It also sets the framework for the training of magistrates.

In delivering its programmes, the JSB provides both *induction* courses, which must be taken before a judge begins to sit, and *continuation* courses, which are offered on a three-yearly cycle. In addition to these regular programmes, the JSB also arranges special programmes. For example there is currently a special programme to introduce the judiciary to the Human Rights Act 1998, prior to its coming into force in October 2000. A special programme was provided, prior to the implementation of Lord Woolf's reforms to the Civil Justice system, on how the new system would work. Most controversial was the programme, in 1995–6, to provide ethnic awareness training to the judiciary—an issue which arose from perceived differences in the ways in which people from different ethnic groups might be treated in the courts.[13] (Following the Stephen Lawrence case, this remains an issue of very great importance for the work of the courts, as well as other actors in the legal system.)[14]

Besides course provision, the JSB also provides written guidance on the running of trials in *Bench Books*—looseleaf volumes of information that the judiciary keep beside them for easy reference while performing their judicial functions. Through its Equal Treatment Advisory Committee (formerly the Ethnic Minorities Advisory Committee) it has been developing advice and training for judges to ensure that parties to

---

[13] Hood, Roger, in collaboration with Cordovil, Graça, *Race and Sentencing : A Study in the Crown Court: A Report for the Commission for Racial Equality* (Oxford: Clarendon Press, 1992).

[14] Sir William Macpherson of Cluny, *The Stephen Lawrence Inquiry Report* (Cm 4262) (London: Stationery Office, 1999).

proceedings in courts or tribunals feel they have been treated equally and not subject to any form of discrimination.

In addition, the JSB has sponsored one or two more practical books, notably the *Guidelines for the Assessment of Damages in Personal Injury Cases*, designed to ensure greater consistency in reaching awards for damages in personal injury cases. It also produces a journal.

Finally, in situations where the resources of the JSB are unable to provide training directly, it nevertheless sets the framework within which judicial training should take place. The clearest example of this occurs with the magistrates. The Magistrates Committee of the JSB does not provide training to JPs directly, but sets the curriculum for such training, which is delivered at the local, MCC level.

The development of the role of the JSB is a fascinating example of the evolution of policy and its implementation. It has not developed out of high-profile parliamentary debate, or the enactment of special legislation. Rather senior officials in the LCD, working with influential members of the judiciary, came to see this as an important facet in the management of a modern judicial system. Pockets of resistance among the judiciary—which undoubtedly existed ten or fifteen years ago—have been replaced by an acceptance, reflected in professional life more generally, that continuing education is a proper, indeed essential, part of professional development. The newly appointed judiciary now expect training; and those in post acknowledge the need for opportunities to reflect on their work.

This is not to say that the model so far developed is perfect. The amount of training which English judges receive is still modest in amount. Unlike the situation in some other jurisdictions, there is no university law school which offers a specialist postgraduate diploma or degree in judicial science. There is always more that can and should be done. Nevertheless, the development of professional judicial studies has been one of the most significant developments in the English legal system in the past two decades. It has not attracted the public attention that it deserves.

THE LAW COMMISSION

The Law Commission was established by the Law Commission Act, 1965 to keep the law of England and Wales under review.[15] It is the most important standing body devoted to questions of law reform. Though independent in character, it falls within the overall responsibility of the LCD. The commission is chaired by a High Court judge, currently Mr. Justice Carnwath. He is assisted by four other commissioners, who in turn are assisted by a small team of research assistants and a small secretariat.

In carrying out its functions it does not attempt to review all the law all the time. Rather it determines, on a regular basis, programmes of work it intends to carry out. At any one time, the commission will be engaged on between twenty and thirty projects, at different stages of development. The main areas of law on which the

---

[15] There is a separate Law Commission for Scotland.

commission works are included in law reform programmes approved by the Lord Chancellor. They include contract, the law of landlord and tenant, the law on transfer of land, criminal law, family law, trusts, the law relating to mentally incapacitated adults, judicial review, and damages. In addition the commission works on other law reform projects which have been referred to it usually (but not exclusively) by the government.

Its mode of work is to start by careful analysis of the existing law, including, where relevant, consideration of how other countries have dealt with the issue in question. It then drafts a preliminary consultation paper setting out a statement of the existing law, explaining why that area of law needs reform, and indicating its preliminary views on which it seeks the comments from members of the public. Having received and reflected on these comments, the commission then develops its ideas into firm proposals for the reform of the law. It will frequently commission the drafting of a bill designed to 'capture' the outcome of these policy formulations.

However, the mere fact that this stage in the law-making process has been reached by no means guarantees that the bill so drafted becomes law. It still has to go through the Parliamentary process discussed in Chapter 3. And no further progress can be made if Parliamentary time cannot be found. Only about two-thirds of the commission's proposals for reform have reached the Statute Book.

In addition to developing specific proposals for law reform, the commission also engages in longer term exercises in codification, consolidation, and statute law revision.

Codification. In most countries whole areas of law are contained in a single code rather than, as in England, being divided between the common law, which is derived from decisions of judges made over the centuries, and statute law enacted by Parliament. It has always been the commission's objective that English law should similarly be governed by a series of statutory codes, to make the law more accessible to the citizen and easier for the courts and litigants to understand and handle. For instance, in family law much of the commission's work has resulted in the production of what is in effect a code, though contained in a series of separate Acts of Parliament. More particularly, since 1968 the commission has had in hand a project to produce a criminal code, such as exists in almost every other country in the world. In 1989 the commission published a Draft Criminal Code and has now embarked upon a programme to produce a series of draft bills, based on the code but incorporating appropriate law reform measures, which will in themselves make substantial improvements in the law. If enacted, these bills will form the criminal code which this country has lacked until now.

Consolidation. In addition to reform projects, the Law Commission also undertakes consolidation exercises, bringing together into a single statute, law that may have become, as the result of considerable amendment by Parliament, highly fragmented.

Statute law revision. The commission also engages in a process of Statute Law revision which involves the repeal of obsolete legislative provisions, many going back hundreds of years. Since 1965, over 5,000 measures have been removed from the Statute Book as a result of this work.

RESEARCH

Unlike many of the other large spending departments, the LCD had until recently a very poor record for research. Specific policy-related research projects were commissioned from time to time. But policy initiatives too often derived from anecdotal evidence, pressure from individual influential judges or groups of judges, powerful professional bodies such as the Law Society and the Bar Council, or the ideas or even prejudices of government ministers or Members of Parliament. It is only over the last three to four years that there has been within the LCD a defined Research Secretariat with control over a (modest) budget dedicated to the development of specially commissioned policy-related research. Initially all the research was carried out by academics or other research agencies on a research contract basis.[16] Recently it was announced that the department will supplement this effort by the creation of an in-house research unit involving the recruitment of researchers to work within the department itself.

Although this research effort does not compare with, for example, the Home Office or the Department of Social Security, at least the LCD is now seen as engaging in a process familiar in other government departments. (Of course, all the research in the world will not help if ministers do not believe that research is needed for the development or non-development of a particular policy. The belief that 'prison works' is often held by Home Secretaries, despite extensive evidence to the contrary.)

It must be right in principle to attempt to develop policy that is going to affect the lives of large numbers of people on the basis of hard information rather than soft anecdote. The present government is very properly committed to the principle of 'evidence-based' policy development. This is very important for the central government, and one that it may be anticipated will develop further in the coming years.

THE ROLE OF THE HOME OFFICE

The other government department that is a major player in the shaping of the institutional framework of the English legal system is the Home Office. It has a central role in relation to the development of the Criminal Justice system. The detail of this is considered further in Chapter 5. However, much of the drive for increased efficiency within the Criminal Justice system, leading to significant changes to the ways in which criminal processes operate, derives from Home Office initiatives.

---

[16] The LCD has been responsible for opening up significant relationships with the academic and research world, which has benefited both the department and the research community. The role of the Socio-Legal Studies Association in these developments has been crucial.

Current proposals to alter the circumstances in which an accused may exercise the right to trial by jury is just one policy initiative driven by the Home Office, rather than the LCD.

Unlike the LCD, which has a relatively focused portfolio of activity, the Home Office has an exceptionally wide remit. In addition to the Criminal Justice system, the Home Office also takes a lead responsibility in relation to a number of other issues which have an important impact on law-making and the role of law in England and Wales. These include: electoral processes; the proposed Freedom of Information Act; data protection legislation and practice; race equality and anti-discrimination legislation; human rights; and the making of local authority by-laws.[17] The Home Office also controls policy development in a number of areas which impact on the system of administrative justice (see below Chapter 6), the most obvious example being that of immigration and asylum.

One of the challenges facing those whose job it is to manage government is to try to ensure that government presents a more or less coherent view of the world. 'Joined-up government' is one of the motifs of the current administration. This is much harder to achieve in practice than the outsider might think. Departmental 'cultures' are a very strong influence on the development of policy and practice and there can be significant 'turf wars' between different government departments. While there are constant calls for better coordination between different parts of the government, these are not always delivered in practice, or not without substantial political impetus. In the context of the English legal system, the Home Office/LCD interface is one where the need for coordination is crucial. Even here, arrangements are not always as coordinated or as harmonious as they should be.

LEGAL SERVICES COMMISSION (FORMERLY LEGAL AID BOARD)

In addition to the role of government in the shaping of the institutional framework within which the law operates, government has also played a crucial role in shaping the delivery of legal services. This is another topic to be considered in more detail later (Chapter 10). The changing framework for the development of policy and provision of legal services may be noted here.

A statutorily based legal aid scheme, which paid fees to lawyers to provide legal services to the poor or those of moderate means, was first introduced in 1949, with the passing of the Legal Aid Act 1949.[18] Initially the scheme was modest in scope,

---

[17] For further detail see the Home Office Home Page: www.homeoffice.gov.uk/

[18] There was a long history of initiatives prior to this development. An excellent account is in Abel-Smith, Brian, and Stevens, Robert, with the assistance of Brooke, Rosalind, *Lawyers and the Courts: A Sociological Study of the English Legal System 1750–1965* (London: Heinemann, 1967).

covering only legal representation in civil cases. Gradually however, during the 1960s and 1970s, the scheme was extended to cover the provision of legal representation in criminal trials, the provision of legal advice and assistance generally, and more specifically for those detained in police stations.

Throughout this period, the LCD made the policy, but the delivery of that policy was by the Law Society. Advice on how the scheme might be improved was offered by the Lord Chancellor's Advisory Committee on Legal Aid and Advice. In addition a number of increasingly influential external pressure groups sought to argue for changes to the scheme, principally through extensions of the scheme. The role of the Legal Action Group was particularly significant.

During the 1980s, voices were increasingly heard that the administration of legal aid by the Law Society—in effect the lawyers' Trade Union—was not wholly proper. Although the Law Society's legal aid work was wholly separate from the normal functioning of the Law Society, there was a danger that the legal aid scheme might be perceived as being run primarily for the benefit of lawyers, rather than members of the public.

In 1989, fundamental reform of legal aid was introduced when the administrative role of the Law Society was ended and replaced by the Legal Aid Board.[19] During the 1990s, the Legal Aid Board developed a number of radically different practices relating to the delivery of legal aid services. For example, the Board introduced a scheme for the 'franchising' of firms of solicitors, whereby they had to demonstrate defined levels of expertise and practice management in relation to the provision of legal aid— in effect, they had to promise to deliver a quality service.

The importance of this development can hardly be overstated. One of the greatest challenges which the Law Society faced in the 1970s and 1980s was devising means to ensure that all members of the legal profession were in fact up to the job of providing quality legal services. The Law Society was unable to achieve this; but—within its defined parameters—the Legal Aid Board did so; it proved very uncomfortable for many practitioners.

As a result of the passing of the Access to Justice Act 1999, the Legal Aid Board was abolished and replaced by the Legal Services Commission, which will have responsibility for two new schemes: the Criminal Defence Scheme and the Community Legal Service. More detail is provided in Chapter 10. While the concept of 'legal aid' was abolished, the new framework builds on the pre-existing legal aid scheme. The changes being made are evolutionary rather than revolutionary in character. But a number of important new principles, not least that certain 'lay agencies' may be able to attract public funding for the provision of certain types of legal service, reinforce the importance of the Legal Services Commission in shaping legal services delivery in the English legal system.

---

[19] Legal Aid Act, 1988, Part II.

OTHER GOVERNMENT DEPARTMENTS

The impacts of other government departments on the legal system are less focused than the examples given above but are nonetheless considerable. Their influence emerges most clearly in considering the shape and extent of the Administrative Justice system (Chapter 6 below). The development of tribunals, inquiries, ombudsmen, and other mechanisms for the resolution of complaints is driven by initiatives from a large number of different government departments.

It is here, perhaps, that the incoherence of government can be most clearly seen. For example, a policy in relation to the development of a tribunal sponsored by one department may be quite at odds with that being developed by another department. Basic questions about the management of tribunals; the role of clerks within tribunals; the appointment of the personnel to tribunals; whether or not they should be full-time; whether or not they should be paid, and if so how much, are all answered differently by different departments. Indeed, unlike the situation with the Criminal, Family, and Civil Justice systems, there has been no tradition of government even trying to develop a coherent strategy for the Administrative Justice system.

At one level this lack of coherence may be a good thing. It enables different practices and processes to be tried. One can argue that the Administrative Justice system provides a test-bed for experimenting with different types of dispute resolution procedure. It may also be argued that each part of that system has a specific task to do, and that therefore there is no need for any overarching framework.

Nevertheless, the LCD is slowly beginning to assert some leadership in this area with the recent creation of a section charged with the development of policy relating to administrative justice. It is likely that, over the coming years, the LCD will emerge as the primary source of ideas for reform and change, as it has done in the other justice systems. However, this will not occur rapidly. And the impact of the tensions between the different cultures of government departments, alluded to above, will be felt even more acutely in this area of activity, unless very clear political leadership is given and a desire to take administrative justice seriously is made manifest.

OTHER STRUCTURAL ISSUES

Despite the pace of change, there are still many important outstanding issues on which there is much current debate.

A Ministry of Justice? The most fundamental issue is whether primary responsibility for the administration of justice should remain, as at present, in the Lord Chancellor's Department, or whether, as is common in many other countries, there should be created a Ministry of Justice, with a minister directly accountable to the House of

Commons. The retention of the Lord Chancellor may seem rather anachronistic, notwithstanding reform of the House of Lords currently in progress. On the other hand, there may be advantage in separating the operation of the courts and the work of the judiciary from day-to-day party political debate.

I am not convinced that practices and procedures could not be developed, even with the chief Minister for Justice becoming accountable to the House of Commons, to ensure the continuation of the fundamental principle of the independence of the judiciary, while at the same time making the operations of the legal system subject to greater Parliamentary accountability. It is arguable that the efficiency of the system might be enhanced by greater interest from Members of Parliament.

Regulation of the Profession. Another of the unresolved issues is the extent to which the LCD should be responsible for standards of professional service delivery by practising lawyers. One of the claims of any professional organization is that they should be able to regulate such standards themselves. But there has been increasing criticism that self-regulation of the legal professions is not working satisfactorily. Currently the Law Society's Office for the Supervision of Solicitors, which deals with complaints against solicitors, has been the subject of fierce attack, not only from politicians but also from other consumer organizations, leading ministers to suggest that government may have to intervene. In both the Courts and Legal Services Act 1990, and the Access to Justice Act 1999, the government has taken powers to intervene in the regulation of the practising legal profession. (See further below, Chapter 9.)

The proper extent of this intervention is extremely controversial. It is important that the legal profession is 'independent'. Too close a regulation of professional activity by government can, and in other countries has, lead to pressure on lawyers not to undertake work that government would not like to see undertaken. On the other hand, one of the ways in which the public today expects governments to act is through the creation of frameworks to guarantee the quality of goods and services. This may be the basis for a way forward—government setting the framework for quality control, but leaving it to others to implement and police that policy. (To an extent the Legal Services Commission has begun to tackle this issue, at least in relation to the provision of publicly funded legal services.)

The appointment of judges. Another controversial area focuses on both the basis for the appointment of judges and the procedural steps for their appointment.[20] Again significant developments have occurred in recent years. (See Box 4.1.) The criteria for appointment, which were once secret, have been in the public domain for at least fifteen years. Most judicial appointments now follow the publication of advertisements inviting applications for judicial appointments. More recently, an annual report on the process has started to be published. There is more transparency in the system than there was a few years ago. And there can be absolutely no doubt that, when it comes to making appointments, successive Lord Chancellors have

---

[20] JUSTICE, *The Judiciary in England and Wales: A report by Justice*, Chairman of Committee, Robert Stevens (London: Justice, 1992).

Box 4.1 APPOINTMENT OF JUDGES: THE REVIEW OF SIR LEONARD PEACH, 1999

In 1999 the Lord Chancellor invited Sir Leonard Peach to review the process of judicial appointments and selection of QCs. He noted that many of the LCD practices had, in recent years, developed in accordance with the best personnel management practice. Thus most judicial appointments were advertised; proper job descriptions and personal specifications had been developed; and there was a very comprehensive system of feedback, on request, to unsuccessful candidates.

In Sir Leonard's view the most controversial aspect of the process was the consultation process. He thought this required a visibility it currently did not have, to ensure that candidates could have confidence that information about them was well founded, and not based on hearsay. To improve the situation Sir Leonard recommended:

- that better value from the consultations would be achieved by a redesign of the consultee forms;
- that candidates should provide more information by way of self-appraisal; and
- that there should be greater opportunity for those who were perhaps not well-known in the main judicial centres to nominate consultees, whose views should automatically be sought.

Sir Leonard did not recommend, as some had argued, that the process should be removed from the LCD. Instead he suggested the creation of a post of *Commissioner for Judicial Appointments*, who would both provide an ombudsman facility for both disappointed individuals and organizations, and undertake a regular audit of applications on a sample basis of current procedures. These would be used to inform recommendations for improvements in process.

He agreed with the current practice that all appointments to full-time judicial office should be preceded by a period as a part-time judge. He strongly recommended that appointments as (part-time) Deputy High Court Judges—who form the pool from which appointments to the highest judicial office were usually made—should be subject to the same formal process of appointment as other part-time judicial appointments. He also recommended that an experiment in self-appraisal for certain (part-time) Deputy District Judges be extended to all part-time judicial appointments. Sir Leonard anticipated that full-time judges would become more drawn into personnel-related issues, such as appraisal and mentoring, which might require specific training from the Judicial Studies Board.

One of the very serious issues he addressed related to equal opportunities, both for women and for members of the ethnic minorities. He made a number of suggestions in this context: for example

- that advocacy experience should not be an essential element in court appointments, rather that experience of the trial and litigation process would be regarded as helpful; and

- that the LCD should be more pro-active in encouraging applications from different groups, for example by encouraging the spread of mentoring and work-experience schemes.

He made a specific recommendation that a disability, which might prevent a person serving as judge till the normal retirement age, should not be a bar to appointment.

Sir Leonard also made a number of more practical suggestions. For example, noting that Judicial Appointments was a big administrative task (in 1998–9, the LCD received 3,719 applications, held 1,423 interviews, and made 634 appointments) he suggested that better use could be made of 'reserve lists'— those who had been approved in principle but where a vacancy was not currently available. He thought this might lead to speedier appointments, particularly where—as sometimes happened in tribunals—vacancies could arise at fairly short notice, reflecting changes in patterns of tribunal use.

appointed to judicial office those with an extremely robust independence of mind and outlook.

Nevertheless, there is still criticism that too much of the process—the development of files about individuals, and the use of those files—is still too secret. It is said that this has the effect of limiting opportunities for appointment to the bench of women and of members of ethnic minority groups. While there have been changes in the balance of judicial appointments, trends which are bound to increase in the coming years, demands for more change, and in particular for the creation of a Judicial Appointments Commission separate from the LCD, are currently loud and will not be silenced by the Peach report. While movement towards a new appointments system outside the LCD will not be rapid, it may be guessed that it will eventually come.

One specific issue relating to the appointment of judges has arisen as a result of the enactment of the Human Rights Act 1998. In a decision in Scotland, *Starrs and Chalmers v. Procurator Fiscal*, determined in November 1999, it was held that part-time judges, who did not have full security of tenure, might not be seen as being fully independent of the Lord Advocate, as their advancement to full-time office was dependant on the Lord Advocate's recommendation. The Lord Chancellor has recently announced that, while not abandoning the use of part-time judges in both courts and tribunals, new arrangements should nevertheless be put in place to enhance their independent status. In future, therefore, part-time judges will be appointed for a period of not less than five years; where appointments are renewable, this will normally be automatic unless limited and specified conditions are met; removal from office will also be only on limited and specified grounds. These grounds will include: misbehaviour, persistent failure to comply with sitting or training requirements, and incapacity. In addition, appointments may not be removed because of changes in operational requirements or to provide for change to create opportunities for the making of new appointments. One particular casualty of the new arrangements is that the post of Assistant Recorder is abolished. All those currently holding that title will be made Recorders.

5

THE CRIMINAL JUSTICE SYSTEM

INTRODUCTION

As indicated in Chapter 2, criminal law is central to the relationship between law and society. It seeks to regulate behaviour; it provides sanctions against those who break those rules. It is intimately linked with key social policy objectives, such as the maintenance of law and order and preservation of the peace, the security of the individual, and the protection of property. It is also linked to other objectives—especially the protection of human rights and individual freedoms. Indeed, one of the great difficulties law-makers face when thinking about the development of rules of criminal law and criminal procedure is how to achieve a proper balance between the provisions of the criminal law and the preservation of liberty and the freedom of the individual. Furthermore, the boundaries of the criminal law change over time. They are not always set by the outcome of purely rational debate and argument; they also reflect the preferences, prejudices even, of politicians. The Criminal Justice system is that branch of the English legal system in which the criminal law is administered.

Any idea that the Criminal Justice system can be understood simply by looking at the work of the criminal courts can be quickly disabused by considering the wide range of agencies involved. They include:

- the police service;
- the Crown Prosecution Service;
- the Serious Fraud Office;
- other investigating/prosecuting authorities;[1]
- magistrates' courts;
- the Crown Court;
- the Appeal Courts;
- the Criminal Cases Review Commission;
- the prison service;

---

[1] For example, the Inland Revenue or the Health and Safety Executive (see Box 5.4).

- the National Probation Service for England and Wales;[2]
- the Criminal Defence Service;
- criminal injuries compensation for victims; and
- other victim and witness care services.

Together, the Criminal Justice system affects large numbers of people.[3] It is a substantial employer. It consumes a great deal of public money: around £12bn a year (or £200 for each man, woman, and child). Over half (£7.5bn) goes on policing, followed by the Prison Service (£1.8bn), criminal legal aid (£0.9bn) and the Probation Service (£0.5bn). These sums are not trivial; yet there is always pressure to spend more. Calls for increased expenditure have to be set in the context of these figures. Opportunities for doing things more cheaply need to be identified as well. The efficiency of the Criminal Justice system—to ensure that its social objectives are met, while at the same time keeping control of expenditure levels—is, as in other areas of social policy, a constant challenge for government.

The Criminal Justice system has been the subject of much political controversy, many official inquiries, and considerable change. To give just a few examples: a Royal Commission on Criminal Procedure reported in 1981; a further Royal Commission on Criminal Justice reported in 1993; and a new review of the criminal courts has just been announced. Nearly every year there is new legislation on some aspect of the Criminal Justice system. Some argue that the system is loaded in favour of those accused of criminal activity and against 'the interest of society at large'. Others point to serious miscarriages of justice and the need to protect the individual from wrongful involvement in the Criminal Justice system. The pace and scope of these changes pose serious and difficult questions about what the limits of government intervention should be. In the pages that follow, each part of the system is considered. First, though, we consider the social theories that underpin the Criminal Justice system.

[2] This is the title proposed in the Criminal Justice and Court Services Bill 2000, currently before Parliament. A proposal to change the name of the service to the 'Community Punishment and Rehabilitation Service' has been abandoned; however the names of the sentences that may be imposed by the courts is being changed. For example, a 'probation order' will become a 'community rehabilitation order' and a 'community service order' will become a 'community punishment order'. These changes are designed to ensure that supervision in the community is not regarded by offenders as a reprieve or a soft option, but a clear mode of punishment with consequences if there is failure to comply with the sentence imposed by the court.

[3] A longitudinal study carried out by the Home Office shows that 34% of *all* males born in this country in 1953 had, by 1993, received at least one conviction for a criminal offence of a more serious nature; the figure for females was 8%. Reported in Taylor, Rick, *Forty Years of Crime and Criminal Justice Statistics, 1958–1997* (London: Home Office, Research and Development Section, 1999).

THEORIES OF CRIMINAL JUSTICE

Just as the social functions of the criminal law may be seen to be quite diverse, so too are the different social theories or models that underpin the Criminal Justice system.[4] From the criminological literature, a number of 'models' of the Criminal Justice system may be identified. These include:

(1) The *due process* model, in which the primary social goal may be said to be 'justice', and where there is an emphasis on fairness, and the rules needed to protect the accused against error and to restrain the exercise of arbitrary power;

(2) The *crime control* model, in which the primary social goal is punishment, and where the focus is on ensuring that the police are able to obtain convictions in the courts;

(3) A *medical model* in which the emphasis is on the rehabilitation of the offender, giving decision-takers discretion to achieve this;

(4) The *restorative justice* model, in which the emphasis is on getting the offender to recognize his or her responsibility in committing the offence and to make amends to the victim;

(5) The *bureaucratic model* in which the emphasis is on the management of crime and criminal, and the efficient processing of offenders through the system;

(6) A *status passage* model, in which the emphasis is on the denunciation and degradation of the offender, involving a shaming of the offender, reflecting society's views of the offender;

(7) A *power model* in which the emphasis is on the maintenance of a particular social/class order, which reinforces that values of certain classes over others.

None of these models offers a uniquely 'correct' interpretation of the Criminal Justice system. The attractiveness of each model will vary, depending on the person looking at the system. The defence lawyer, or the defendant, will take a different view from the policeman, or the prosecutor, the victim, or the Home Secretary. Thinking about these models, however, both highlights the tensions and conflicts that—perhaps inevitably—exist in such a complex sector of the justice system. It also helps to identify the assumptions that are all too often left unstated in considering developments in the Criminal Justice system. The reader will wish to reflect, in the light of these models, on how recent developments in Criminal Justice fit into the models thus identified.

---

[4] The following is derived from the excellent book by King, Michael, *The Framework of Criminal Justice* (London: Croom Helm, 1981).

UNDERSTANDING THE CRIMINAL JUSTICE SYSTEM

To gain some overall understanding of the Criminal Justice system, it is necessary to break the total structure into more manageable parts. The approach adopted here is to look at the system in three stages:

- pre-trial stage;
- trial stage; and
- post-trial stage.

Each of these stages is further subdivided.

1. THE PRE-TRIAL STAGES

Before any alleged criminal gets anywhere near a courtroom, a number of very important preliminary steps will be taken, each of which may affect the outcome of the case, indeed whether a case ever reaches court at all. The following analysis of the stages that an allegation of criminal activity may go through before a trial is reached will not happen in practice as neatly as this; but it should help the reader see the overall structure of the Criminal Justice system more clearly. (See also Diagram 5.1.)

THE COMMITTING, REPORTING, AND RECORDING OF A CRIME

It may be obvious that the first step in any criminal process is that some criminal act should have been *committed*. However, by itself that will (save in the most exceptional circumstances) not be sufficient to launch any kind of criminal process. Unless the offence is *reported* to the authorities, either by the victim, or by some other person who has seen the incident, or has come to realize that some criminal activity has taken place, no further action will follow. (On criminal statistics, see Box 5.1.)

The agency to which most crime is reported is the police. But many other agencies also have criminal law enforcement responsibilities. For example:

- local authorities have particular responsibilities in the area of environmental pollution or public health;
- certain central government departments have responsibilities for investigating a wide variety of potential criminal activity—for example social security benefit fraud, tax evasion, and other types of fraudulent commercial activity;
- Health and Safety agencies have duties to prosecute breaches of health and safety legislation (for example unlawful emissions of radioactive material);

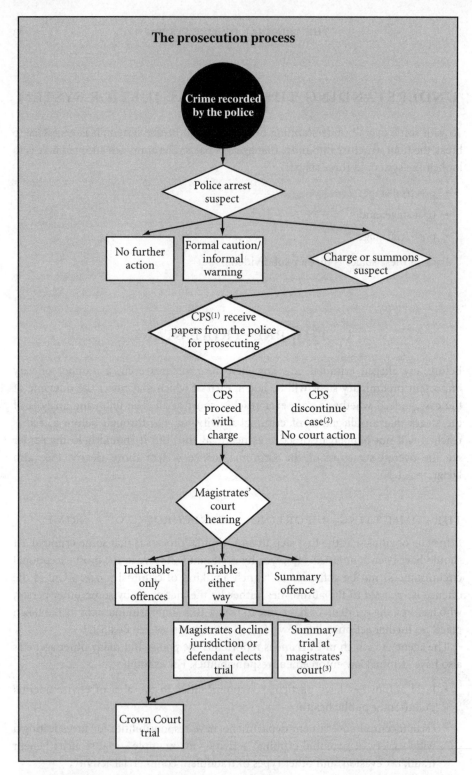

Diagram 5.1 (1) Although the majority of prosecutions are handled by the Crown Prosecution Service, certain offences are still prosecuted by the police, whilst some are by private organizations or government agencies such as the Inland Revenue. (2) A case will be under continual review, and may be discontinued at any stage before the hearing at the magistrates' court, or the prosecution may offer no evidence. In addition, the charge may be altered up to the final decision of the court. (3) Magistrates may commit to Crown Court for sentence.

- in very rare circumstances, an individual him- or herself may commence a criminal prosecution, but this is not common.

Indeed, although the police are the largest single player, the total number of criminal offences committed each year which are dealt with by bodies other than the police exceeds the total offences reported to the police. Nonetheless, for present purposes we concentrate on the role of the police.

Research shows quite clearly that, if the victim of a crime is unwilling to report a crime and to push the police to investigate it, then in all save the gravest situations no effective further action will be taken in relation to that alleged offence.[5] The initial act of reporting is crucial to any further action.

Furthermore, if the police are perceived as being unsympathetic in any particular context, then this may reduce the likelihood of alleged offences being reported. For example, some years ago the police were perceived—whether rightly or not—as being unsympathetic to female victims of alleged rape. The police took this criticism seriously and made strenuous efforts to demonstrate that this was not the case. Insofar as the criticism had validity, the police were determined to change their practices. At the time it could be predicted that the number of reported rape cases would increase. This has indeed happened over recent years. It may well be that the increase in numbers of alleged rapes is the result of more rapes occurring. But at least some of the increase is likely to be attributable to a more realistic pattern of reporting and recording, which brings more cases to the attention of the authorities.

Another example is domestic violence. There is a widespread assumption that the police are reluctant to get involved in domestic issues. Whether or not this perception is correct, it is very likely that the numbers of cases of domestic violence known to the police is considerably smaller than the total number of incidents that actually take place. Similar comments could be made in relation to the reporting of crimes which have racial implications.

Even if an alleged offence is reported, the police may not think that there is sufficient information to justify the *recording* of the alleged incident. If the matter is not recorded, no further action will be taken.

Finally, even if a crime is both reported and recorded, no effective further action will necessarily result. Many reports of petty theft, for example, are not taken further by the police—they do not have the resources to carry out the required investigations.

THE INVESTIGATION STAGE

Once a crime has been reported to the relevant agency (still using the police as the main example) the next stage is the investigation. In the case of major incidents this will involve the consumption of considerable resources with large numbers of police spending a lot of time on an investigation. In less important cases, the investigation stage may be extremely cursory. (There will be cases where the conceptually distinct

[5] Cretney, Antonia and Davis, Gwynn, *Punishing Violence* (London: Routledge, 1995).

Box 5.1 CRIMINAL STATISTICS[6]

One technical point needs to be made in this context. Most press reports about levels of crime are based on data published by the police of incidents of crime reported to and recorded by them. There are at least two problems with this data, as a measure of levels of criminality in the community.

First, as is the case with all data, its value is dependent on the quality of the input. I do not suggest that the police in any way deliberately fail to enter data correctly, though there is always the possibility of error in data collection. But some reporting practices may distort patterns of criminality. The thief who steals a crate of milk bottles from outside a front door may be recorded as having stolen one item (the crate); or twelve items (each individual bottle). In statistical terms this is a very considerable difference. There is also always some pressure on the police to relate their crime figures to arguments for resources. If they judge that more resources will be available to fight crime if trends are upwards, this may—even if only subconsciously—lead to an increasing trend in the figures; if they judge that success in reducing crime will be rewarded this might equally encourage a downward pressure on figures.

Second, the figures relate to reported and recorded crime. Many factors influence reporting and recording. For example if insurance companies insist on theft from cars or property being reported this may lead to an increase in the rate of recorded crime; conversely a relaxation in their practices may lead to a reduction in recorded crime.

It is not argued here that the figures for recorded crime do not reflect trends in criminality in the community. But there is a need to be cautious about drawing the simple conclusion, as is usually done in the media, that published statistics of recorded crime represents 'the crime figures'. It is more complex than that.

Corroboration of the points made here can be found in the *British Crime Survey*,[7] in which a sample of the population is interviewed about their experience of crime as well as the Criminal Justice system. Although this survey by no means covers the totality of the population, the sample of 24,000 people is drawn on the basis of accepted practices for creating social survey data bases. The conclusions to be drawn from the British Crime Survey are that a very different picture of criminality and the individual experience of crime can emerge when compared with the picture presented by the *Criminal Statistics*.

processes of reporting and investigating will in practice be blurred. The police may gain intelligence that a criminal act is being planned. This will lead to the investigation of the matter in advance of the commission of the offence. If the offence is actually committed, the preliminary intelligence gathering may also result in the gathering of

---

[6] These are prepared by the Home Office and published annually by the Stationery Office.

[7] This is also undertaken by the Home Office. The eighth such survey since 1982 is being carried out in 2000.

sufficient evidence to justify the arrest of the person or persons concerned and their being charged with the commission of an offence.)

For the criminal investigation bodies to be able to do their work, they need special powers. In the case of the police, their powers were the subject of major reform in 1984, with the enactment of the *Police and Criminal Evidence Act 1984* (PACE). The statutory powers of the police are accompanied by important *Codes of Practice*, which should also be observed by the police.[8] The principal powers enabling the police to carry out their functions are:

- the power to stop and search;
- the power to arrest;
- the power to detain;
- the power to question;
- the power to enter and search premises.

The precise order in which these powers are used in any particular case will naturally depend on the circumstances. The extent of police powers, how they are interpreted and applied by the police, and the balance between those powers and the liberty of the individual is a constant source of controversy.

Stop and search

The powers of the police to stop and search people or vehicles are contained in section 1 of the Police and Criminal Evidence Act 1984. The law provides that a constable must have reasonable grounds for believing that, by exercising his/her powers, stolen goods, or an offensive weapon, or a knife or other bladed or sharply pointed article, or articles adapted for use in burglary, theft or obtaining by deception, or a vehicle that has been taken without authority, will be found.

These general powers are supplemented by other powers to stop and search to be found in other specific Acts of Parliament—for example those relating to drugs, firearms, or alcohol at sporting events. The Criminal Justice and Public Order Act 1994, section 60 also created an extensive power to stop and search 'in anticipation of violence'. However this power may not be exercised unless a police superintendent has authorized its use in a particular locality.

In exercising these powers, the police are required to follow procedures set down in section 2 of PACE, which, among other things, requires the officer to give his/her name, state why the search is taking place, and to record that the stop and search has occurred (unless this is not practicable).

It will be appreciated that the language of the legislation gives considerable room to the individual police officer to decide whether or not the conditions for carrying out a

---

[8] There are 5 Codes of Practice: Code A on Powers of Stop and Search; Code B on Search and Seizure; Code C on Detention, Treatment and Questioning of Persons; Code D on the Identification of Persons; and Code E on Tape Recording.

stop and search are met. The exercise of the power has been controversial, in particular because of evidence that black people are more likely to be stopped and searched
than whites. (See Box 5.2.)

The power of arrest

Broadly there are two types of power of arrest—with warrant, and without warrant.

- An arrest *with warrant* takes place under the authority of a warrant issued by a
  magistrate. A warrant may be issued after information has been given to the
  magistrate, on oath, that the person named has or is suspected of having
  committed an offence.

- There are a number of powers to arrest *without a warrant*. PACE, section 24 gives
  the police (and other members of the public) power to arrest without warrant
  persons who have committed or are suspected of committing an 'arrestable

Box 5.2 STOP AND SEARCH IN LONDON

This is one of the most controversial of all police powers, not so much for the
power itself, as for the manner of its operation. The criticism is frequently made
that, in exercising these powers, the police tend to focus particularly on the
young, and more particularly on black youth. This has very considerable
implications for race relations and the effective policing of many urban areas.

The use of stop and search powers in London has been the subject of a recent
research report.[9] This seems to demonstrate that there is a link between the
exercise of the power of stop and search and levels of criminality in the community. In particular, it was found that the majority of arrests for possession of
offensive weapons and going equipped to steal were the result of the exercise of
stop and search powers. There was also a link between stop and search and
arrests for crimes relating to drugs.

The report found that there were problems in the ways in which the powers
were used, but that in general their use was supported by the public at large.

As regards the impact of arrests on particular ethnic groups, taking the Metropolitan Police area as a whole, the impact of the use of the power on different
ethnic groups was less than previously thought. Eighty-eight per cent of all
searches were in the 13–37 age group, and the ratio of those stopped and
searched was 1.6 black to 1.0 white; however in particular areas of ethnic concentration, the figures look rather different. The report argues therefore that
basic data on resident populations can be seriously misleading.

In short, there was evidence that if the police take a 'softly, softly' approach to
stop and search, levels of crime rise. The conclusion drawn is that, while the
power is an important one, it is one that must be used sensibly and with care.

[9] FitzGerald, Marian, *Final Report into Stop and Search* (London: Metropolitan Police, 1999).

offence'.[10] PACE section 25 also gives a power to arrest without warrant where 'general arrest conditions' are met.[11]

In addition, there are a number of specific powers to arrest without warrant under particular Acts of Parliament—for example the Mental Health Act 1983. Finally there is a common law power to arrest where a breach of the peace is taking place or is reasonably anticipated.

For an arrest to take place without a warrant, the person making the arrest must make it clear, by words or action, that the person arrested is under compulsion. The person arrested must be informed of the ground for the arrest, either at the time of arrest or as soon as possible thereafter or where it is not practicable to provide the information before the person to be arrested runs away. There is no legal power simply to detain persons for questioning without first making an arrest.[12]

An arrest is the first stage in a process that may eventually lead to a criminal trial. Research suggests that, despite the legal framework created by PACE, a very large number of arrests lead to no further action being taken, which raises the question of the extent to which police practice on arrest conforms to the legal rules relating to arrest.

Detention

Once a person has been arrested, that person may be detained in a police station to enable further investigation (including questioning of the person) to be carried out. One of the principal changes brought about by PACE was that a detailed set of statutory provisions was put in place to regulate the time a person could be detained in custody. Under Part IV of the Act, arrangements must be made for a police officer, known as the custody officer, to keep the detention under review. The police have, in general, 24 hours in which they must either charge the arrested person with an offence, or release the person, either with or without bail. Exceptionally, authorization for detention without charge for up to 36 hours may be given.

Once charged the person may be further detained and must be brought before a magistrates' court as soon as practicable. They will decide whether the person can then be released on bail, or remanded in custody.

[10] This is defined as an offence, such as murder, where the penalty is mandatorily fixed by law, or for which a person may be sentenced to a prison sentence of five years or more: in short the most serious offences. There are also a number of offences, e.g. indecent assault on a woman, which though not meeting these criteria, are defined as 'arrestable'—PACE s. 24(2).

[11] The 'general arrest conditions' include: that the name of the relevant person cannot be ascertained; that a name or address is not thought to be real or satisfactory; that the constable has reasonable grounds to believe that arrest is necessary to prevent the person causing damage to himself, or to others, or to property; committing an offence against public decency; causing unlawful obstruction of the highway; or to protect a child or other vulnerable person.

[12] In practice, this does happen. When a person is said, in a news bulletin, to be 'helping the police with their inquiries', this is an indication that they have not been arrested, but nonetheless 'persuaded' to attend the police station 'voluntarily'.

PACE also sets out in detail, in Part V of the Act,[13] provisions for the treatment of those who have been detained. In most situations, a person detained is entitled to have someone informed of that fact, and to have access to legal advice, which gives the right to consult privately a solicitor at any time. There are powers to delay these rights where this is thought necessary, for example to prevent evidence being destroyed. The statutory rules and Code also set out in detail the physical conditions in which people should be detained; these include details about the provision of drinks and refreshment.

Questioning

The powers to question suspects detained by the police are the subject of detailed guidance in Code C. The police regard the power to question as crucial, since in their view, questioning often leads to the suspect providing a confession, which in turn leads to considerable savings later in the criminal process, as many of those confessing will plead guilty.

There are two particular problems: 'induced' confessions; and false confessions.

Induced confessions are, as the name implies, confessions that have arisen from the police offering 'incentives' to confess—for example, early release of a suspect on bail, the suggestion that a confession may lead to less serious charges being made against the alleged criminal, or that in some other way the outcome will be less serious than it would otherwise be. Such inducements can colour the veracity of the confession.

Rules of evidence which operate in court are designed to ensure that induced confessions are not made, by preventing such evidence from being presented in court. Many police practices, for example the tape recording of interviews, or the requirement to issue a formal caution to those who might be charged with an offence, are designed to eliminate improper police behaviour. It seems unlikely that the police will never seek to induce a confession, for example in a location where there are no tape recorders. Furthermore the present form of the 'caution'[14] provides some incentive on people to make statements at an early stage.

False confessions are more problematic. Contrary to common sense and expectation there have been cases where a person being questioned by the police 'confesses' to a crime that he has not in fact committed. This can arise from the considerable pressure people are under when detained in a police station. This was one of the issues which led to the establishment of the Royal Commission on Criminal Evidence and Procedure in 1979.[15]

---

[13] Supplemented by *The Code of Practice for the Detention, Treatment and Questioning of Persons by Police Officers* (Code C) (London: HMSO, 1995).

[14] 'You do not have to say anything. But it may harm your defence if you do not mention when questioned something which you later rely on in court. Anything you do say may be given in evidence.' This form of words provoked much criticism when introduced as it was argued that it undermined the right of silence, one of the principal sources of procedural protection for the accused.

[15] See Irving, B., *Police Interrogation: A Study of Current Practice*, Research Study No. 2 for the Royal Commission on Criminal Procedure (London: HMSO, 1980).

Entering and searching premises

The last general power available to the police (and indeed other crime investigation agencies) is the power to enter and search premises for evidence, and where relevant to seize that evidence. Many specific Acts of Parliament give power to grant warrants to the police for particular purposes, for example, investigating drugs offences, or theft. Section 8 of PACE creates a general power enabling magistrates to grant search warrants for evidence relating to a serious arrestable offence. As with other police powers, these statutory provisions are supplemented by a Code of Practice.[16] Certain types of material are excluded from this provision, for example: items subject to legal privilege,[17] and certain other categories of excluded material.[18]

There are also circumstances where the police are empowered to enter and search premises without a warrant: for example to arrest someone suspected of committing an arrestable offence, or to save life and limb, or prevent serious damage to property.[19]

COMMENT

There can be no doubting the powers that the police have over the ordinary citizen. The range of powers, considered in outline above, may be seen to provide a sensible code, enabling the police to go about their business of investigating crime and catching suspects. Nevertheless, there are always concerns, backed by specific examples of police malpractice, which demonstrate that the police act beyond the powers given to them. This in turn means further controls on police behaviour to prevent the exercise of powers beyond the legally prescribed limits are essential.

Where examples of the planting of evidence, or the use of oppressive questioning techniques are demonstrated, some critics argue that use of illegally obtained evidence is endemic to police practice. Others, including the police themselves, argue that such abuses are simply the result of individual 'rotten apples' in the police barrel, and that so long as steps are taken to remove the rotten apples, the basic activities of the police are undertaken within both the letter and the spirit of the law.

The principal sanction for the police failing to act within the scope of their legal powers is that any evidence obtained improperly may not be able to be given in court. The police are aware that during the investigative/information gathering stage these rules of evidence will be applied should a case reach court and be contested. These rules should shape the ways in which evidence is obtained by the police. Failure to follow these rules can result in the evidence improperly obtained being declared inadmissible by the trial judge. (But as is noted later, the law of evidence gives judges

---

[16] Code of Practice for the Searching of Premises by Police Officers and the Seizure of Property found by Police Officers on Persons or Premises, Code B (London: HMSO, 1995).

[17] Principally communications containing legal advice from a professional legal adviser to his/her client.

[18] For example, personal records and journalistic records. There is a procedure whereby a circuit judge may be asked to make an order granting access to such material or in an extreme case to grant a warrant to search for this sort of material: PACE, s. 9 and Sched. 1.

[19] PACE s. 17.

considerable discretion as to whether or not evidence should be excluded.) In addition, failure to follow the Codes of Practice can result in disciplinary proceedings
being taken against individual police officers.

As in other aspects of professional and public life, there is now much more formal
accountability than was the case some years ago. The overall efficiency of police forces
is the responsibility of Her Majesty's Inspectorate of Constabulary. The creation of
the Police Complaints Authority has resulted in new mechanisms for individuals to
pursue grievances against the police. In addition, a number of cases are taken by
individuals against the police each year, for example seeking damages for false
imprisonment or damage to property.

Suggestions, made by some, that police activity is characterized by wholesale malpractice and corruption do not appear to be justified. Many who have incidental
brushes with the police find they operate strictly to the book and in a perfectly proper
fashion. However, it is also likely to be the case that there are more circumstances than
those which hit the headlines in which the police do not behave strictly according to
the book. There seems rather less doubt that, when relations between the police and
members of ethnic minority communities are in question, the police do not always
exercise their powers as they should.

NEXT STEPS

Once the first two stages are completed, the police have four choices (see Diagram
5.1). They may:

- take no further action, for example where insufficient evidence has been
  obtained;
- give an informal warning;
- issue a formal caution from a senior police office—this should only follow an
  admission of guilt and informed consent by the offender (or his/her parents or
  guardian in the case of a juvenile);[20]
- charge (or summons) the person with having committed a particular offence,
  and then refer the case on to the prosecuting authorities.

In practice very many reported and recorded crimes are dealt with in the first three
of the ways listed above. It is statistically much more likely that a case will end at this
point and not proceed to formal prosecution. Those who argue that the Criminal
Justice system should be based on the 'due process' model will realize that, in this
majority of cases, the formal protections of that model are effectively not available to
the accused.

If a person is charged with an offence, a further decision will then need to be taken
whether the person charged is to be detained in custody or released on bail. (See Box
5.3.)

---

[20] 60% of offenders under the age of 18 were cautioned for indictable offences in 1997.

Box 5.3 BAIL OR CUSTODY

A fundamental principle of the Criminal Justice system is that a person is deemed to be innocent until proved guilty. It is wrong to deny an innocent person his liberty. Yet consideration of the real world suggests that some accused of crime are simply too dangerous to be allowed to remain at liberty until any case against them has been determined. They have to be remanded in custody, either for their own good or for the good of society at large.

Decisions about whether to release someone on bail (i.e. subject to a requirement that they surrender to custody at a specified time and place) can be taken at any stage in the criminal trial process until the final determination of the last appeal. Thus bail may be granted by the police, magistrates' courts, Crown Courts, the High Court and the Court of Appeal (Criminal Division). The granting of bail, by whichever agency is involved, is subject to the principles laid down in the Bail Act 1976. The act creates a statutory presumption that bail should be granted unless specified circumstances exist which mean that bail should not be granted. These make it easier to justify remanding in custody persons charged with an offence that might result in a sentence of imprisonment, than those which would not. In some cases, there is no discretion. For example those charged with a homicide offence, or rape, or attempted rape currently cannot be released on bail if they have a previous conviction for such an offence.[21]

In practice the vast majority of those against whom criminal proceedings are taken are granted bail. Nevertheless there are those who argue that bail is granted too readily. In particular, there is disquiet about the numbers of crimes committed by people while they are out on bail. Notwithstanding these fears and the apparent policy of the Bail Act, numbers of those remanded in custody awaiting trial, or sentencing, or an appeal, have increased sharply over the years and have exacerbated the problem of prison overcrowding. This has led policymakers to consider other options, such as the electronic tagging of defendants so that the authorities can keep track of those persons even though they have not been detained in custody.

THE DECISION TO PROSECUTE

Even if a potential criminal investigation has reached the stage where a criminal act has been investigated, and a charge has been preferred against a suspect who has been arrested, or a summons has been issued against a suspect, there still remains the question of whether or not an actual prosecution will be taken forward. The decision whether or not to pursue a prosecution is taken, not by the police, but by staff

---

[21] In *Caballero v. United Kingdom*, the European Court of Human Rights, following a concession on the point made by the UK government, held that the automatic denial of bail was a breach of Article 5 of the European Convention on Human Rights (*The Times*, 29 February 2000).

employed in the Crown Prosecution Service (CPS). (For other prosecuting authorities, see Box 5.4.)

The CPS is a public service, headed by the Director of Public Prosecutions (DPP), and answerable to Parliament through the Attorney General. It was established in 1986, following enactment of the Prosecution of Offences Act 1985. Before then, the decision to prosecute was usually taken by the police themselves.[22] However, this led to the criticism that in some cases which had involved miscarriages of justice, the inter-relation of the investigation process and the prosecution process had resulted in the police exercising their powers to prosecute inappropriately. The Royal Commission on Criminal Procedure, which reported in 1981, recommended that there should be a separation of the investigation function from the prosecution function, to introduce an element of independence into the latter.

This was extremely controversial. There can be no doubt that, at least in the early years, the police in particular were very unhappy. The CPS was also confronted with many public challenges. It was said that they employed poor quality staff; their work was hampered by poor quality administration; and their decisions were often criti-cized. However, notwithstanding these early criticisms, the role of the CPS has been retained and there are now fewer complaints, at least in the mass media, about their role in the Criminal Justice system.

The basic procedure is that, after the police have investigated a crime, and charged (or summonsed) the suspect, they pass the papers to the CPS. One of their lawyers—a Crown Prosecutor—reviews the papers to decide whether or not to go ahead with the case. The prosecutor's decision is based on two tests set out in the *Code for Crown Prosecutors*: Is there is enough evidence? Is it in the 'public interest' to prosecute? A case has to pass both these tests before the CPS will start or continue a prosecution.

The evidence test

The prosecutor first sees if there is enough evidence to provide a 'realistic prospect of conviction'. This process requires an assessment both of the amount of evidence which is available, and also its quality—is it evidence which will be able to be put before a court? If there is not enough and the police say that there is no more evidence or no real prospect of any more becoming available, the case will be stopped. Nonetheless, the CPS will ask the police to look at the case again if more evidence should become available.

The public interest test

If a prosecutor thinks that there is enough evidence to start or continue a prosecution, she will then consider whether a prosecution is needed in the public interest. This means that the prosecutor must think carefully about all the factors for and against a

---

[22] There remain a number of instances where the decision to prosecute remains with the police and other prosecuting authorities. There are also a number of situations in which the decision to prosecute is taken by the Attorney General. The large bulk of decisions to prosecute are however taken by the CPS.

prosecution, and assess in each case whether a prosecution should go ahead. Some of the public interest factors which the CPS take into account are set out in the *Code for Crown Prosecutors*. For example, a prosecution is likely to be needed if:

- a weapon was used or violence was threatened during an offence;
- the motive for the offence was any form of discrimination; or
- the offence was committed against a person serving the public such as a police officer.

The CPS is required to act in the public interest, and not just in the interests of one person. Crown Prosecutors must always think very carefully about the interests of the victim of the crime. This is an important factor when prosecutors decide where the balance of public interest lies.

Notwithstanding the general approach of the CPS there are still cases where the CPS comes under heavy criticism, either from the police or from a victim (or her family). Particular problems arise in very emotive cases, which may have attracted considerable media publicity, where there is therefore a great pressure to prosecute, but where the evidence to satisfy the tests sketched out above may just not be there. In making their decisions, the CPS will not always reach conclusions that will attract universal approval.

The CPS employs a considerable number of staff who work in different parts of the country on a regional basis. There is also a group, known as 'Central Casework' who deal with especially important cases, such as deaths in police custody, cases involving the Official Secrets Act 1911, or cases involving terrorism.

Monitoring

Because of concerns about the consistency of the quality of the work of the CPS, an Inspectorate was established in 1996 to monitor the quality and consistency of decision-taking across the country, and to try to ensure the spread of good practice. Initially, the creation of the Inspectorate was the result of executive action; recent legislation has, however, put the existence and powers of the authority onto a statutory footing.[23] Particular incidents may, additionally, be the subject of special inquiry.[24] (See also Box 5.6.)

THE TRIAL STAGE

As will already be appreciated, there are many reasons why criminal offences do not all result in an offender being brought before the courts. Even when a case is so brought,

---

[23] Crown Prosecution Service Inspectorate Act 2000. This followed a recommendation in the Glidewell Report, *Review of the Crown Prosecution Service* (1998). The Inspectorate publishes an annual report on its work.

[24] See for example, His Honour Gerald Butler QC's report, *Inquiry into CPS Decision-Making in Relation to Deaths in Custody and Related Matters* (London: Stationery Office, August 1999).

Box 5.4 OTHER PROSECUTING AGENCIES

As noted in passing above, there are many other prosecuting agencies apart from the police. Local authorities, the taxation authorities, and the social security authorities are just some of the other public bodies that have the legal powers both to investigate criminal activities and to bring prosecutions before the courts. Limits on space prevent any detailed discussion here.

One particular agency, in relation to which a short note will be provided, is the work of the *Serious Fraud Office*. This was established by the Criminal Justice Act 1987.[25] Its establishment was designed to increase the capability of the authorities to investigate serious and complex fraud cases. The Director of the SFO is appointed by the Attorney General, and she works with a dedicated staff appointed by herself. In this area, the investigation and prosecution functions have been kept together. The Director and by extension her staff have wide powers to require those under investigation (and others believed to have relevant information) to answer questions and to furnish information. It focuses on the most serious fraud cases; other cases are pursued in the normal way through the Fraud Investigation Group within the CPS.

The workload of the SFO is not extensive but is very intense. For example, during the reporting year ending April 1999, it worked on the investigation or prosecution of 94 cases; but the total value of the sums involved was well in excess of £1bn. During the same year, 18 trials involving 38 defendants were concluded. The principal defendants were convicted in all but one of those trials.

the public image of what then happens is likely to be far removed from the typical case. The impression given in the news media or in drama series is that prosecutions result in full-scale trials in the Crown Court. The reality is quite different. The vast bulk of criminal trials are disposed of in the magistrates' court, and the vast bulk of them—both in the Crown Court and in the magistrates' court—are determined on the basis of a plea of guilty. The trial is a statistical rarity.

All prosecutions start in the magistrates' court. Whether they finish there depends on how the case is classified. (For classification of criminal cases, see Box 5.5.) The most serious cases—indictable offences—are forwarded ('committed') to the Crown Court for disposal. The vast majority of criminal cases—summary cases—are disposed of in the magistrates' court. Cases which are triable either way, i.e. either summarily or on indictment, are determined in the appropriate court, once a decision on the classification of the case has been made.

Criminal Trial Courts have two principal functions:

- dealing with the case, which includes determining guilt where the defendant has pleaded not guilty, as well as deciding on the correct sentence; and

---

[25] Following the *Report of the Roskill Committee on Fraud Trials* (London: HMSO, 1986).

Box 5.5 CLASSIFICATION OF CRIMINAL CASES

There are four potential classes of criminal case.

1. Offences triable only on indictment. These are the most serious cases, such as murder, manslaughter, and rape. If the defendant pleads not guilty, these cases must be tried in the Crown Court, before a jury.

2. Offences triable summarily. These are all offences created by statute, where the statute provides that they are summary offences. These cases must be determined by magistrates, and there is thus no right to trial by jury. There have been some attempts at reclassifying certain offences as summary only, in particular, small thefts; but political arguments about 'taking away rights to a jury trial' have made change difficult.

3. Offences triable either way. These are offences, also created by statute, where the act provides that they may be dealt with either summarily or on indictment. In such cases, the accused currently chooses how he wishes to be tried, before magistrates or before a jury. Opting for trial in the Crown Court exposes the accused to the prospect of more serious sentences, as the Crown Courts have wider powers of sentence than the magistrates' courts, though the latter can commit a case to the Crown Court where they think their powers of sentence are inadequate. (See further below.)

If the provisions of the extremely controversial Criminal Justice (Mode of Trial) Bill 2000 are enacted into law, the position will change. The decision on place of trial will be removed from the accused and given to the magistrates.[26]

4. Summary cases triable on indictment. In specific cases an accused may have a charge that he has committed a summary offence 'tacked on' to a charge that he has committed an indictable offence. These can now both be dealt with in the same trial in the Crown Court.[27]

• ensuring that, so far as possible, the trial is fair.

They may also have to deal with other procedural questions, such as whether or not to grant bail or remand a person in custody. (See above Box 5.3.)

Dealing with the case

In cases where an accused person has pleaded not guilty, the court has to hear the evidence, in the light of that evidence reach findings of fact, in the light of those findings determine whether the accused person is or is not guilty of the alleged crime,

---

[26] A measure recommended by the Royal Commission on Criminal Justice, 1993, and the Review of Delay in the Criminal Justice System, 1997. A *National Mode of Trial Guidelines* will be issued to assist magistrates in their decision-taking. At the time of writing the bill had been withdrawn from the House of Lords, where it had started its progress, and the government had re-introduced the measure in the House of Commons.

[27] Criminal Justice Act 1988 s. 40; see also s. 41.

and if found guilty, pass an appropriate sentence. In the magistrates' courts, all these functions are performed by the magistrates. In the Crown Court, the findings of fact and thus the question of guilt are determined by the jury. However, before the jury starts its work, it is provided with a 'summing-up' of the case by the trial judge, an exercise designed to help the jury focus on the issues they have to decide. If a conviction results, then, subject to further pleas in mitigation and reports on the accused from other agencies such as the Probation Service, sentence is by the presiding judge.

Although many think that the function of the court is to determine the truth about the events that have led to a person appearing in court, in practice the function of the trial is rather different. The prosecution must prove 'beyond reasonable doubt' that the accused committed the offence alleged. The function of the defence, therefore, is to throw sufficient doubt on what the prosecution is alleging so that the burden of proof is not discharged. If that burden of proof is not discharged, the defendant must be acquitted.

In cases where the defendant pleads guilty, the only issue for the court, again subject to pleas in mitigation made on behalf of the accused, and other reports, e.g. from social workers or probation officers, is to determine sentence.

Ensuring the fairness of the trial

Fairness is at the heart of the 'due process' model of Criminal Justice. A great deal of the law of criminal procedure and evidence is designed to ensure that the accused gets a fair trial. It is, however, in this context that many of the tensions between the due process model and the crime control model may be seen. A number of initiatives have been taken in recent years which have shifted the balance from the former to the latter. The question is whether the balance has now gone too far. The full detail of the relevant law is beyond the scope of this book. However two examples will be briefly considered: evidence and disclosure.

Evidence. The law on criminal evidence is designed to ensure that only relevant material is put before the court and to prevent material being put before the court which would be unfairly prejudicial to the defendant. Among the rules which exclude evidence in a criminal trial are:

- *the rule against hearsay evidence.* In general, only evidence given by witnesses in court is admitted. What others said to a witness cannot be admitted, as the person who made the statement cannot be challenged (cross-examined) about its veracity;

- *the rule preventing the giving of information about a person's past record.* In general, it is not permitted to tell the court about the person's history, particularly criminal record, unless the accused wishes to challenge the veracity of a prosecution witness, say a policeman.

- *the rule relating to 'similar fact' evidence.* The fact that a person may have been involved in some other activity similar to the events in the present case is not usually admitted, since it is seen as not directly related to what the prosecution has to prove in the instant case.

Many of these rules are not absolute, and judges and magistrates have to exercise judgement as to whether the exceptions to the rule operate in the particular case so as to allow evidence that would otherwise not be admissible to be admitted.

In some circumstances, there are precise rules of law which relate to the admissibility of evidence. For example, where it is proposed to rely on a confession, section 76 of PACE requires the prosecution to demonstrate beyond reasonable doubt that the confession was not made by oppression of the person who made it, or as a result of inducements made to the person giving it which might render the confession unreliable.

Section 78 of PACE also gives the judge/magistrate a general discretion to exclude evidence that would otherwise be admissible and relevant 'where the admission of the evidence would have such an adverse effect on the fairness of the proceedings that the court ought not to admit it'. Evidence obtained by the police in breach of the rules relating to questioning and interrogation can fall into this category.

The coming into force of the Human Rights Acts 1998 may well result in further judicial pronouncement to ensure that the rules of criminal evidence and procedure conform to the provisions of the European Convention on Human Rights, in particular Article 6, which is designed to ensure the right to a fair trial.

Disclosure. A separate issue relates to the question of what evidence should be disclosed by the prosecution to the defendant and vice versa. (See Box 5.6.) One of the

---

Box 5.6 DISCLOSURE OF EVIDENCE

The Royal Commission on Criminal Justice was appointed in 1991 against a background of cases where there had been clear miscarriages of justice: the 'Guildford four', the 'Maguire seven', the 'Birmingham six', and the Judith Ward cases are amongst the best known. In addition, the courts in a number of cases had been developing the (then) common law relating to disclosure. The result had been to place increased responsibility to disclose on the police, which at the same time provided opportunity to the defence to mount fishing expeditions, to find out what information the police had. The Royal Commission sought to strike a balance between the duties of the prosecution and the rights of the defence. The Royal Commission proposed that there should be a new scheme for disclosure enshrined in statute, accompanied by a Code of Practice, or a more detailed Statutory Instrument.

In May 1995, the then government published a consultation paper, which led to the Criminal Procedure and Investigations Act 1996, which provides for the following scheme:

(a) The investigator (usually the police but not necessarily) is under a duty to preserve material gathered during the investigation and make available to the prosecutor material falling into defined key categories, plus a list of other material which has been acquired.

(b) The prosecutor is under a duty to serve on the defence the material on which the prosecutor intends to rely to found her case.

(c) The prosecutor is under a duty also to disclose certain material on which the prosecution did not intend to rely, which falls into specified categories or which would otherwise undermine the prosecutor's case. The act also provides that a list of non-sensitive unused material must also be provided. This is known as the 'primary prosecution disclosure'.

(d) The defence has to provide sufficient particulars of its case to identify the issues in dispute. Failure to disclose can be the subject of (adverse) comment during the trial. The act makes this procedure mandatory in trials on indictment, voluntary in summary trials. This is known as 'defence disclosure'.

(e) The prosecutor is then required to disclose any additional unused material which would assist the particular line of argument disclosed by the defence—known as the 'secondary prosecution disclosure'.

Any disputes about disclosure are to be resolved by the court in a pre-trial hearing.

The main features of the process are: (i) that it is statute based; (ii) that it puts the responsibility on the prosecution to decide what should be disclosed; (iii) that it requires, for the first time, that the defence should make disclosure of its case before the start of the trial.

The accompanying *Code of Practice* (made under the authority of Part 2 of the act) requires the appointment, in any criminal investigation, of an 'officer in charge', plus a separate 'disclosure officer' who will be responsible for the administration of the investigation, including the operation of the disclosure scheme. The 'investigator'—the police or other officer doing the investigation—is made responsible for retaining material gathered or generated by the inquiry. The disclosure officer prepares the schedule of unused material, together with a list of any sensitive material (e.g. relating to national security, or information given in confidence). The disclosure officer must send these schedules to the prosecutor, accompanied by copies of any material relating to the unreliability of witnesses or confessions, or containing any explanation by the accused for the offence. Once the defence statement is filed, the disclosure officer is to look at all the files again and draw attention to any which might assist the defence. He must then certify to the prosecutor that, to the best of his knowledge and belief, the duties imposed by the code have been complied with.

In a recent decision by the European Court of Human Rights, it was held where the prosecution withheld evidence because it was claimed to be immune from disclosure on the grounds of public interest, that the failure to put it before a trial judge so as to permit him to rule on the question of disclosure deprived an accused person of the right to a fair trial.[28]

It will be realized that the effectiveness of these arrangements depends to a large extent on the willingness of the particular individuals, on both the investigation and prosecution side, to operate the scheme in accordance with the statutory provisions and code of guidance. A recent report by the Crown Prosecution Service Inspectorate[29] gives a disturbing account of routine failures to follow the rules.

most significant causes of serious miscarriages of justice arises when the prosecution withholds evidence which it has acquired during the process of its investigation but which weakens the case which the prosecution is seeking to build against the accused. This was a central issue considered by the Royal Commission on Criminal Justice, which reported in 1993. As a result of, though not fully accepting, its recommendations, the former Conservative government introduced a new legal regime relating to disclosure, contained in Parts 1 and 2 of the Criminal Procedure and Investigations Act 1996. Disputes about whether or not documents should or should not be disclosed are also resolved by the court, at a pre-trial hearing.

MAGISTRATES' COURTS [30]

Magistrates' courts have a long history. They have a distinct character in that, although subject to nationally determined guidelines, they operate at a local level. They also depend very heavily on volunteer/lay persons to determine decisions. Much of the claim to legitimacy for the magistrates is that benches are composed of persons who come from the community affected by the alleged criminal activity. (For types of magistrates' courts, see Box 5.7.)

Functions

All criminal trials start in the magistrates' courts. In carrying out their judicial function, there are two distinct types of procedure which they control: *Committal Proceedings* and *Summary Trials*. In addition they have responsibility for enforcing non-custodial penalties, especially fines.

[28] *Rowe and Davis v. United Kingdom* (*The Times*, 1 March 2000).

[29] Crown Prosecution Service Inspectorate, *Report on the Thematic Review of the Disclosure of Unused Material*, (London: CPS, 2000).

[30] For an introduction to the principles on which magistrates' courts are managed, and on proposals to change that system, see above Chapter 4 pp. 66–9. The magistrates' court also has responsibilities in certain family matters. These are considered below in Chapter 7.

Box 5.7 TYPES OF MAGISTRATES' COURTS

There are two distinct types of magistrates' courts which operate in England and Wales: the *lay justices'* courts, and the *stipendiary magistrates'* courts.

Lay justices' courts are made up of (usually) three lay persons (i.e. persons with no specific legal qualifications) known as Justices of the Peace, JPs, who sit and determine criminal cases, with legal advice on their powers given to them by the *Justices' Clerk*, a specially appointed official who is legally qualified. JPs provide their services on a voluntary basis; they receive expenses, for example for travel and subsistence, and, where appropriate, can claim a loss of earnings allowance. Apart from that, however, they are unpaid. By far the majority of magistrates' courts are lay justices' courts.

Stipendiary magistrates courts are run by stipendiary magistrates, who sit on their own, rather that in panels of three. As their name implies they are paid a salary ('stipend') and are professionally qualified lawyers who will have been in legal practice before being appointed as a stipendiary magistrate. 'Stipes', as they are informally known, have, in the past, only sat in those areas of the country which have been designated by the government as areas which should have a stipendiary magistrates' court. These tend to be large urban areas, such as parts of London, Manchester, Liverpool, and so on. However as the result of a recent change in the law, they are now able to sit in any magistrates' court in the country, thus giving court managers greater flexibility in the use of this source of judicial manpower.[31]

Stipendiary magistrates are being 'rebadged' as *District Judges (Magistrates' Courts)*, a change of title designed to reflect their professional status as a judge.[32]

Committal proceedings

These take place where the nature of the case is such that it has to be tried in the Crown Court, either because it must be tried on indictment or the decision has been made, in the case of an offence triable either way, that the trial should be on indictment. The function of committal proceedings is to ensure that the magistrates are satisfied that there is a case for the defendant to answer. It used to be the case that committal proceedings were fully aired in the press and other mass media; but this led to the criticism that such publicity made it difficult to find members of a jury who had not heard about the case. The law was therefore changed; publicity to committal proceedings can only be given where the defendant permits this. It is only very rarely that magistrates find there is no case to answer.

In 1998, just over 75,800 cases were committed to the Crown Court for trial (down from over 91,000 in 1997). Much of this decrease is attributable to a change in procedure whereby accused persons are required to enter a plea—guilty or not

---

[31] Access to Justice Act 1999, s. 78 and Sched. 11.
[32] Access to Justice Act 1999, s. 78.

guilty—in the magistrates' court.[33] Thus those who would have been sent to the Crown Court for trial and who then pleaded guilty are still being committed to the Crown Court but only for sentence, not for trial. (On sentencing generally, see further below.)

Summary trials

All other prosecutions are dealt with summarily, that is to say by the magistrates themselves. In 1997–8 some 1.8m defendants were proceeded against in the magistrates' courts. The vast majority of prosecutions are dealt with in this way. And the vast majority of these cases are determined by a plea of guilty, rather than following a trial.[34]

Referrals for sentence

In all cases where guilt is established, whether or not there is a trial, the magistrates have to impose a penalty. The powers of magistrates to impose sentences are strictly limited. However they do have power to refer a case to the Crown Court where they think that their powers of sentence are inadequate in the particular case. The number of cases referred to the Crown Court has increased sharply in recent years, rising from around 11,500 cases in 1987, to nearly 30,000 in 1998. (Even in 1997 the figure was only 14,800.) The reason for this large jump is the result of the procedural change noted above which requires the accused person to indicate how he will plead (guilty or not guilty) before any decision as to which court should hear the case is made.

Fine enforcement

In many cases where the penalty imposed is a fine, the magistrates have to follow this up with enforcement proceedings.

Youth court

When dealing with young offenders, the magistrates' court is technically known as the *youth court*. (This is considered in Box 5.8.)

CROWN COURTS

Jurisdiction and organization

Crown courts are the forum in which the most serious criminal cases—cases tried on indictment—are disposed of. Crown Courts are divided into three tiers located in

---

[33] Criminal Procedures and Investigations Act 1996, s. 49 introducing the Magistrates' Court Act 1980, s. 17A.

[34] In 1997, 81% of cases taken to the magistrates' courts by the CPS pleaded guilty; 7% pleaded not guilty; and 12% were dealt with in the absence of the defendant: *DIGEST 4—Information on the Criminal Justice System* (London: Home Office, 1999).

Box 5.8 YOUTH JUSTICE

A vast amount of criminal activity is carried out by people, mainly men, at a relatively early age in their lives. 'Juvenile delinquency' and measures to try to deal with it—not, it has to be said, with conspicuous success—have been on the policy agendas of governments for many years. There have been major tensions between the desire to prevent juvenile crime and deal with those young persons found guilty of criminal activity, and the desire not to blight young lives unnecessarily by giving them criminal records which may prevent them entering the job market or otherwise disadvantaging them.

There have also been fierce debates about where the responsibility for youth crime should lie—with the individual, with their parent(s), or with the wider society which is said to fail to provide the educational and employment opportunities that might make them more productive members of society.

The issue was most recently reviewed by government in 1997, in the White Paper *No More Excuses*.[35] This has already led to two new Acts, the Crime and Disorder Act 1998, and the Youth Justice and Criminal Evidence Act 1999. These contain a number of new initiatives which have been put in place, not only to process young offenders (those under the age of 18) through the Criminal Justice system more quickly, but also to try to demonstrate to them the effect their actions have had on the lives of others.

The Crime and Disorder Act 1998, for example, saw the creation of *youth offending teams*—multi-disciplinary agencies brought together at the local level to devise effective programmes to prevent offending and re-offending by young people. Their work is kept under review nationally by a new Board, the *Youth Justice Board*. The Board is also responsible for funding offending prevention schemes.

In addition, the 1998 act replaced the non-statutory policy whereby police could merely decide to caution a young offender, with a new statutory 'final warning' scheme. The act provides that once an offender has received this, any further offence will lead to criminal proceedings in court.

When dealing with young offenders, magistrates' courts are technically known as *youth courts*. When sitting as a youth court, magistrates are subject to special procedural rules, designed to ensure that cases are dealt with as speedily as possible. Magistrates were also given a special range of sentencing options under the act of 1998. These included powers to make a *reparation order*,[36] an *action plan order*,[37] a *child safety order*,[38] and a *parenting order*.[39] These schemes

---

[35] Cm 3809 (London: Stationery Office, 1998).

[36] For example, requiring the offender to write a letter of apology to a victim, or to clean up graffiti, or repair criminal damage.

[37] A three-month programme of community-based intervention combining punishment, rehabilitation and reparation, designed to address specific causes of offending.

[38] Also known as a curfew order, to protect children under the age of 10 from the risk of involvement in crime. This might involve requiring the child to be at home at particular times or to stay away from certain people or places. The government is currently considering raising the age limit to 16.

[39] Which could require parents to attend counselling and guidance sessions, and to ensure their children attend school.

were introduced on a pilot basis initially, but are being extended to the country as a whole from April 2000.

For the most serious cases, a new sentence, authorized by the act of 1998, will be introduced from April 2000—the *detention and training order*, providing for a single custodial sentence for all 10–17 year olds.[40]

In addition, as a result of the Youth Justice and Criminal Evidence Act 1999, magistrates may refer first-time offenders to a *youth offender panel*.[41] This is intended to work with the young offender to establish a programme of behaviour for the young offender to follow. The programme is explicitly based on the theory of 'restorative justice', to ensure that the offender takes responsibility for the consequences of his offending behaviour; makes restoration to the victim; and achieves re-integration into the law-abiding community. Whether these objectives will be achieved is, as yet, too early to determine. It must also be questioned whether the theory of restorative justice is the only theory behind the new programme; other 'justice models'—including the 'crime control' and the 'bureaucratic'—appear to be in play as well.

about ninety centres around the country. These centres are further grouped into six circuits.[42]

- First-tier courts are courts in which High Court judges, circuit judges, and recorders sit. They have higher levels of security to deal with the most difficult prisoners. The full range of criminal work, together with High Court civil work (see Chapter 8) is dealt with in these courts.

- Second-tier courts are the same, though no civil work is conducted in them.

- Third-tier courts are presided over only by circuit judges or recorders.

The offences dealt with in the Crown Court are themselves divided into four classes, in directions given by the Lord Chief Justice.[43] The aim is that the most serious offences are dealt with by the most senior judges. Distribution of business is the responsibility of the presiding judges—judges specially nominated in each circuit to have responsibility for the efficient running of trial lists.

The Crown Court also has powers to sentence persons convicted in the magistrates' court, where the magistrates have decided that their own powers of sentencing are

[40] It replaces the sentences of a *secure training order* and *detention in a young offender institution*.

[41] The power to refer is only available in the youth court. A young offender tried in the Crown Court may, however, on conviction be referred to the youth court for sentence in a case where the trial judge regards that as appropriate.

[42] Midland and Oxford; North Eastern; Northern; South Eastern; Wales and Chester; and Western. The 'Old Bailey' is the name given to the Central Criminal Court in London, a Crown Court in the South Eastern Circuit.

[43] The latest amendment to the directions was made on 10 January 2000 (*The Times*, 18 January 2000).

inadequate. In addition, the Crown Court hears appeals from decisions of the magistrates' court.

Workload

Committals for trial. According to the latest *Judicial Statistics*, the Crown Court had just under 76,000 cases committed to it to be dealt with (a 13 per cent drop on the previous year's figure); it actually dealt with nearly 78,000 cases in the same period, thereby reducing the number of cases outstanding at the end of the year. Of the cases dealt with, only 27,000 were after a plea of not guilty—i.e. just over a third. However a considerable number of trials were 'cracked trials', that is cases originally listed for trial, but where the accused changed his plea from not guilty to guilty, very often on the day of the trial. There were over 17,000 cracked trials in 1998.

Of those pleading not guilty to all charges, nearly 64 per cent were acquitted; this represents nearly 20 per cent of the total number of defendants dealt with by the Crown Court during the year. Of these, only 35 per cent were acquitted as the result of a verdict of not guilty by the jury; 65 per cent were either discharged by the judge or acquitted on the direction of the judge. Of those convicted after pleading not guilty, 80 per cent were convicted by the unanimous decision of the jury; only 20 per cent were convicted on the basis of a majority verdict.

Committals for sentence. Nearly 30,000 committals for sentence were made; just over 28,000 were dealt with. This was a doubling of the previous year's figure, and was the result of the coming into force of the Criminal Procedure and Investigations Act 1996, which made the change to procedure in the magistrates' court noted above, p. 103.

Appeals. Just over 16,000 appeals from magistrates' courts were made, and a similar number were dealt with. Of these, 43 per cent resulted either in the appeal against conviction being allowed or in the sentence being varied. The rest were either dismissed (33 per cent) or abandoned, or otherwise disposed of (24 per cent).

Hearing times. The average hearing times were:

- for not guilty pleas, 9.4 hours;
- for guilty pleas, 1.1 hours;
- for sentence, 0.6 hours;
- for appeals, 1.0 hours.

Comment

- The most obvious point is that, as with magistrates' courts, trials following a plea of not guilty are a statistical rarity.
- A significant percentage of those who plead not guilty are ultimately acquitted, though far more are on the direction of the judge rather than by a jury verdict.
- The newspapers may give the impression that cases in the Crown Court take significant amounts of time, particular where there is a full trial. Although trials

take very much longer than other forms of disposal, on average they last only two sitting days.

- The 'success rate' in appeals might be seen as raising some questions about the quality of magistrates' decisions, though the total number of appeals is a tiny proportion of the total number of cases dealt with by the magistrates.

ISSUES IN THE CRIMINAL JUSTICE TRIAL SYSTEM

Charge and plea bargaining

The high level of guilty pleas in both the magistrates' and Crown Courts may suggest that the police and prosecution only allow the strongest cases to come before a court. But it might nonetheless seem surprising that in a system where the theory is that all are innocent until proved guilty, so few accused actually take advantage of the due process model of Criminal Justice and submit the evidence presented by the prosecution for testing before either the magistrates or a jury.

Of course there will be cases where the evidence is so overwhelming that a guilty plea is the only sensible option for the accused. But in less clear-cut cases, at least part of the answer to this puzzle arises from the fact that those within the Criminal Justice system work quite hard through various forms of bargaining to ensure that accused persons plead guilty. This saves considerable amounts of court time (as the statistics for average hearing times set out above clearly show) and thus expense and other resources. There are various practices which may occur to assist the accused in deciding what plea to enter.

First, there may be a negotiation between the prosecutor and the defence about the charge to be proceeded with before the courts. If the accused is willing or can be persuaded to plead guilty to a charge which carries a less severe penalty, the prosecution may then decide not to pursue an alternative charge which could arise from the same factual situation, which might attract a more severe penalty.

Secondly, there may be an indication that if a plea of guilty is entered, then, in passing sentence, the judge may reduce the sentence he might otherwise have imposed. Direct negotiations between defence lawyers and judges on sentence, commonplace in the USA, do not take place here. Further, the decision in R v. Turner[44] makes it clear that judges may not indicate the sentence he or she is planning to impose, nor indicate how that sentence might change were the defendant to plead guilty. However, at the end of a hearing, the Criminal Justice and Public Order Act 1994, s. 48(2) requires a judge to give reasons for any reduction in the sentence from what would be the normal expectation for the offence in question, taking normal sentencing guidelines into account. It is therefore known that in practice judges allow a discount of between 25 per cent and 33 per cent in cases where the defendant pleads guilty.

The formal legal position on these practices is that undue pressure must not be put

---

[44] [1970] 2 QB 321.

on defendants to enter any particular plea, as this may lead the innocent to plead guilty to a crime they did not commit. In other words, such practices do not fit with the due process model of the Criminal Justice system. The reality is, however, that justice is frequently negotiated, a practice justified for the added efficiency that it brings to the system, thus fitting the crime control model. The extent to which such practices should be condoned is the subject of considerable debate in the Criminal Justice literature.

Jury trial

A second issue of considerable current importance relates to the use of juries to determine the facts in Crown Court trials. There are three issues which should be considered separately. Are juries competent to decide cases? To what extent should the accused be entitled to choose trial by jury, in those cases where a choice is open to them? Should the classification of indictable offences (for which the right to trial by jury arises automatically) be altered?

The competence of juries. Jury trial is perceived by many as one of the great strengths of the English Criminal Justice system. There is an enormous literature on the jury, asserting its importance as a defender of civil liberty and a bulwark against oppression by the State. Indeed, the use of juries may be said to legitimate decision-taking in the Criminal Justice system by enabling decisions to be taken by ordinary lay people. This reinforces the independence of the judicial system in this context and thus fits with the constitutional separation of the courts from other decision-making bodies.

There have certainly been historically significant, if rare, cases where juries appear, despite the weight of evidence, to have acted on their conscience to protect civil liberty by finding persons not guilty of crimes which may be said to have significant political overtones. The example of the acquittal of Clive Ponting is often cited. Ponting was a former civil servant, accused of offences under the Official Secrets Act after he had passed confidential documents relating to the sinking of an Argentinian battleship during the Falklands War in 1982 to a Member of Parliament. Despite a ruling from the judge that Ponting had no authorization to pass the documents on, and that there was no other lawful justification for his action, the jury acquitted him. It was assumed that the jury had decided that the moral arguments in favour of his doing what he did outweighed the legal arguments that what he did was unlawful.

Important changes to the constitution and functions of juries have been made over the years. Thus the range of persons entitled to sit as jurors is now significantly wider than it was before 1972, when occupation of a house with a prescribed rateable value was one of the criteria for selection.[45] This has led to profound changes in jury com-position, certainly in terms of their class composition. Since 1981, selection for jury service has been by random selection using a computer. Perhaps the most significant

---

[45] Changes were made in the Criminal Justice Act 1972.

change occurred in 1967, when the ability of juries to determine cases on the basis of majority verdicts was introduced.[46]

Despite the arguments in favour of jury trial, which have considerable force, little is actually known about how they function. Direct research into the work of the jury has never been permitted. The only research currently available is through the use of 'surrogate' juries dealing with hypothetical situations.

There have been a number of suggestions that in particular types of case—lengthy and complex fraud trials are given as the prime example—juries as traditionally constituted are not best suited to determining facts. This has led to alternative proposals being adopted, for example judges sitting with a panel of lay assessors, or such cases being heard by a panel of judges rather than just a single judge. (There are significant dangers in allowing facts to be found from disputed evidence by a single adjudicator.)

Although some believe that juries are too ready to acquit defendants, there are actually no serious proposals that jury trial should be abolished. Such a step would be seen as politically unacceptable, and as too great a move from the due process model to the crime control model of Criminal Justice.

Choice of mode of trial. A quite distinct issue, though a matter of considerable controversy at the time of writing, is the question of who should have the right to choose jury trial in those cases which are triable either way. The present government believes, following the Royal Commission on Criminal Procedure's report in 1993, that the decision should be made by the magistrates before whom all such cases initially come, and not left to the discretion of the accused. By definition, the categories of case in which this choice arises are less serious than the indictable offences in which the right to trial by jury arises automatically. On this basis, it might be thought that the impact of such a change on the individual would not be very great. On the other hand, powerful voices assert that this change involves a fundamental issue of principle which, once conceded, will further undermine the due process model of Criminal Justice. The outcome of the government's proposals are, at the time of writing, far from certain.

Should the classification of indictable offences be altered? There is a quite distinct argument that the present classification of offences allows some to be tried by juries in situations where this does not seem warranted by the seriousness of the offence. There have been examples of this happening in recent years.[47] There have other attempts, for example, to reclassify certain types of minor theft as summary offences, thereby denying those accused of them the right to trial by jury. The recently announced review of the Criminal Justice system under Lord Justice Auld may well revisit this question. Proposals for change are always countered by the 'thin end of the wedge' argument, that any step in this direction will encourage governments to take further steps in the same direction, thereby reducing the scope of jury trial still further.

---

[46] See now the Juries Act 1974, s. 17. Majority verdicts are subject to an important *Practice Direction* [1967] 1 WLR 1198 and [1970] 1 WLR 916 which regulates their use. Current data on the use of majority verdicts is given in the text above.

[47] The Criminal Justice Act 1988 reclassified a number of motoring offences as summary only.

REPRESENTATION

New proposals for the creation of a Criminal Defender Service, to replace criminal legal aid for representation of criminal defendants in court are discussed below, at Chapter 10, p. 231.

SENTENCING (SEE DIAGRAM 5.2)

In the same way that the Criminal Justice system as a whole may be seen to depend on a variety of conflicting social theories, so too should the social theories which underpin sentencing policy and practice be better understood. The literature on theories of sentencing is extensive. Ashworth has classified the main approaches under five main headings:

- desert (retributive) theories;
- deterrence theories;
- rehabilitative theories;
- incapacitative theories; and
- restorative (reparative) theories.

Desert or retributive theories take as their focus the idea that punishment is a natural or appropriate response to crime, at least so long as it is proportionate to the crime committed. It is assumed that a person who commits a crime deserves to be punished; and that society is entitled to see that retribution is exacted from the offender. The problem of determining whether sentences are in fact proportional to the offence is, of course, a matter on which there can be great room for debate—and often is when the press criticize judges for apparently light (occasionally over-harsh) sentencing.

Deterrence theories offer a slightly different view. Here the perspective is on deterring future offending behaviour by punishing the offender currently before the authorities. Such a theory would then justify harsher penalties being imposed on an offender who has committed the same offence on more than one occasion than would be the case for a first offender. The research literature does not offer great confidence that, in practice, policies of deterrence work. Nonetheless they are very important politically, and indeed have led to the adoption of mandatory sentences for certain categories of repeat offenders.

Rehabilitative sentencing focuses on the offender and efforts to change his behaviour so that he can become a full and productive member of society. It may be assumed that offenders are in some way unable to cope with life and thus need professional support to change. It involves elements of diagnosis and treatment; it also implies that particular decisions need to be tailored to the individual offender.

Incapacitative sentencing focuses on the need to identify particular individuals or groups who are likely to do serious harm in the future, and who therefore need to be removed from society ('incapacitated') to prevent such harm occurring. The

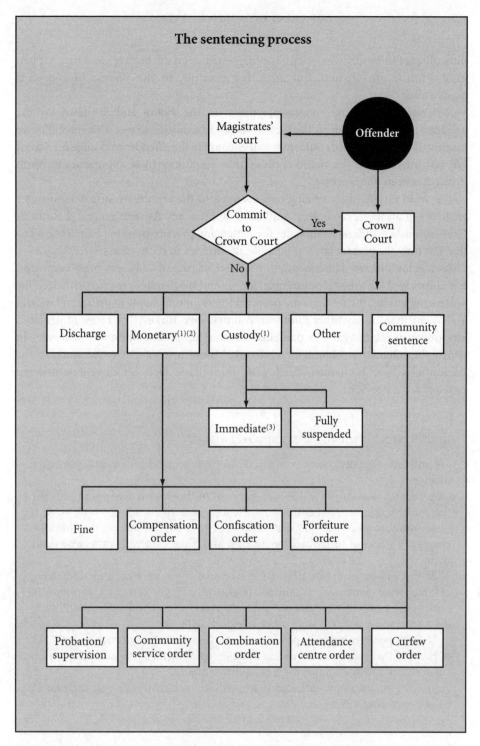

Diagram 5.2 (1) Magistrates' courts and the Crown Court differ in their powers to award monetary and custodial penalties. (2) May either be the sole penalty or in association with another disposal. (3) Includes detention in a young offenders' institution and unsuspended imprisonment.

difficulties of imposing what may be severe penalties on the basis of what may happen in the future are obvious, but arise, for example, in the context of convicted paedophiles.

Restorative approaches concentrate more on the victim and the need for the offender to make amends to the victim. Restorative justice shares with rehabilitative models the belief that such outcomes will encourage the offender to change his way of life, but the focus on the victim is distinctive. The use of these approaches in youth justice has been noted above.

The wide variety of sentencing options open to the criminal courts demonstrates elements of all these, often very conflicting, approaches. As with general theories of Criminal Justice, different rationales for sentencing practice need to be understood so that not only the present law but possible alternatives to it can be assessed.[48]

Sentencing practice is frequently the subject of (usually adverse) press comment, not always well informed. For example, judges and magistrates are often criticized for sentencing too lightly. Yet there are proportionately more people in prison in England and Wales than in any other European country, save Turkey. The range of penalties has grown in recent years. In particular various forms of 'community sentence', in which the offender is obliged to undertake some form of reparative work in the community, have been introduced. (For some basic facts on current sentencing outcomes, see Box 5.9.)

Box 5.9 SENTENCING: SOME BASIC FACTS[49]

1.4 million offenders were sentenced in 1997 for indictable and summary offences.

At magistrates' courts in 1997, 35 per cent of those sentenced summarily for the more serious triable-either-way offences were fined, 29 per cent given a community sentence, 23 per cent sentenced to a conditional or absolute discharge, 10 per cent to immediate custody, and 3 per cent were otherwise dealt with.

At the Crown Court in 1997, 61 per cent of those sentenced for indictable offences were sentenced to immediate custody, 27 per cent to a community sentence, 4 per cent were fined, 3 per cent received an absolute or conditional discharge, and 5 per cent were otherwise dealt with.

163,000 persons began supervision under the probation service in 1997, 73 per cent of them under court orders and the remainder for pre- and post-release supervision during or following a custodial sentence.

93,000 persons were sentenced to immediate custody in 1997, an increase of 61 per cent since 1992.

[48] The powers of the courts to sentence offenders are being consolidated in the Powers of Criminal Courts (Sentencing) Bill 2000, taking up recommendations of the Law Commission.

[49] Data taken from *Information on the Criminal Justice System in England and Wales*, ed. Barclay, G. C. and Tavares, C. (London: Home Office, Research, Development and Statistics Directorate, October 1999).

Over this period, the number of juvenile offenders aged 14 to 17 sentenced to custody rose by 58 per cent, young adult offenders aged 18 to 20 by 43 per cent, and adults by 65 per cent.

The average custodial sentence length for male offenders convicted of indictable offences was 15.8 months in 1997, well above that for 1994 and 1995 (14.8 months).

The numbers sentenced to immediate custody for summary offences rose from 4,600 in 1987 to 22,000 in 1997.

THE POST-TRIAL STAGES

APPEALS[50]

Those convicted in a magistrates' court can appeal to the Crown Court, either against conviction or against sentence. Similarly appeals from the Crown Court can be made to the Court of Appeal (Criminal Division).

In 1996, there were 10,440 appeals against conviction, and 14,190 appeals against sentence to the Crown Court from the magistrates' courts. Of these, 33 per cent of the appeals against conviction were allowed; 43 per cent against sentence were, similarly, allowed.

The total numbers of appeals were, respectively, 26 per cent and 16 per cent lower than the figures for 1995, possibly reflecting the coming into effect of the Criminal Appeals Act 1995, which enabled magistrates to re-examine cases to rectify mistakes without reference to the Crown Court.

The Court of Appeal dealt with 2,400 appeals against conviction, and 7,250 appeals against sentence from the Crown Court. Of these 11 per cent against conviction and 19 per cent against sentence were allowed. There were in total 9 per cent more appeals in 1996 than in 1995. 12 per cent of all offenders convicted at the Crown Court appealed.

It is now also possible for a reference to be made to the Attorney General by the prosecution on the basis that a sentence is too light. In 1997, there were seventy such references, which resulted in increased sentences being imposed by the Court in forty-three cases.

CRIMINAL CASES REVIEW COMMISSION

One of the most serious challenges facing the Criminal Justice system is ensuring that miscarriages of justice do not occur. Notwithstanding the opportunities for appeal

---

[50] Data from Home Office Statistical Bulletin, 3/98, reported in *Information on the Criminal Justice System in England and Wales*, ed. Barclay, G. C. and Tavares, C. (London: Home Office, Research, Development and Statistics Directorate, October 1999).

and the outcomes from appeal, there may always be cases where the full facts have not emerged at trial or on subsequent appeal, possibly because there have been failures by the police or prosecution to put evidence before the court, or disclose it to the defence.

The Criminal Cases Review Commission was established in 1997.[51] It will usually consider only those cases that have been through the normal judicial appeal process. Since it started undertaking casework (at the end of March 1997) it has received over 2,600 applications. On average four new cases are received every working day. Reviews of 961 had been completed by the end of June 1999; of these only 52 had been referred back to the Court of Appeal. Reviews are conducted by case review managers. There is serious concern that levels of work and insufficient staff numbers are leading to unacceptable delays.

Decisions on the outcomes of the work of the case review managers are taken by the Commission. The Commission has fourteen members, appointed from a variety of backgrounds. Any decision to refer a case back to the Court of Appeal must be taken by a committee of at least three members.

The function of the Commission is to consider whether there would be a real possibility that a conviction, finding of fact, verdict, or sentence would not be upheld by the Court, were a reference back to be made. In relation to reviews of convictions, there has to be either an argument or evidence which had not been raised at the trial or on appeal, or other exceptional circumstances; in relation to sentencing, again there has to be legal argument or information about the individual or the offence which was not raised during the trial or on appeal.

PAROLE AND THE WORK OF THE PAROLE BOARD

Even though the court may have imposed a custodial sentence in a particular case, this does not mean that the convicted person will serve the whole period of the sentence. Sentences are subject to review by the Parole Board. This body has been in operation since 1968.[52] Its primary function is to make risk assessments which will inform decisions as to whether prisoners can be released back into the community early. While protection of the public is a matter of paramount concern, the board seeks to enhance the rehabilitative effect of prison in cases where that seems possible. The responsibilities of the board vary, depending on different types of case.

Determinate sentence cases

Where a convicted person has been sentenced to a fixed term of imprisonment, it is now provided (since 1 October 1992) that a prisoner becomes eligible for parole

---

[51] Criminal Appeal Act 1995, Part II. This followed recommendations from the Royal Commission on Criminal Justice, 1993. It has recently had its powers extended to enable it to consider cases where the verdict of 'guilty but insane' was reached: Criminal Cases Review (Insanity) Act 1999. Although this verdict was abolished in the mid-1960s, there is a small number of people whose cases were so determined, who might wish to take advantage of these new provisions. Since 1964 the verdict in such cases is 'not guilty by reason of insanity': Criminal Procedure (Insanity) Act 1964.

[52] It was established under the provisions of the Criminal Justice Act 1967.

halfway through his sentence (backdated to include any time spend in custody on remand before the trial).[53] Thus a prisoner sentenced to four years on 2 January 1994, who had also spent six months in custody on remand, became eligible for parole on 2 July 1996—the parole eligibility date (PED).

Six months before the PED, officers of the Parole Board begin gathering the information together to enable a panel from the Parole Board to take an initial decision on whether the prisoner may or may not be suitable for parole. The prisoner will also be interviewed by a Parole Board member. In addition to written reports, the panel is required to take into account *Directions* made by the Home Secretary. These give guidance on particular issues on which the panel must be satisfied before finding in favour of the prisoner. In the reporting year 1998–9, over 78 per cent of prisoners received the result of this preliminary review at least two weeks before their PED.

The decision to grant parole is formally one for the Secretary of State. But he has delegated his decision-taking powers to the board in all cases where the prisoner was sentenced for a period of less than fifteen years.[54]

Whether or not prisoners are released following a Parole Board review, determinate prisoners are automatically released two thirds of the way through their sentence. However, all those released either after a parole decision or under the automatic process remain subject to supervision by the Probation Service and are subject to recall either for reoffending or for other breaches of the probation supervision until 75 per cent of the period of the sentence has expired. Although the supervision of the Probation Service ends at that point, the remaining 25 per cent of the sentence can be reactivated if the person is subsequently committed for another criminal offence.

The latest Annual Report from the board records that over 6,000 cases were dealt with in 1998–9; that parole was awarded in nearly 40 per cent of cases; and that the rate of recall of parolees to custody for committing another offence was only 4 per cent.

Life sentences

The Parole Board also has important responsibilities in relation to life sentences. In dealing with them, a distinction is drawn between *mandatory* life sentences, where the judge had no option but to impose a life sentence (as in the case of a conviction for murder), and *discretionary* life sentences, where this was the sentence that the judge decided was appropriate.[55]

The starting point is a decision on *the tariff*. This is the minimum period which the prisoner is to serve. The tariff for mandatory lifers is currently fixed by the Home Secretary, taking into account a recommendation of the trial judge, though this practice has recently been the subject of adverse judicial rulings, both in the House of

---

[53] For those sentenced before 1 October 1992, the date of eligibility for parole arose one third of the way through the sentence.

[54] Until 1998 the upper limit for Parole Board decisions was sentences of less than seven years.

[55] This group includes those sentenced under the provisions of the Crime (Sentences) Act 1997, which gives the court power to impose a life sentence where a person has been convicted for a second serious offence. It also includes those under the age of 18 who have been convicted of murder.

Lords and in the European Court of Human Rights.[56] The tariff in other cases is set by the trial judge.

Three years before the expiry of the tariff, the case is reviewed by the Parole Board who consider whether or not a prisoner is suitable to be moved to the more relaxed regime of an open prison.

On the expiry of the tariff, the Parole Board considers whether the prisoner is suitable for release on licence. If release on licence is recommended, the prisoner will still be subject to supervision by the Probation Service, for at least four years. At that point (or later) the Home Secretary may decide that the supervision requirements can be lifted. However, the prisoner remains liable to recall and for the balance of his sentence to be reactivated for the rest of his life, should there be reason for so doing, such as subsequent offending.

If the Parole Board concludes that on the expiry of the tariff, release would not be appropriate, the case is reviewed normally every two years.

Procedure

The process of reaching these decisions does, however, vary. In the case of *mandatory* lifers, the decision-taking process is very similar to that for determinate sentences. Reports are prepared; an interview is held by a member of the Parole Board with the prisoner; and a decision is reached on the papers. Mandatory lifer panels are specially constituted to include a judge and a psychiatrist. Again the panel is required to take into account *directions* prescribed by the Home Secretary. The actual decision is always taken by the Home Secretary; the Parole Board panel can only make a recommendation.

For *discretionary* lifers, the process of review involves the compilation of a dossier of reports. But there is then a fundamentally important difference. An oral hearing (rather like a tribunal hearing) is listed before a discretionary lifer panel of the Parole Board (which includes a judge and a psychiatrist). The prisoner is entitled to legal representation at this hearing. At the conclusion of the hearing, the panel may rec-ommend transfer to open prison conditions, or may in appropriate cases direct release.

The Parole Board considered 753 life sentences cases in 1998–9. Release on life licence was agreed in 22 per cent of them.

---

[56] *In R. v. Secretary of State for the Home Department, ex parte V. and T.* [1998] AC 407, the House of Lords held that it was unlawful for the Home Secretary to set a tariff relating to young persons which did not take into account the provisions of the UN Convention on the Rights of the Child. The European Court of Human Rights has now held *T. v. United Kingdom; V. v. United Kingdom* (*The Times*, 16 December 1999), that setting a tariff is a sentencing function which should not be carried out by a member of the executive arm of government but by an independent tribunal. It has recently been announced that the Lord Chief Justice will fix the tariff.

THE PLACE OF THE VICTIM

One of the ways in which the Criminal Justice system has been transformed in recent years is through increased recognition of the victim of crime. As has already been noted, the position of the victim is fundamental to the whole Criminal Justice system since, if the victim does not report a crime, no further steps are usually taken in the criminal process. Further, as also noted, the viewpoint of the victim is one of the factors taken into account by the CPS in reaching a decision as to whether or not to prosecute a case. There are respects in which sentencing policy reflects the impact which the criminal activity may have had on the victim. Much of the activity in the youth justice system is designed to make the offender aware of the victim's perceptions of what he has done. The Home Office has sought to bring support for victims (and witnesses) together in its *Victims' Charter* (published in 1997).

Three particular developments may be briefly noted: victim support schemes, the criminal injuries compensation scheme and compensation orders.

Victim support schemes. There are now 365 local victim support schemes with 15,000 volunteers offering help to over 1 million victims. In the Crown Court, there are another 1,500 volunteers helping over 100,000 victims and witnesses who have to attend court. These do a great deal of work trying to reassure the victims of crime that they have not been targeted, but are simply the victims of opportunistic criminal activity. They also help victims and other witnesses cope with the stress and strain of appearing in court.

It is still argued that more should be done to inform victims about outcomes, particularly where the police or prosecuting authorities determine not to pursue a case. It is also argued that more information should be provided to victims when a person who has been sent to prison is released from prison. It seems inevitable that there will be continued developments in these areas in coming years.

The criminal injuries compensation scheme. This has been in operation for many years. Originally established through the use of prerogative powers, it has now been put on a statutory footing. It is a state-funded scheme administered by the Criminal Injuries Compensation Authority (formerly Board) which in 1998 delivered around £201m in compensation for some 45,000 claimants. The scheme is limited to those victims who have been injured as the result of violent criminal activity directed towards them. Critics point out that other negative consequences of being the victim of crime are not thus compensated.

Compensation orders. In addition to this statutory scheme, it may also be noted that since 1972 the criminal courts have had power to order those convicted of crimes to pay compensation to their victims. These powers have been developed so that there are circumstances in which a compensation order may be imposed as the sole penalty. Since 1988, the courts have been required to consider making compensation orders in defined groups of cases involving death, injury, loss, or damage, and to give reasons where an order is not made. And since 1991 the limits on the sums which magistrates may order to be paid in compensation have been increased. These developments may be seen as more reparative forms of outcome for the Criminal Justice system.

A STRATEGIC APPROACH TO CRIMINAL JUSTICE?

Underpinning many of the particular facets of the Criminal Justice system set out above has been the recognition by government of the need for a more integrated approach to dealing with crime. Numerous initiatives have been taken in recent years to try to deliver this. Three examples are considered here.

1. The *Trials Issues Group* (TIG) brings together representatives of all those working in the Criminal Justice system to iron out inter-agency difficulties and to improve the working of the system generally. It has been in existence for some nine years and meets monthly. Members of TIG focus on the practical and operational, rather than the conceptual. It grew out of an acceptance that the participants in the Criminal Justice system are heavily interdependent, that simply apportioning blame for the problems in the system was sterile, and that no progress could be made without some give and take. Thus its members are expected to take an objective attitude, to be as cooperative as possible, and not to seek to defend their corners come what may.

TIG members are drawn from organizations across the Criminal Justice system including the Lord Chancellor's Department, the judiciary, the Home Office, the Crown Prosecution Service, the Police, the Magistrates' Association, the Justices' Clerks' Society, the Probation Service, the Law Society, and the Bar Council. TIG has a number of sub-groups which draw in participants from outside the main group in order to work through projects suitable to be taken forward on an inter-agency basis. Examples of previous projects include:

- the development of new style case files to reduce police administrative forms;
- joint performance management as a means of improving the quality and timeliness of case preparation by the police and prosecution;
- the development of new standards for witness care to improve the treatment of witnesses; and
- introduction of new streamlined procedures for finalizing minor road traffic cases.

TIG has a permanent Projects Team drawn from the Crown Prosecution Service, the police, the Home Office and the Lord Chancellor's Department. Its members combine their TIG functions with other duties in their home organizations.

2. The *Criminal Justice Strategy* started with the publication in December 1998 of a Public Service Agreement (PSA) setting out what the public should expect from the Criminal Justice system.[57] This has more recently been supplemented by a *Strategic Plan for the Criminal Justice System for 1999–2000 to 2001–2002*. The government has set two aims for the strategy:

- to reduce crime and the fear of crime and their social and economic costs;
- to dispense justice fairly and efficiently and to promote confidence in the rule of law.

It is the second of these that is most relevant to this work.

In relation to this, the government is seeking to reduce substantially time taken for the disposal of cases, particularly those involving persistent young offenders.[58] A number of processes should be available in the next few years, to take advantage of increased investment in IT:[59]

- records initially built in the police station (incorporating information about previous convictions taken from a national database) can be passed electronically to the CPS for a decision on prosecution;
- if the prosecution goes ahead, the file can then be forwarded electronically to the defendant's lawyers;
- the court listing officer uses information—provided electronically—to find a date when witnesses are able to attend court;
- the Court's video-conferencing facility is used for deciding preliminary issues, such as remanding in custody without the need for attendance at court;
- requests for pre-sentence reports can be forwarded by e-mail to the Probation Service;
- information about driving offences can be obtained direct from the DVLA;[60]
- information about a convicted person including previous convictions can be forwarded to prisons to enable a full risk assessment to take place;

[57] Part of the White Paper *Public Services for the Future: Modernisation, Reform, Accountability* (Cm 4181) (London: Stationery Office).

[58] In 1996, the Audit Commission estimated that people under 18 committed 7 million offences a year; the government argues that dealing quickly with this group will indicate the seriousness with which young offending is regarded. A 'fast track' experiment in North Hampshire has nearly halved the time for dealing with young offenders.

[59] Electronic case files are currently being piloted in the Stockport police force.

[60] At present it is estimated that around 170,000 cases are adjourned each year, with all the knock-on consequences of increased costs and delays in other cases, simply because magistrates' courts cannot directly access driving records.

- similarly electronic means can be used to assist probation officers, or those taking decisions on parole.

This will not happen overnight, but indicates ways in which current procedures within the Criminal Justice system should operate much more efficiently than is presently the case.

3. A further review of the Criminal Court system was established by the Lord Chancellor at the end of 1999. Chaired by Lord Justice Auld, it has to 'review . . . the practices and procedures of, and the rules of evidence applied by, the criminal courts at every level, with a view to ensuring that they deliver justice fairly, by stream-lining all their processes, increasing their efficiency and strengthening the effective-ness of their relationships with others across the whole of the Criminal Justice system, and having regard to the interests of all parties including victims and witnesses, thereby promoting public confidence in the rule of law'.

Given the other attempts to increase efficiency in the Criminal Justice system that have been taken in recent years, it may be wondered why this further initiative has been thought necessary. In its press announcement the government noted that, for the first time, the work of the Crown Courts and of the magistrates' courts would be considered together. It also stated that the review would complement the review of the Civil Justice system undertaken by Lord Woolf and which recently led to a major reform of the Civil Justice system. (See below Chapter 8.) It is not possible to antici-pate, at the time of writing, the likely outcome of this new review, but is another indication of the need for improved planning and coordination.

6

THE ADMINISTRATIVE JUSTICE SYSTEM

INTRODUCTION

Although the Criminal Justice system, discussed in the previous chapter, is institutionally extremely complex, the primary focus of the system—on the regulation of forms of social behaviour, and dealing with those who transgress the rules—is clear. By contrast, the very concept of 'administrative justice' is controversial, meaning different things to different people. Indeed, traditional analyses of the legal system, focusing exclusively on criminal and civil law, have failed to recognize any separate system of administrative justice. Discussion of administrative justice gets wrapped up in general discussion of the Civil Justice system.

In part, this failure to acknowledge a distinct system of administrative justice reflects the continuing influence of the nineteenth-century writer A. V. Dicey, who argued that there should not be a separately identifiable body of *droit administratif* (administrative law). He thought that this would result in public officials and others who worked for public bodies being given legally preferential treatment and thus offend against the fundamental principle of the rule of law, that all should be treated equally before the law.

A hundred years on, the reality is that the state plays a large part in the regulation of society; there is a vast array of institutions employing individuals who provide public services on behalf of those institutions. Although there may still not be a conceptually distinct branch of the law which may be described as administrative law, as there is for example in many of the countries in continental Europe, understanding the modern English legal system involves recognizing the concept of administrative justice.

The primary focus of this chapter is on the range of institutions in which administrative law is practised. First, however, we reflect on the nature of administrative law and the role it plays in modern society.

THE ROLE OF ADMINISTRATIVE LAW:
AUTHORITY AND VALUES

As already noted, one of the features of the twentieth century—and one likely to continue into the twenty-first—has been the significant role of government in developing and implementing a vast range of social policies. Legitimacy for the activities of public officials in implementing those social policies depends on law. Administrative law:

- provides authority for public servants to deliver government policy, whose legitimacy is enshrined in the laws (primary, secondary, and tertiary—see Box 3.2) passed through the Parliamentary system;
- authorizes the raising and expenditure of public funds;
- sets limits to the powers of public officials;
- creates the institutional mechanisms for calling public officials to account; and
- provides means for the redress of individual grievances or resolution of complaints by the citizen.

In addition to the functional attributes of administrative law, administrative justice embraces certain *values* or *principles*, which should underpin good administration by state officials, or those who deliver services on behalf of the state. These include: openness (or transparency); fairness; rationality (including the giving of reasons for decisions); impartiality (independence) of decision-takers; accountability; the prevention of the exercise of arbitrary power and the control of discretion; consistency; participation; efficiency; equity; and equal treatment.

These underlying values of administrative justice are not wholly consistent one with another. There may be circumstances in which openness may properly yield to confidentiality; where fairness of process may conflict with the efficient reaching of a decision. Each of these values is to an extent contingent upon the context in which it is asserted. One of the challenges for those who govern, and for those who criticize the role of government, is to achieve an appropriate balance between these conflicting objectives.

The details of any particular area of substantive public law (for example the statutory rules relating to the provision of social security benefits) are not for discussion here. Rather the focus is on the mechanisms of accountability which exist to keep officials in check and provide means of resolving disputes when things go (or are alleged to go) wrong. But the reader should reflect on the tensions between the different values in administrative justice in the context of particular administrative activities—for example, the collection of taxes; or the granting of planning permissions; or the payment of social security benefits.

ADMINISTRATIVE JUSTICE:
THE INSTITUTIONAL FRAMEWORK

There is a great variety of bodies which make up the institutional framework for administrative justice. They include:

- the courts;
- tribunals;
- inquiries;
- ombudsmen;
- complaints procedures.

Each of these is considered below. It will quickly be realized that this is another area in which there has been very rapid development in the last thirty to forty years. It is one of the most dynamic areas of the English legal system.

This way of conceptualizing the framework of administrative justice is not wholly orthodox. Practising lawyers tend to think of 'administrative law' as, in essence, the special process available in the High Court known as *judicial review*. Academic lawyers go beyond this court-focused approach to include in their analyses comments on other mechanisms for the resolution of disputes. But the treatment tends to be somewhat superficial, and even here the balance is normally tilted in favour of the court's role.[1] There are perfectly good reasons for this:

(1) The *qualitative* importance of the law of judicial review is clear. It is the reported decisions of judges in the Divisional Court[2] and above that have developed the jurisprudence of judicial review. The fundamental principles, of procedural 'fairness', and for limiting the exercise of discretionary power by officials, are the creation of the courts. The range of persons permitted to bring proceedings by way of judicial review has been expanded. The numbers of bodies and institutions subjected to the principles of judicial review have been significantly widened. The grounds on which judicial review may be sought have also been developed. Judicial review provides the legal background against which the Administrative Justice system must operate. This is largely the work of the courts—judges asserting their constitutional function of independence over the executive.

(2) Second, it is in the courts that practising lawyers earn good money and develop formidable reputations. With rare exceptions, legal aid is not available to pay for legal representation before tribunals or other dispute resolution/grievance handling fora.

---

[1] There are honourable exceptions: Harlow, Carol and Rawlings, Richard, *Law and Administration*, 2nd edn. (London: Butterworths, 1997).

[2] Following publication of the report by Sir Jeffrey Bowman in March 2000, *Review of the Crown Office List*, the Lord Chancellor has announced that he is accepting the recommendation that the Divisional Court should be renamed 'the Administrative Court'. The existing name is, however, retained in this chapter.

There is therefore little incentive for practitioners to get to know about the wider world of administrative justice.

(3) The work of this wider range of bodies is often not the subject of formal published documentation. Thus the legal scholars have found it hard to access the material needed for a full review of the administrative justice system as a whole.

Nevertheless, concentration on judicial review—a procedure that brings about 4,000 cases before the courts each year—means that other procedures for the delivery of administrative justice are not paid the attention they are due. For example, the social security tribunal system (from April 2000 known as the Unified Appeal Tribunal) currently handles in excess of 300,000 appeals a year; immigration adjudicators disposed of 38,000 immigration appeals in 1998, and the Immigration Appeals Tribunal dealt with another 15,700 appeals;[3] Mental Health Review Tribunals currently deal with around 35,000 cases a year. Many other examples could be given. The various ombudsmen that now exist handle thousands more cases in a year. And the variety of complaints procedures available under the general umbrella of the concept of the citizen's charter deal with countless other grievances. *Quantitatively* these other mechanisms are far more significant than the courts. This account seeks to redress the balance.

The reason for making this argument arises, however, not just from a desire to be different. What the Administrative Justice system—taken as a whole—provides is a vast test bed for the development and evaluation of new procedures:

- decisions being taken on the papers;
- decisions by three- (or more) person tribunals;
- decisions with informal procedures;
- decisions with formal procedures;
- procedures involving the unrepresented and inarticulate;
- decisions based on the use of inquisitorial procedures.

It is one of the great wasted opportunities that those who have sought in recent years to introduce change into the Civil Justice system should have paid such scant attention to what goes on in practice in the Administrative Justice system. It provides a rich source of ideas as to how things might be done differently. Those who, in the past, may have looked down their noses at the Administrative Justice system as 'not being proper courts', should think again. It is here that alternative systems are to be found, which in many cases work extremely well.

---

[3] *Judicial Statistics Annual Report 1998* (Cm 4371) (London: Stationery Office, 1999).

THE COURTS

The heart of the Administrative Justice system is found in the Divisional Court of Queens Bench, where the fundamental principles of *judicial review* have been developed, particularly since the mid-1960s.[4] The essence of judicial review is straightforward. Public officials must act within the constraints of the law. If they do not, the courts will declare a decision to be unlawful. In general the judges limit themselves to this; they will not usually substitute their own decision for that of the original decision-taker.

The primary tasks of the judges in a judicial review case are:

- *To interpret statutory provisions.* There are many situations, particularly when a new piece of legislation has been passed, when the law may need clarification. Deciding the limits of the law, and whether or not a person acted within the law or outside it, is one of the tasks of the judges.

- *To control discretion.* In some situations the legislation has been drafted in a deliberately vague fashion, in order to give officials some flexibility in the application of the law to the particular case. Where a statute states that the minister 'may' act in a certain way, or reach a 'reasonable' decision, these are examples of the granting of discretionary power. In this context the judges have developed the principle that the exercise of discretion must not be 'unreasonable'.[5]

- *To determine the validity of secondary legislation.* The courts have resisted the temptation to decide, as does the Supreme Court in the USA, that particular items of legislation are unlawful, though it has recently been decided that they should do so if an item of British legislation is contrary to the law of the EU.[6] However, the courts have long asserted the power to declare secondary legislation unlawful, on the basis that the statutory instrument was beyond the powers of the minister as established by the primary Act of Parliament.[7]

- *To determine the fairness of procedures.* The courts have also been determined to develop fundamental principles of fairness in the lower courts, in other tribunals and in a range of other contexts in which decisions affecting the citizen are made. Where these principles apply, the person must know the basis of the case against her, and have an opportunity to be heard.

- *To prevent bias.* In addition, the judges have insisted that adjudicators in the courts and other fora must not be 'biased', in the sense that they must not have a personal interest in the outcome of any particular case.

---

[4] Woolf, Lord and Jowell, Jeffrey (asst. ed. Le Sueur, A. P.) *Judicial Review of Administrative Action*, 5th edn. (London: Sweet & Maxwell, 1995).

[5] *Associated Provincial Picture Houses Ltd. v. Wednesbury Corporation* [1948] 1 KB 223.

[6] *Factortame v. Secretary of State for Transport (No. 2)* [1991] 1 AC 603.

[7] *R. v. Secretary of State for Trade and Industry, ex parte Thomson Holidays* (*The Times*, 12 January 2000); and *R. v. Secretary of State for the Environment, Transport and the Regions and Another, ex parte Spath Holme Ltd.* [2000] 1 All ER 884.

Judicial review has not developed in a vacuum. It is a response to the fact that people no longer accept official decisions as easily as they once did. The reasons for this are complex: better public education; a more 'consumerist' society; the development of this type of legal activity by legal practitioners. But government has also expanded its activities. There has been huge growth in the power of the state. It seeks to regulate large tranches of human activity. It is not surprising that the use of judicial review, or the threat of such use, should now be part of the 'politics' of modern public administration.[8]

One of the outcomes of the developments of judicial review is that there has been an increased use by pressure groups of the courts for testing the validity of legislation or its interpretation. 'Test cases', or as it is known in the US 'cause lawyering', have become a part of contemporary legal practice.[9] The scope of the work of the courts in determining the limits of governmental power will expand significantly with the coming into force of the Human Rights Act 1998 in October 2000.

TRIBUNALS

The adjudicative fora in which the vast majority of disputes between the citizen and the state get resolved are known collectively as tribunals. Some, such as the General Commissioners of Income Tax, trace their history back to the late eighteenth century. But the vast majority are the creation of the twentieth century, reflecting the increasing involvement of the state in the lives of its citizens.

For the first twenty to thirty years of that century, there was considerable concern about the use of tribunals as a mechanism for the resolution of disputes. It was argued that only courts had the constitutional authority to perform this function. It was, perhaps, one of the advantages of the lack of a written constitution that, despite this claim, there was no written constitutional principle that *required* all dispute-resolution bodies to have the status of 'court'. In fact, the development of tribunals was a pragmatic response to the problems caused for the court system when, at the end of the nineteenth century, jurisdiction to deal with disputes arising under the Workmen's Compensation Acts was given to the county court. This had the result of completely drowning those courts in work, thereby preventing them from efficiently dispatching other business. When the National Insurance Act 1911 was enacted, with the creation of the first social security benefits, appeals against decisions were not to the courts, but to a tribunal, the sportingly named *Committee of Referees* with a further right of appeal to the equally sporting *Umpire*.

Criticism of the use of bodies other than the courts for resolving disputes led to fierce criticism, not least from the then Lord Chief Justice, Lord Hewart, who in 1929

---

[8] On the 'tactical' use of judicial review, see Bridges, Lee, Meszaros, George and Sunkin, Maurice, *Judicial Review in Perspective* (London: Cavendish, 1995).

[9] Prosser, Tony, *Test Cases for the Poor: Legal Techniques in the Politics of Social Welfare* (London: Child Poverty Action Group, 1983); Sarat, Austin and Scheingold, Stuart, *Cause Lawyering and Professional Responsibilities* (New York: Oxford University Press, 1998).

published his famous polemic *The New Despotism*. This resulted in the establishment of the Committee on Ministers' Powers, under the chairmanship of Lord Donoughmore, which in 1932 reported that, in their view and subject to safeguards, tribunals were a necessary if not desirable part of the fabric of the English justice system.

The issue was revisited after the second World War when, in 1955, a further committee under Sir Oliver Franks was established to review Tribunals and Enquiries, in the wake of a scandal known as the Crichel Down affair. The report of his committee was published in 1957. By this time many more tribunal systems were in existence. Franks accepted that, subject to basic principles of openness, fairness, and impartiality, tribunals should be accepted as a part of the adjudicative structure. Since that time, there has been no serious discussion about the need for tribunals. Indeed, their number has continued to grow (alongside other institutional developments, to which we shall come below). The position of tribunals is likely to become even more secure following the enactment of the Human Rights Act 1998, since Article 6 of the European Convention on Human Rights requires the existence of courts or tribunals to determine a person's civil rights.

There are currently at least eighty different tribunal systems in existence. They come in a bewildering variety of forms.

Structure

Some are 'two-tiered' tribunal systems. For example in social security, appeals go first to the *Unified Appeal Tribunal*,[10] which may consist of between one and three members—depending on the type of case. From there a case may go, with leave and on a point of law only, to the *Social Security Commissioners*. The Commissioners usually sit on their own, but for the occasional difficult case they may sit in a tribunal of three. There is a similar structure with *Employment Tribunals* (formerly Industrial Tribunals), with a second-tier appeal to the *Employment Appeal Tribunal* consisting of three people, a judge and two lay assessors. In immigration, cases are heard at the first tier by an *Adjudicator* sitting on his/her own. There may then be an appeal to the *Immigration Appeal Tribunal* which usually comprises three people (though this practice is changing). In all these cases, there is the possibility of further challenge on a point of law in the courts.

Other tribunal systems are 'one-tier': examples include the *Mental Health Review Tribunal*, the *Valuation Tribunal*, and the *Rent Assessment Committee*. In other words, there is only one level of appeal or review within the statutory framework. Any further challenge has to be direct to the courts.

Personnel

Although the label 'tribunal' may imply a body of three people, as has already been noted in passing, some are made up of less than three people; one-person tribunals are becoming increasingly common as government departments seek to cut the costs

---

[10] See Social Security Act 1998.

of Administrative Justice. Other tribunals may have more than three persons involved, particularly tribunals which deal with matters relating to the National Health Service.

Qualifications

Most tribunal systems these days have legally qualified persons to act as the tribunal chairs. But this is not universal—for example *General Commissioners for Income Tax* who determine tax cases, and *Valuation Tribunals*, which determine property values, operate only with lay persons on the tribunal. In such cases it is usual for the clerk to the tribunal to be legally qualified (rather like the justices' clerks who assist benches of lay magistrates).

In other tribunal systems, there is more professional expertise sitting around the table. Most commonly there is legal expertise; but where relevant, there may be a valuer, or an accountant, or medical expert. In cases where the tribunals operate with professionally qualified adjudicators, whether lawyers or other professionals, the clerk will perform more of an administrative or clerical role, not giving advice to the tribunal.

Process

Tribunals operate under a bewildering variety of procedures. Some only take evidence on oath or after affirmation, given by the witness or party to the proceedings; others do not use the oath. Some sit in court rooms—or rooms set out like court rooms. Others are established in much more informal contexts, such as school rooms or hotel rooms. Some large tribunal systems operate their own tribunal accommodation; others have to rent or borrow space as occasion demands. (It is remarkable—given the extent of the Administrative Justice system, and the numbers of tribunals it comprises—that towns do not have 'Administrative Justice centres' to match the criminal court centres and civil court centres that are commonly found.)

Many tribunal systems make extensive efforts to deal with appellants who—as the result of a lack of availability of legal aid—either have to represent themselves or have to rely on lay advocates. The social security system, for example, prides itself on its 'enabling role'. Unlike the adversarial approach of the courts, where the judges tend to take a back seat while the argument, for and against, is presented by advocates for both sides, tribunals take a more interventionist role, seeking to draw relevant information from the parties by appropriate questioning. It is in this variety of forensic methods that much of the potential innovation of the tribunal system is to be found, and from which the courts—if they knew what went on in the best-run tribunals—might have much to learn.[11]

It is sometimes suggested that tribunals offer 'informal' as opposed for 'formal' justice. This gives the wrong impression, certainly if informal implies a lack of organ-ization or discipline. The primary advantage of a tribunal as opposed to a court is that

---

[11] Mr Justice Lightman has recently argued, in a lecture to the London Solicitors' Litigation Association, on 9 November 1999, that the judges in the ordinary courts should adopt a more interventionist approach. This merely reflects what has long happened in many tribunals.

there is a lack of rigidity of process, though the person running the tribunal must have a very clear grasp of who is to speak, and when, and ensure that everyone has their say. The relevant information can thereby be obtained which should allow the tribunal to come to a fair and proper decision. The fact that no strict order of procedure is followed does not matter.

Management

Management of tribunals also varies enormously. Many systems have presidents who operate at national level, often through a regional structure, for example social security, employment, and—a more recent example—the *Special Educational Needs Tribunal*. These tribunal systems tend to be well organized, with comprehensive programmes of training for members and chairmen, monitoring and evaluation of performance, and the use of other modern management techniques.

In other cases, such as *Education Appeal Committees*, the tribunals are organized at the local authority level, with very little central direction. Others operating on a regional basis are mental health, rent assessment, and valuation. These tribunals systems tend to be less advanced in the development of training programmes and the use of other management techniques and seem less well resourced for the tasks they are required to perform.

Reporting of decisions

A final respect in which tribunal systems differ relates to the ways in which important decisions get reported. Many of the two-tier systems have the means of publishing significant decisions from the upper tier. Some of these reports are published commercially—as in the case of employment cases; others are published regularly by the government department in question—such as immigration reports, or tax cases. Others appear on a more hand-to-mouth basis, such as the reported decisions of the social security commissioners. Other tribunal systems have no formal reporting mechanisms. (This may need to change once the Human Rights Act 1998 is in force.)

This wide variety of structure and process poses an obvious question: is this 'system' with all its variation the best way of running this part of the Administrative Justice system? Would there be scope for greater efficiency if there was to be some restructuring? Or have the individual procedures—developed to deal with particular sets of issues—provided the most efficient method of delivering a service to the public?

The fact is that there has been no review of the system as a whole for over forty years, and there has never been a formal audit of the present structure. It is likely that, were we to start from scratch today, we would not introduce the system that we currently have; but would this be an argument for moving, for example, to the much more structured system to be found in Australia? These questions are taken up in the 'overview' section at the end of this chapter.

INQUIRIES

The historically conceptual distinction between a tribunal and an inquiry was that, whereas a tribunal usually had the statutory authority to reach a final decision which, subject to any right of appeal, determined the dispute before it, an inquiry was a process of information gathering, in the light of which a government minister would reach a determination of the issue under dispute.

In practice, this distinction has become somewhat blurred. Mental Health Review Tribunals, for example, when dealing with mental patients who have been detained in a mental hospital as a result of a court order, can only make a recommendation to the Home Secretary that a patient should be released from hospital; it is the Secretary of State (or more usually his officials) who make the final decision. Conversely in the sphere of the inquiry, many inquiries now result in a decision being reached, rather than a report to a minister which would form the basis for the decision.

Planning inquiries and related procedures

The principal use of the inquiry as an institution in the Administrative Justice system is now found in the context of the planning process. In a geographically small country with a substantial population, it has long been accepted that the state has an interest in determining how land should be used. The competing interests of urban dwellers, rural dwellers, industrialists, scientists, the pursuers of leisure interests, the providers of transport systems and other utility providers (gas, electricity, water)—to give just some examples—are attempted to be held in balance through the planning process, which takes the decisions on how land is to be used.

The bulk of planning decisions are taken by local authorities, acting as local planning authorities, though some strategically key decisions—for example over the siting of a new airport—may be 'called in' for determination by the Secretary of State within central government.

Once a planning decision has been reached, rights of appeal are provided. But whereas in other contexts, a tribunal has been established to deal with appeals, in the planning context, appeals are dealt with by way of inquiry, supplemented by two additional procedures: written representations and hearings. All these procedures are dealt with by a special team of decision-takers, known collectively as the 'Planning Inspectorate'. Originally, planning inspectors did not reach decisions in planning appeals; they held inquiries and in the light of their findings made recommendations to the Secretary of State in central government. Thus these procedures were 'inquiries' in their original sense. As a result of changes in the law, however, planning inspectors now have the authority to make the final determination in all save the most complex or important cases, where they still make recommendations to the Secretary of State. In the majority of cases, the functions of the planning inspectorate are indistinguishable from the functions of the normal tribunal.

As noted in passing, planning inspectors have three mechanisms for reaching determinations:

- written representations;
- hearings; and
- inquiries

Statistically, the inquiry is the least frequently used mode for determining planning appeals.[12]

- *Written representations* are, as the name implies, a means for dealing with an appeal purely through written representations. This is the speediest and cheapest of the procedures and is particularly suitable for the determination of relatively small matters, such as an extension to a dwelling.
- *Hearings* involve the appellants and the local planning authority in a hearing before a planning inspector, but the process is rather consciously 'low-key'. Planning inspectors are trained to run hearings proactively, to try to avoid the need for the use of expensive legal representation. The inspector will shape the nature of the hearing by assisting the parties to identify the issues that need to be addressed. Typically, the hearing is used in cases slightly more significant than those dealt with by written representation, but not as large-scale as those going to inquiry.
- *Inquiries* are much more formal. They are used primarily for the major planning issues that have to be determined in particular areas of the country. (Inquiries are also used in the context of determining the shape of the local planning authorities' local plans—which provide the background against which individual planning applications are determined.)[13] Inquiries involve hearing a wider range of persons with an interest in the decision—for example, environmental groups, or trade associations—than written representations or hearings. Procedurally they are more formal, with the parties usually using barristers or solicitors to represent their interests. Inquiries can take a very long time; the public inquiry into the fifth terminal at London Heathrow Airport took over five years to complete.

Particular and ad hoc inquiries

In addition to planning inquiries, which are held on a regular basis, many other particular forms of inquiry are put in place as the need arises, for example, inquiries into serious rail accidents or other disasters.

In addition, the government may use an *ad hoc* inquiry to deal with the aftermath of a particular incident. Recent examples include the inquiry into events at the Bristol

---

[12] In 1998–9, 9,405 planning appeals were determined by written representations; 2,446 by hearing, and only 938 by inquiry. In the same period, the Secretary of State made 15 decisions following written representations, 14 following a hearing, and 61 following an inquiry: *Council on Tribunals Annual Report, 1998–9* (London: Stationery Office, 1999).

[13] Inquiries into local plans are very time consuming; in 1998–9, some forty local plan inquiries were handled by the Planning Inspectorate.

Children's Hospital, or the Scott inquiry into the Arms for Iraq affair. The Council on Tribunals recently issued advice on matters that government should take into account when establishing such *ad hoc* inquiries.[14]

REVIEW

Another form of process for the redress of grievance is review, whereby officials within the department that has taken the initial decision are required to review that initial decision to see whether or not it is correct, or should be revised. The reviewer may in some cases be the initial decision-taker; in others the reviewer is another official, usually more senior in the hierarchy. Reviews may seem to lack the independence that characterizes an appeal to a tribunal or an inquiry.[15] But they do provide an easy and quick means of rectifying a decision where something has clearly gone wrong. Reviews are found in two basic forms: the formal and the informal:

- *Formal* reviews are those which are required by law to be carried out. In some cases, as with Child Benefit Appeals or Disability Benefit Appeals, statutory review was a preliminary stage which all appeals had to go through before the decision could reach a tribunal.[16] In other cases, such as housing benefit reviews, or review of decisions relating to the Social Fund, there is no tribunal process available at all—all appeals go through the review process, in both cases a two-tier review process.

- *Informal* reviews are those that are not required by law but which officials nonetheless carry out as part of their routine administrative procedures. In the case of social security appeals, for example, any appeal by a social security claimant against a decision of the Benefits Agency triggers an internal official review to check whether the decision appealed against is or is not correct. There is evidence that more cases are revised in favour of claimants at this stage than at the appeal stage.[17]

Reviews as a feature of the Administrative Justice system have been the subject of considerable criticism. In the same way that, in the context of Criminal Justice, decisions by the police to deal with suspects administratively—for example by issuing a caution—are criticized for undermining the 'due process' model of Criminal Justice, so too is review seen as hostile to a 'due process' model of Administrative Justice. Thus Sainsbury argues strongly that the review process is objectionable in principle, in that there cannot be independence where reviews are conducted essentially within the

---

[14] Council on Tribunals, *Advice to the Lord Chancellor on the Procedural Issues arising in the Conduct of Public Inquiries set up by Ministers*, July 1996 (published as an appendix in the Annual Report, 1995–6).

[15] A view that would certainly be challenged by the Social Fund Commissioner who runs the Independent Review Service.

[16] This type of formal review has now been abolished and replaced by *informal* review: Social Security Act 1998.

[17] See Baldwin, John *et al.*, *Judging Social Security* (Oxford: Clarendon Press, 1992).

organization that made the initial decision. He also objects to review on the practical ground that, by introducing another layer of decision-taking, this may have the effect of denying claimants the right to appear before a tribunal to hear their case—at least in those cases where review is a preliminary to appeal before a tribunal.[18]

Against this, others suggest that models of Administrative Justice based not just on due process but also on other principles such as cost-effectiveness and efficiency might result in the conclusion that review is not so objectionable. Harris argues that reviews are a pragmatic and sensible way of ensuring that mistakes are corrected without the expense and delay of a tribunal hearing, and can be organized so as to meet the objection that they lack independence.[19] In addition, Scampion thinks that— when well organized—review has all the hallmarks of independence and due process in any event.[20]

While the theoretical objections can perhaps be overstated, the review mechanism—in its various guises—will undoubtedly remain in the repertoire of the dispute-resolution procedures of the Administrative Justice system, and should thus be seen as a part of that system. The question is not so much whether review should be part of the system at all; rather consideration needs to be given to those cases where review is appropriate, and those where it is not.

Practical experience suggests that the primary reason why decisions taken by officials are often found to be wrong is not because the official has misunderstood the law to be applied to the case in question, but because the factual information on which the decision is based is in some respect wanting. It should therefore make sense to find ways of getting at the relevant facts other than by the relatively expensive and drawn-out process of a tribunal hearing. In this context, review may be a valuable form of procedure. However, if the way in which the review works is that no effort is made to see whether new evidence is forthcoming, or that those who might have a case to take to a tribunal become so disheartened that they fail to pursue their claims in full, then the review may not be fulfilling a helpful role in the repertoire of Administrative Justice procedures.

OMBUDSMEN

The Parliamentary Ombudsman

The ombudsman concept was introduced into the United Kingdom from Scandinavia in 1967. The first ombudsman was and still is formally known as the 'Parliamentary Commissioner for Administration' (PCA), though he now describes himself

[18] Sainsbury, R., 'Internal Reviews and the Weakening of Social Security Claimants' Rights of Appeal', in Richardson, G. and Genn, H. (eds.), *Administrative Law and Government Action* (Oxford: Clarendon Press, 1994).

[19] Harris, M., 'The Place of Formal and Informal Review in Administrative Justice', in Harris, M. and Partington, M. (eds.), *Administrative Justice in the 21st Century* (Oxford: Hart Publishing 1999).

[20] Scampion, J., 'New Procedures', in Harris, M. and Partington, M. (eds.), *Administrative Justice in the 21st Century* (Oxford: Hart Publishing 1999).

as the *Parliamentary Ombudsman.* Following devolution, he also holds the posts of *Scottish Parliamentary Commissioner for Administration* (the Scottish Commissioner) and *Welsh Administration Ombudsman.*

The ombudsman's function is to investigate complaints and allegations of *maladministration* in central government departments which may result in injustice. He also has important functions—that will change once the Freedom of Information Bill becomes law—to deal with complaints about failures by government departments to provide information about their work, contrary to the *Code of Practice on Access to Official Information.*

Two particular features of the Parliamentary Ombudsman's jurisdiction should be noted. First, members of the public are not entitled to complain directly to the PCA;[21] they must get their complaint referred to the Ombudsman by a Member of Parliament (in Scotland, a Member of the Scottish Parliament). MPs are not actually obliged to refer cases on, if they think they can deal with the matter themselves. The reason for the existence of this filter is that, when the ombudsman concept was introduced, there were those who argued that it might undermine the primary responsibility of Parliament and its members to call Ministers (and their officials) to account. The 'MP filter', as it is known, was not part of the original Scandinavian ombudsman concept, where direct access of the public was permitted.

Second, the Parliamentary Ombudsman cannot order that any particular consequence should follow a finding of maladminstration. He can only 'persuade' a government department, for example, to pay compensation to an aggrieved citizen. Again, in other countries, the ombudsman has power to enforce his decisions.

The Health Service Ombudsman

Since first established, the jurisdiction of the ombudsman has broadened considerably. The same person also holds the three separate posts of Health Service Ombudsman for England, for Scotland, and for Wales. As Health Service Ombudsman he investigates complaints about failures in National Health Service (NHS) hospitals or community health services, about care and treatment, and about local NHS family doctor, dental, pharmacy, or optical services. Any member of the public may refer a complaint direct—i.e. not necessarily through a Member of Parliament—to one of his offices, though normally only if a full investigation within the NHS complaints system has been carried out first.

Besides investigating and, where appropriate, redressing grievances, the ombudsman sees his function as also to improve the quality of administration. He thus endeavours to ensure that his reports contain general guidance on good practice from which government departments may learn. Summaries of his investigations are published regularly, and are also now available on the internet. He also produces an Annual Report which is submitted to the Select Committee of the House of

---

[21] There is now an exception: complaints to the Welsh Administration Ombudsman do not have to be referred though a member of the Welsh Assembly.

Commons, to the Scottish Parliament or to the National Assembly for Wales, as appropriate. The Select Committee regularly sees the Parliamentary Ombudsman, as well as senior civil servants from departments that have been criticized by him. Thus Parliament is kept informed about the ombudsman's work and the impact it has had on government departments.

Local Government Ombudsmen

The ombudsman concept has been extended to local government. There are now three Local Government Ombudsmen covering all local authorities in England, plus one each for Wales and Scotland. They investigate complaints against principal councils (not town, parish, or community councils) and certain other bodies in England, Scotland, and Wales. By law, some kinds of complaint cannot be considered. Examples are personnel complaints and complaints about the internal running of schools.

As with other ombudsmen, the objective of the Local Government Ombudsmen is to secure, where appropriate, satisfactory redress for complainants and better administration by local authorities. Indeed, since 1989, they have had power to issue advice on good administrative practice, drawing lessons from the cases they have handled. To date, six guidance notes have been published: on setting up complaints procedures; good administrative practice; council housing repairs; local authority members' interests; the disposal of land; and remedies, when things have gone wrong.

The government is currently engaged in a review of these public sector ombudsmen with a view to seeing whether there should be any restructuring of the present arrangements, or any changes to their procedures or powers.

Others

A more recent development is that increasingly, ombudsman, or ombudsman-type, offices are being created which are much more specialist in nature. For example, in areas of particular relevance to this book, there is now a *Legal Services Ombudsman* with powers to investigate complaints about services provided by lawyers; the *Police Complaints Authority*, which—as the name implies—deals with complaints against the police; and the *Independent Housing Ombudsman*, which deals with complaints against (primarily) registered social landlords (formerly called housing associations).

The rise of private sector ombudsmen

Over the last ten years or so, a new and peculiarly British phenomenon has emerged. A considerable number of private sector industries have set up their own sector-wide ombudsman schemes to deal with those customer complaints that cannot be resolved within a particular company. These schemes include the Banking Ombudsman, the Insurance Ombudsman, the Building Societies Ombudsman, even the Funeral Directors Ombudsman. By contrast with the PCA and the other public sector ombudsmen, where the levels of complaints has been relatively low, many of these private sector ombudsmen have had large caseloads to deal with. They are offering a 'mass-market' dispute resolution procedure, as opposed to the more 'Rolls-Royce' work of the PCA.[22]

Much of this work will move closer to the Administrative Justice system once the Financial Services and Markets Act 2000 is in force. The act provides for the creation of the Financial Services Ombudsman scheme which will bring together a number of currently separate private sector schemes (for example Banking, Insurance, and the Personal Investment Authority), who in future will operate within a statutory, as opposed to an industry self-regulating, framework.

Process

A common feature of all ombudsmen's procedures is that they operate on what might be described as an 'inquisitorial' or 'investigative' basis. The complaint is made; the relevant ombudsman's staff investigate the complaint, taking further evidence both from the government department concerned and the complainant. In the light of the investigation a conclusion is reached as to whether or not there was in fact maladministration. Many investigations result in a finding that the department in question behaved perfectly responsibly, and the complainant was being unreasonable. Where there was a finding of maladministration, there is comment on whether the action of the department was appropriate. Again, many findings of maladministration lead to no more that the writing of a letter of apology, which is often all that the complainant wanted in the first place. Usually there is no possibility of an oral hearing (though the Pensions Ombudsman is required to offer this). This may change following the coming into force of the Human Rights Act 1998.

The European Ombudsman

In addition to developments in England and Wales, the ombudsman concept now also extends to the work of the European Union, with the creation of the European Ombudsman in 1995. He has been issuing annual reports on his work since 1996. He operates on the basis of *The European Ombudsman Implementing Provisions*, dated October 1997, which came into force in January 1998.

These not only set out in general terms the principles on which the Ombudsman will carry out his work, but also list the various powers he has when determining cases: these include the possibility of making critical remarks where no more general conclusions can be drawn from the case under investigation, and the making of a report with draft recommendations, where it appears that some more general lessons may be learned.

In addition, and unlike the national ombudsmen in England and Wales, the European Ombudsman has a very broad power to instigate his own-initiative inquiries. One fruit of this, to date, has been the preparation of a set of draft recommendations,

---

[22] Williams, T. and Goriely, T., 'A Question of Numbers: Managing complaints against rising expectations', in Harris, M. and Partington, M. (eds.), *Administrative Justice in the 21st Century* (Oxford: Hart Publishing, 1999).

which have been put both to the European Commission and to the European Parliament and Council of Ministers, relating to the adoption of a *Code of Good Administrative Behaviour*. His reason for doing this was the result of reflecting on many of the individual complaints he had received, which indicated that maladministration might have been avoided had clearer information been available about the administrative duties of Community staff towards its citizens.

At the time of writing it is not clear whether the Commission and the various agencies of the EU will be persuaded to adopt this recommendation.[23] However it has received broad support from the European Parliament and seems in tune with the general spirit of the Amsterdam Treaty which sought to ensure that 'decisions are taken as openly as possible and as closely as possible to the citizen'.

THE CITIZEN'S CHARTER/SERVICE FIRST

Another development in the field of administrative justice, and one that has not attracted the attention it deserves, was the introduction of the concept of the Citizen's Charter, now 'rebadged' as *Service First*. In contrast with the ombudsman, where the concept has moved from the public sector to the private, the Citizen's Charter concept has gone the other way. Private sector ideas about standards of customer care and service delivery, and modes of responding to failures in those standards, have been brought into the public sector.

Though the initial introduction of the Citizen's Charter, in 1991, by the government of Mr Major, was seen at the time as rather gimmicky, it has provided another impetus to promoting service standards in the public sector, through the concept of the 'Customers' Charter' and the related 'Chartermark' awards, and for dealing with customer complaints.[24] In May 1999, the British Standards Institute published a British Standard (BS 8600:99) dealing with the effective management and handling of complaints.

As part of the New Charter Programme nine principles for public service delivery have been promulgated. They include:

- Setting standards of service;
- Being open and providing full information;
- Encouraging access and promoting choice;
- Treating all fairly;
- Putting things right when they go wrong;
- Innovating and improving.

These principles provoke two immediate reflections. First, it seems surprising that

---

[23] A draft Code of Good Administrative Behaviour is attached to the Ombudsman's Report.

[24] The Service First website provides links to the complaints procedures of nearly fifty central government departments and agencies; this does not include any of the health service or local government procedures.

those engaged in the delivery of public services should need to be provided with such a set of principles at all. They seem to be obvious and rather commonsense in content. However, if it is the case that those who deliver public services do not already satisfy these principles, then no harm can be done by issuing them, and indeed as they develop some considerable good may flow from them. Second, and more specific, although most public-sector activity is bounded by rules of law which empower officials to take action, there is no mention of the need for officials to obey the law in performing their administrative tasks.

To date, not all the initiatives that have been taken are necessarily as effective as might be wished. Some of the Customer Charters[25] set standards of service that do not appear to be particularly demanding. But other targets—for example, relating to the time for dealing with matters or responding to queries from the public—have become tougher in recent years. Insofar as the concept of Administrative Justice embraces issues relating to the proper and efficient delivery of service standards, then this is another development which, for all its current limitations, should be regarded as significant in the Administrative Justice system. Service First should certainly be better understood by students of the Administrative Justice system.

OTHER BODIES HANDLING COMPLAINTS

It might be thought that with the creation of ombudsmen to deal with issues at a high level, and with the more recent development of a wide variety of complaints resolution procedures in individual government departments, there were now adequate means for the redress of citizens' complaints. In fact, other bodies and procedures have been created with more specific remits than those of the ombudsmen but more general authority than an internal complaints procedure. It is only possible to give examples here.[26]

- The *Adjudicator* investigates complaints from people and businesses about how the Inland Revenue (including the Valuation Office Agency), Customs and Excise, and the Contributions Agency of the Department of Social Security have handled their affairs. The Adjudicator does not look at issues of law or of tax liability, because there are tribunals who resolve these problems. But she does look into excessive delay, mistakes, discourtesy of staff, and the use of discretion.

- The *Independent Case Examiner for the Child Support Agency* investigates complaints about maladministration by the Child Support Agency, when clients are dissatisfied with the outcome of the agency's internal complaints service.

- Similarly the *Independent Complaints Reviewer to HM Land Registry* investigates complaints about the Land Registry. Her role is to establish whether there has

[25] Again the Service First website provides links to a number of these—currently in excess of forty can be taken directly from the web.

[26] Links to many of these other complaints-handling mechanisms can be found at the website of the British and Irish Ombudsmens' Association.

been maladministration on the part of the agency in the conduct of matters giving rise to complaints. These include failure to meet standards of service, quality, speed, and performance. Where appropriate she makes recommendations aimed at putting matters right for an individual complainant and improving Land Registry services in the future.

- The *Prisons Ombudsman* considers complaints from prisoners about their treatment in jail, and can consider both the merits of particular cases and the procedures that have been followed by prison staff.

Other bodies include the *Subsidence Adviser* who considers the ways in which the Coal Authority and private mining companies handle claims for mining subsidence damage; and the *Waterways Ombudsman* which deals with complaints against British Waterways, where internal complaints have failed.

In a slightly different category was the *Visa Monitor*, who had a general responsibility for examining the case-handling of those from abroad who were seeking visas to come to this country, who was appointed during a period when visa applicants had no right of appeal against the refusal of a visa application. This post was rather innovative in that she did not have to wait for an individual to make a complaint or in some other way commence proceedings. She acted proactively, and had power to look at case files, visit visa offices abroad, talk to staff, and to those seeking visas. She presented an Annual Report on her findings about this aspect of the work of the Immigration and Nationality Department of the Home Office.[27]

'COLLECTIVE' ADMINISTRATIVE JUSTICE—REGULATORS OF PRIVATIZED UTILITY PROVIDERS

Yet another context for the resolution of disputes arises from the process of the privatization of most of the main utility providers—water, gas, telecommunications, for example. Following privatization, the provision of services by state monopolies was, in the main, replaced by the same provision but now by private monopolies. Thus new regulatory offices—including OFWAT, OFGEM, and OFTEL—were established to regulate these new industries to prevent abuse of market power in the setting of prices, and to create the conditions in which other suppliers might come into the market to provide the competition essential for consumer protection. These regulatory offices have also had some responsibility for the development of procedures for dealing with individual customer complaints, and also complaints from others wishing to enter particular market sectors. The complaints-handling work of these bodies has been discussed in detail by McHarg.[28]

---

[27] See Anson, E., in Harris, M. and Partington, M. (eds.), *Administrative Justice in the 21ˢᵗ Century* (Oxford: Hart Publishing, 1999).

[28] McHarg, A. T., 'Separation of Functions and Regulatory Agencies: Dispute Resolution in the Privatised Utilities', in Harris, M. and Partington, M. (eds.), *Administrative Justice in the 21ˢᵗ Century* (Oxford: Hart Publishing, 1999).

Again this is not the place to consider the work of these industry regulators in any detail. But their existence does need to be noted and the fact that they too now play a part in the overall framework of Administrative Justice.

'PRIVATE' ADMINISTRATIVE JUSTICE—REGULATION OF THE PROFESSIONS

A final area in which the presence of institutions of Administrative Justice may be said to exist is in the regulation of the professions. Here private bodies, such as the Law Society (for solicitors) or the General Medical Council (for doctors) exercise statutory powers relating to the regulation of their professions, designed to enhance the quality of service provision and the protection of the public. In carrying out these functions, they and other professional regulators tend to operate through varying forms of tribunal, before which the doctor or lawyer is required to appear to answer the case against him or her.

This is a little researched[29] and thus poorly understood part of the Administrative Justice system. But again its existence should be noted in any overview of that system.

OVERVIEW OF THE ADMINISTRATIVE JUSTICE SYSTEM

THE COUNCIL ON TRIBUNALS

The most well established of the bodies which keep the Administrative Justice system under review is the Council on Tribunals. Created in 1959 under the authority of the Tribunals and Inquiries Act 1958, the council has the statutory responsibility to advise and report to the Lord Chancellor. Its primary function is to consider and keep under review the work of the tribunals and inquiry systems under its jurisdiction; to comment on drafts of procedural regulations, on which the council must be consulted; and to deal with such other matters as may be referred to it.

It has over the years interpreted its remit broadly, and indeed government departments have used it more broadly than this. For example, the council is regularly consulted on proposals to establish new tribunals, or to introduce changes to existing tribunals, for example by changing their procedural rules or by expanding the range of cases which may go before the tribunal.

In addition the council has prepared a number of reports relating to general issues about the operation of tribunals and inquiries: for example, in 1991 it produced a major analysis (currently under revision) of the procedural rules that might be

---

[29] For a notable exception see Smith, Russell G., *Medical Discipline: The Professional Conduct Jurisdiction of the General Medical Council, 1858–1990* (Oxford: Oxford University Press, 1994).

adopted by tribunal systems.[30] In 1997 it produced another report on the independence of tribunals, reasserting the importance of this fundamental principle in the operation of tribunals.[31]

A particular feature of the *modus operandi* of the council is that it has, in the vast majority of the tribunal systems under its authority, a statutory right to attend hearings. Members of the council make around 120 visits a year to different tribunals and inquiries in all parts of the country. Members produce reports for consideration by the council on what they have seen, which, while not amounting to a full research survey, provide a powerful source of information about both good and bad practice in the system.

As a result of these visits many items of concern to the council have emerged, which have been translated into proposals for change: for example:

- the need for training of tribunal chairs and members;
- the importance of the role of the clerk and administrative support generally in ensuring the smooth running of tribunals;
- the need for an adequate level of resource to enable the work of the tribunals to be done effectively.

Indeed, the annual reports of the council provided a rich repository not just of information about developments in the Administrative Justice system, but also of the principles and practices which should be adopted in that system. The obvious limitation of the work of the council is implicit in its name; its focus is limited to the tribunals and inquiry system over which it has been given a supervisory function.

THE BRITISH AND IRISH OMBUDSMEN ASSOCIATION (BIOA)

As the ombudsmen concept has developed from the original Parliamentary Commissioner to the vast array of both private and public sector ombudsmen that now exist, the BIOA was founded in 1995. Its principal purpose is to ensure that only those bodies that subscribe to certain procedural standards use the label 'ombudsman'. In particular, the importance of ombudsmen in the private sector of the economy, being funded by that sector (for example the Building Societies, or the Insurance Industry), remaining truly *independent* of their paymasters is an important function for the BIOA. They have also undertaken other activities, such as developing principles for the training and procedures to be adopted by individual ombudsmen systems.

One feature particularly worthy of note—and which, surprisingly, does not exist in other parts of the English legal system—is the link with that other common law jurisdiction, Ireland. (Though not strictly relevant to this book, there would be some advantage in thinking of other areas of the justice system where there might be opportunities for the British and the Irish to learn from each other.)

---

[30] *Model Rules of Procedure for Tribunals*, Cm 1434 (London: HMSO, 1991).
[31] *Tribunals: Their Organisation and Independence*, Cm 3744 (London: HMSO, 1997).

A STANDING CONFERENCE ON THE RESOLUTION OF CITIZENS' GRIEVANCES?

As will be realized from the coverage in the main part of this chapter, there remain other areas of the Administrative Justice system, as here defined, which fall outside the remit either of the Council on Tribunals or the BIOA. For this reason there have been calls for some more wide-ranging body or institute which might keep the Administrative Justice system, taken as a whole, under review. For example in Australia there is an Australian Institute of Administrative Law, with a wide membership drawn from throughout that great continent.

In the British context, there have been similar calls, the most recent being for the creation of a Standing Conference on the Resolution of Citizens' Grievances (SCROCG) which might take on the role of looking at the Administrative Justice system in the holistic sense indicated above; to explore the extent to which there may be gaps in provision, or over-provision; to argue for the provision of sound statistical information to provide proper management information about the development of administrative justice, and so on.

More specifically there are a number of developments which, in the context of individual tribunals or other dispute-resolving fora, may seem justifiable but which need to be seen in the round. For example, there is considerable pressure in a number of tribunal systems to move from three-person to one-person tribunals; there is pressure to do as much decision-taking on the basis of the papers only without hearings; there are very considerable resource pressures which have led to the reduction or even withdrawal of essential administrative services, such as the provision of clerks; provision of training is still very patchy; the use of accommodation for tribunals and other fora is often less efficient than it should be.

The coming into force of the Human Rights Act 1998 in October 2000 is also likely to highlight other issues which will impact on the Administrative Justice system. And although the Freedom of Information Bill has been criticized for its rather timid approach to the greater provision of information to the public, this too would seem to have considerable potential for making an impact on the Administrative Justice system.

These are the sorts of structural issue that should be kept under general review, which present arrangements do not permit. It would also help if the Lord Chancellor's Department were able to assert more forcefully its claims to be leading policy development in this area within the central government machinery. And, as with the Select Committee on the Parliamentary Commissioner for Administration, it would also help if a Select Committee of the House of Commons were to take a more specific interest in the structure and workings of the Administrative Justice system as a whole.

Although not going this far, the Lord Chancellor has recently announced, following a recommendation in Sir Jeffrey Bowman's Report, *Review of the Crown Office List* (March 2000) that there is to be a full review of the tribunal system, looking in particular at the interface between tribunals and the Administrative (Divisional)

Court. This will be the first official review of the tribunal system since the Franks Committee reported in 1957.

AUDIT AND QUALITY CONTROL

The discussion of Administrative Justice so far has focused on the wide variety of fora, ranging from the courts to informal complaints-handling procedures, available to the citizen dissatisfied with some aspect of public administration. There are now many avenues for objection for challenging the legality of a decision, or the use of a discretionary power, or the process by which a decision was made.

Other mechanisms have also been introduced to try to ensure quality of performance and the provision of good public services which provide value for money. As Ison has argued, if officials get the initial decision right, then the consumers of public services should be better satisfied and have less need to use the myriad of appeal and complaints mechanisms outlined above.[32] (Indeed, one of the criticisms that can be made of many of these processes—the ombudsmen are perhaps an exception—is that there is rather little institutional commitment to the idea of considering what *general* lessons might be drawn from the resolution of the *individual* appeal or complaint. Indeed, the very process of encouraging disputes to be resolved on an individual basis may disguise structural questions which, if addressed by the government department or other agency, might have prevented the problem arising in the first place.)

Among the alternative techniques now used to try to achieve these more general objectives are:

- the use of audit to ensure that value for money in the provision of public services is achieved;

- the use of inspectorates to ensure the quality of service provision;

- the provision of benchmarking statistics to provide baseline data against which performance by public sector agencies may be measured; and

- the conclusion of public service agreements, designed to encourage the modernization of service delivery, support proposals for reform, and increase accountability by the setting of clear aims and objectives.[33]

The time has come to consider the importance of the application of these techniques to the Administrative Justice system.

[32] Ison, T. 'Administrative Justice: Is It Such a Good Idea?', in Harris, M. and Partington, M. (eds.), *Administrative Justice in the 21st Century* (Oxford: Hart Publishing, 1999).

[33] See *Public Services for the Future: Modernisation, Reform, Accountability* (Cm 4181) (London: Stationery Office, 1998).

7

THE FAMILY JUSTICE
SYSTEM

INTRODUCTION

The role of law in regulating family relationships is particularly controversial. Some argue that the law should have little part to play; how people structure their lives are essentially matters of private choice and personal morality. Others argue that 'society' has a legitimate interest in the arrangements that people make, particularly where children are involved, since it is in these arrangements that the foundations for the continuity of society are laid. Current trends suggest that law is likely to become more rather than less involved in family matters, especially if a broad view is taken of the scope of family policy and the arrangements that might be needed to underpin that policy. (See Box 7.1.)

For present purposes, the principal functions of the law relating to the family may be defined as:

(1) To define the rules for the validity of marriage;

(2) To prescribe the bases on which marital relationships may be brought to an end through divorce or nullity;

(3) To deal with the consequences of divorce and other relationship breakdown, in particular questions of responsibility for children, financial support, and the division of property rights;

(4) To provide a framework for the protection of children;

(5) To provide a framework for dealing with issues of domestic violence.

The last two of these items are not dependent on the existence of a marriage, the first two are. The third is largely dependent on the existence of a marriage, though there is limited though complex involvement of the law on the breakdown of *de facto* relationships.

The extent to which the law should be involved in the regulation of *de facto* relationships is currently the subject of considerable debate. For example there is fierce argument about the extent to which, if at all, the provisions for distributing property on the breakdown of a marriage should or should not apply to (hetero-sexual) *de facto* relationships where parties have lived together as a family, but

Box 7.1 SUPPORTING FAMILIES

The scope of family policy

Lawyers tend to think of the Family Justice system as the place where issues are resolved when things have gone wrong with a relationship. The government's Green Paper *Supporting Families,* published in November 1998, makes it clear that family policy must be seen much more broadly than that.[1] While purporting to acknowledge the limits of the law, the government nevertheless stated that it wished to focus on five key issues, where it claimed government can make a difference:

- ensuring all families have access to the advice and support they need;
- improving family prosperity and reducing child poverty through the tax and benefit system;
- making it easier for families to balance work and home;
- strengthening marriage and reducing the risks of family breakdown;
- tackling the more serious problems of family life, such as domestic violence, truancy, and school-age pregnancy.

Much of the detail of the Green Paper therefore focuses on, for example, developing the role of health visitors and other advice-givers; creating a National Family and Parenting Institute to provide government with advice on best practice; using social security and tax policy to enhance the finances available to families; improving incentives to employers to adopt 'family-friendly' employment policies; enhancing maternity and paternity leave entitlements; tackling issues of social exclusion to ensure that families with problems do not miss out on the opportunities open to the majority. This approach includes dealing firmly with juvenile crime, as well as other issues such as truancy from school. Many of these policies imply the creation of new law or the amendment of existing law.

Despite evidence of the increasing numbers of families created by those in long-term relationships who are not married, the government still argues that marriage is the preferred context for bringing up children. It proposes a number of measures to enhance marriage, including:

- Providing couples intending to marry with a clear statement of what their new status means in terms of extra rights and also extra responsibilities;
- Making 'pre-nuptial' written agreements about property legally binding for those who wish to make them;
- Improving arrangements to help people prepare for marriage. This will include a wider role for registrars to give better support to marrying couples; allowing couples more time to reflect before they marry; and requiring both partners to attend the register office to make the first arrangements before marriage;

---

[1] The document is available on the Home Office website: http://www.homeoffice.gov.uk

- Enhancing and modernizing the service provided by registrars, who now perform the majority of marriages in Britain;
- Helping to support marriages in difficulty, including strengthening marriage counselling before divorce;
- Reforming information meetings before divorce to increase the chance of saving more marriages;
- Helping with relationship problems at the birth of a child;
- Encouraging baby-naming ceremonies to help parents make a public, long-term commitment to their children and bring together friends and the wider family.

Despite the government's assertion that families do not want to be nannied, this seems a pretty detailed list of suggestions.

Nevertheless there are also striking omissions. Nothing is said about the impact on families of bereavement; nor of a partner being sent to prison. More generally nothing is said about the resources that might be needed to set up the proposed institute or to develop the role of health visitors. A summary of responses to the consultation paper was published in 1999.[2] However, current indications suggest that detailed changes to the law are not imminent.

without formally getting married. Even more controversial are questions of the extent to which, if at all, those involved in homosexual relationships might be subject to analogous principles.

SOCIAL TRENDS

Social statistics[3] demonstrate quite clearly, first, that the link between marriage and the creation of children is not as strong as it was twenty-five years ago. In 1997, over one third of all live births occurred outside marriage. Even so around 80 per cent of those births were registered by both parents of the child, and of these 75 per cent were registered by both parents living together at the same address. By contrast the number of births registered by a sole parent has remained relatively constant, at under 10 per cent over the period 1974–97.

Second, there has been a sharp decline in the incidence of marriage. In 1996 there were 185,000 first marriages, half the figure in 1970. Overall (taking into account second and subsequent marriages) there were 309,000 marriages in 1997, the lowest figure since 1917. Of this total just under half were religious ceremonies, though for second and subsequent marriages over 80 per cent were civil ceremonies.

Third, between 1970 and 1998, the number of divorces more than doubled, from

---

[2] (London: Stationery Office, 1999).
[3] *Social Trends, No. 29* (London: Stationery Office, 1999).

around 80,000 to 166,000. Of these, 147,000 divorces involved children—around 150,000 in total. Twenty-five per cent of children born since 1979 are estimated to have been affected by divorce before reaching the age of 16.

Given these social trends, it seems clear that this is an area of law that must develop in response to changing societal attitudes. For example:

- general social attitudes in relation to children born 'out of wedlock' is now wholly different from the situation before World War II, and indeed for some time after;

- the stigma on couples living together without being married, very significant two generations ago, is much reduced (though still strong amongst those over the age of 60); and

- the emphasis on the proof of 'fault' as the basis of obtaining a divorce, though not entirely disappeared, is certainly less significant than it was thirty years ago.[4]

Public discussion of how the law on family relationships—whether in marriage or outside—should develop tends to focus on what might be good for the parties to those relationships; much of the government's *Supporting Families* paper illustrates this point. However, it should not be forgotten that the state has a considerable interest in encouraging relationship stability and responsibility, particularly where there are children. New arrangements for the provision of child support for example were 'sold' by politicians on the basis that they would reinforce parental responsibility for children; but they were also designed to cut the social security bill for maintaining children. Similar observations can be made in relation to the new provisions relating to the division of pension rights on divorce. The more that ex-partners are enabled to provide for themselves, the less potential financial liability falls on government.

The bases on which substantive family law should develop in future are beyond the scope of this book. However, three particular issues have emerged in the last twenty years as factors which should influence not only the structure of the Family Justice system, but also the roles that people who work within that system should perform.

- First, there has been the important realization that if a marriage (or indeed other long-term relationship) does break down, the process of bringing that relation-ship to a formal end should—wherever possible—reduce the inevitable feelings of stress, rejection, and failure that accompany such a process, rather than add to them.

- Second, there is now a widespread acceptance, given statutory recognition, that the welfare of the child must be protected wherever possible.

- Third, there is much greater awareness of the problem of domestic violence and other forms of abuse which occur in the family home. There have been a number

---

[4] To the dismay of many, the government has recently announced that implementation of Part 11 of the Family Law Act 1996, which would have taken this process further, is to be indefinitely postponed.

of legal developments designed both to assist victims of such abuse, and also to send the broader educational message that such behaviour is not acceptable.

These issues have informed much of the institutional development of the Family Justice system, and the attitudes of those who practice within it.

FAMILY JUSTICE:
THE INSTITUTIONAL FRAMEWORK

Unlike the position in some other countries, England and Wales has no specialist family court. Rather there is a complex set of arrangements with different courts having a range of powers to determine the different issues that may arise in family law. The idea of a separate family court structure—often proposed by experts in the field—has not to date been accepted by the government. Nevertheless it is accepted that, in most areas of family work, the relevant judiciary should ideally be specially suited to the particular tasks they have to perform.

In many instances they are required to undertake specialist training before they can determine family cases, particularly those relating to children. The training embraces not only instruction on the law and legal procedures, but also issues relating to the theories of child development and principles of social work. The difficulty of resolving cases relating to children, in particular, can hardly be overstated, since the outcome of such cases may be that children are removed from one parent and transferred to another, or are removed from the parent(s) altogether and placed under the care and supervision of others. Special educational measures for judges have been designed to ensure that decisions taken are as appropriate as possible.

CHILDREN

From October 1991 (when the Children Act 1989 was implemented) there has been a common jurisdiction across all the tiers of the court structure for dealing with issues relating to children. The structure is designed to enable cases to be disposed of at the most appropriate court level. Three levels of courts need to be considered:

- *Family Proceedings Courts*
- *The county court*
- *The High Court*

FAMILY PROCEEDINGS COURTS

The lay magistrates who sit in Family Proceedings Courts (as magistrates' courts are called when they deal with family matters) are drawn from specially selected family panels, the members of which have all been trained and receive on-going training. The stipendiary magistrates who sit in family proceedings are also specially trained. In this jurisdiction they sit with lay justices. Family Proceedings Courts have jurisdiction to deal with both public and private law matters relating to children. (For the distinction between public law and private law cases, see Box 7.2.) All public law cases start in

---

Box 7.2 PUBLIC LAW AND PRIVATE LAW CASES

In relation to children, an important distinction must be drawn between 'public law' cases and 'private law' cases. *Public law* cases are those brought by public authorities—in particular the social services departments of local authorities— or other agencies such as the NSPCC, who may be seeking orders from the court relating to the care, supervision, or emergency protection of children. *Private law* cases are those brought by private individuals, usually the parents of the child, seeking orders relating to the child in the context of a divorce or the separation of the parents.

One of the principal objectives of the Children Act 1989 was an attempt to try to ensure that the voice of the child was heard. To assist in this, in most public law applications, the court will appoint a *guardian ad litem* to assist the child, unless the court is satisfied that this is not needed to protect the interests of the child. The role of the *guardian ad litem* is to ensure that the court is fully informed of facts relevant to determining the best interests of the child. She also seeks to ensure that the court is made fully aware of the child's feelings and wishes. *Guardians ad litem* are appointed from special panels—fifty-four in England, and a further five in Wales. Membership of the panels is drawn from qualified social workers, who may be either self-employed or employed by a local authority; or from employees of a voluntary organization; or probation officers. In defined cases, the *guardian ad litem* is also required to appoint a solicitor to act for the child, to ensure proper legal representation.

In private law cases, where the *guardian ad litem* cannot be appointed, a somewhat analogous role is played by the court welfare officer. National Standards for Probation Service Family Court Welfare Work were brought into effect at the beginning of 1995.

If the proposals in the Criminal Justice and Court Services Bill 2000 are enacted into law, the currently separate *Guardians ad litem* service and the Family Court Welfare Service (part of the Probation Service) will be merged into a new 'Children and Family Court Advisory and Support Service'—a non-departmental public body, accountable to the Lord Chancellor.

the Family Proceedings Court.[5] (Despite their name, Family Proceedings Courts do not deal with divorce.)

This is a busy jurisdiction, with over 14,000 public law applications being made in the Family Proceedings Court in 1998, and nearly 33,000 private law applications being made during the same period.

COUNTY COURTS

County courts are divided into four distinct categories:

- Non-divorce county courts, with no power to deal with any family law matters;
- Divorce county courts, which can issue all private law family proceedings but from which, if a matter is contested, it is referred to a family hearing centre for trial;
- Family hearing centres which can issue and hear all private law family cases whether or not they are contested;
- Care centres, with full powers to deal with all private law and public law matters.

The circuit judges and district judges who deal with matters relating to children under the Children Act 1989 have to be specially nominated[6] for family work by the Lord Chancellor, and will not be so nominated without receiving special training and guidance. They are formally known as 'nominated care judges'.[7] Those circuit judges who are so nominated have full powers to deal with all public and private law matters. District judges who have been nominated as care judges can hear uncontested public law cases, and contested private law cases. In addition to the nominated care judges there is also a group of 'circuit family judges' who can deal with private law matters, but not public law matters.

The county court also has a large caseload. In 1998 it received over 80,000 private law applications, plus another 3,000 public law cases.

THE HIGH COURT

Although there are no formal training requirements for those High Court judges who do family work, nonetheless they sit in a separate Division of the High Court known as the Family Division. There are sixteen such judges, plus a President, specially appointed to give the appropriate leadership to the work of this specialist group of the

---

[5] They may be transferred to a county court where this would minimize delay, or would enable proceedings to be consolidated with other proceedings, or where the matter is exceptionally grave, complex, or important.

[6] One exception is that circuit judges who are not 'nominated' can still hear cases involving requests for injunctions arising from allegations of domestic violence and some other matrimonial work.

[7] There are also 'designated family judges' who, besides undertaking normal judicial duties as nominated care judges, also chair local Family Court Business Committees and Family Court Forums—both mechanisms for improving working relationships between the courts and their users.

judiciary. The smallness of their number enables them to operate in a 'collegiate' style with a fair degree of common purpose and approach.

The High Court has power to hear all cases relating to children. It has exclusive power to decide matters relating to wardship, whereby the court assumes responsibility for the child, taking over from the parents. It also hears appeals from Family Proceedings Courts. The workload of the High Court is numerically trivial by comparison with the other two courts—just 115 public law and 219 private law applications in 1998. But its more important decisions will be reported and thus develop the jurisprudence of the Family Justice system.

ORDERS

The Children Act 1989 provides for a wide range of orders which can be made by the courts. They include:

- *Care/supervision orders*
- *Emergency protection orders*
- *Exclusion requirements*
- *'Section 8' orders*

Care/supervision orders

These are made on application by either a local authority or the NSPCC.[8] Before an order may be made, the court must be satisfied either that a child is suffering or is likely to suffer significant harm, and that the harm or likelihood of harm is attributable to

(1) the care given to the child; or

(2) the likelihood of the care not being what it would be reasonable to expect a parent to give a child;

or that the child is beyond parental control.
If the court is so satisfied, it may make an order

(i) placing the child in the care of a designated local authority; or

(ii) putting the child under the supervision of a designated local authority or probation officer.

Such orders cannot be made in relation to a child who has reached the age of 17 (16 if the child is married).

The effect of a *care order* is to impose a duty on the local authority to keep the child in care, to exercise parental responsibility over the child, and to determine the extent

---

[8] The National Society for the Prevention of Cruelty to Children. It is the only 'authorized person' under the terms of the Children Act able to bring such proceedings.

to which a parent or guardian may meet his or her parental responsibility towards the child.[9]

The effect of a *supervision order* is to impose a duty on the supervisor to advise, assist, and befriend the child, and to take the necessary action to give effect to the order, including whether or not to apply to vary or discharge it.

Emergency protection orders

These may be made where the court is satisfied that there is reasonable cause to believe that a child is suffering, or is likely to suffer, significant harm if not removed to accommodation provided by the applicant, or does not remain in the place where she is currently living. Emergency protection orders may be sought where anyone, including a local authority, believes that access to a child is being unreasonably refused.

Exclusion requirements

From October 1997, the courts have had power to order the exclusion of a suspected abuser from a child's home, where ill-treatment of the child is alleged, and either an interim care order or an emergency protection order has been made. A power of arrest can be added to the exclusion requirement, so that anyone in breach may be instantly arrested. Before an exclusion requirement can be ordered, the court must be satisfied that there will still be a person remaining in the premises with the child, and that that person has agreed to care for the child and has consented to the exclusion requirement.

'Section 8' orders

Orders made under section 8 of the Children Act include:

- *residence* orders, determining where the child should live;
- *contact* orders, deciding who the child may see;
- *prohibited steps* orders, to prevent a defined action(s) taking place; and
- *specific issue* orders, dealing with particular aspects of a child's upbringing.

Nearly 87,500 private law applications resulted in the making of a section 8 order, as compared with a mere 1,600 or so arising from public law applications. The vast bulk of section 8 orders relate to residence and contact.

---

[9] The impact of placing children in care, particularly in care homes run by the authority, can be extremely severe. See Tribunal of Inquiry into Child Abuse in North Wales: *Lost in Care: Return to an Address of the Honourable the House of Commons dated 15th February 2000 for the Report of the Tribunal of Inquiry into the Abuse of Children in Care in the Former County Council Areas of Gwynedd and Clwyd since 1974 [Waterhouse Report]: Summary of Report with Conclusions and Recommendations in Full.* (HC1999–2000 201)(London: Stationery Office, 2000).

ADOPTION

The other main activity of the courts in relation to children concerns adoption, a process whereby the rights, duties, and obligations of a child's natural parents are legally extinguished and are vested, by order of the court, in the adoptive parents. It is essential that the court is satisfied that the adoptive parents are suitable and have consented to the adoption. Where possible it is also necessary to obtain the consent of the parents (including, since 1991, any guardian with parental responsibility), though this may be dispensed with if there is evidence that the natural parent has persistently ill-treated the child or that consent is being unreasonably withheld.

Once again, the primary objective of the courts is to safeguard and promote the welfare of the child. This includes taking the views of the child into account. In 1998 some 5,000 applications for adoption orders were made. Just over 4,600 orders were actually made, 50 per cent being to the child's step-parents.[10]

MATRIMONIAL MATTERS

The other principal work of the courts in the context of the family relates to the dissolution of marriages. For these purposes the courts are the county courts, save those designated as *non-divorce county courts*. Family Proceedings Courts do not deal with the dissolution of marriage.

There are two ways in which a marriage may be dissolved: divorce and nullity. *Divorce* is by far the most frequently used procedure. To obtain a divorce, the petitioner must prove that the marriage has broken down irretrievably. This can be demonstrated by proof of: adultery; behaviour which the petitioner cannot reasonably be expected to live with; desertion for at least two years; two years' separation where the respondent consents; five years' separation where there is no such consent.[11] Most applications for divorce are dealt with in the county court.[12] Evidence of irretrievable breakdown is usually considered by a district judge. If proved to the satisfaction of the judge, a provisional measure, the *decree nisi*, will be made. The divorce only becomes final after a final decision, the *decree absolute*. The existence of this two-stage process is to provide an opportunity, albeit infrequently used, for second thoughts. Most cases are disposed of on the basis of paper evidence without the need for a hearing.

---

[10] A new review of the law of adoption has recently been announced by the prime minister.

[11] These grounds for divorce were to have been replaced by Part II of the Family Law Act 1996; shortly before these provisions were due to come into effect, however, the government announced that they were subject to indefinite postponement.

[12] Except for the 'non-divorce county courts'—see above p. 150.

Where children are involved, the court must also be satisfied with the arrangements for their welfare. These must be written down and, if possible, agreed between the parents. If agreement is not possible, the judge may order the parents to come to court so that the issues may be resolved. If the issues are uncontested at this point, the judge may issue a *section 8 order* (see above).

The divorce caseload is enormous.[13] In 1998, nearly 166,000 petitions for divorce were filed; over 144,000 decrees nisi were made, and over 141,000 decrees absolute were made.

Nullity is the other mode of dissolving a marriage. However this can only be used where there is proof that the marriage either was void in the first place (for example because one of the parties was under the age of 16, or was already married), or was voidable (for example because one of the parties was pregnant by someone else at the time of the marriage, or the marriage was not consummated due to incapacity or wilful refusal). To obtain a decree of nullity, a two-stage process, similar to the divorce process, must be gone through. By contrast with divorce, this mode of dissolution is very infrequently used: 505 petitions filed in 1998; 281 decrees nisi, and 267 decrees absolute.

Judicial separation is an alternative procedure, for those who do not wish to or who for some reason cannot get divorced. It does not terminate the marriage, but legally absolves the parties to a marriage from the obligation to live together. Just over 900 petitions were filed in 1998; 519 decrees were granted.

ANCILLARY RELIEF

Ancillary relief is the term given to the powers of the court to make orders related to divorce or other matrimonial proceedings. These relate to maintenance (periodical payments to an ex-spouse) and to lump sum payments or property orders (usually dealing with the matrimonial home). As with divorce, the courts for these purposes are the county courts.

The power of the courts to deal with maintenance orders relating to the children of the marriage have largely been taken over by the child support system (see below). Since April 1993, most new applications for maintenance have been dealt with by the Child Support Agency. Initially there was a plan to transfer existing court orders to the agency, by a process that was due to start in April 1996. However the controversies and operational chaos that have surrounded the agency have led to an indefinite deferment of this plan. Thus the courts still have to make a number of orders relating to the maintenance of children. In 1998, just over 8,000 such orders were made.

---

[13] Numbers of divorces have grown enormously over the last fifty years, reflecting both changes in social attitudes and changes in the law. Even in 1968 only 54,000 petitions were filed. The peak was in 1990, when 191,615 petitions were filed.

In addition, the court's jurisdiction to make maintenance orders for spouses has remained in place, with around 9,000 such orders being made in 1998. (A similar number of applications for spousal maintenance were dismissed.)

The courts made over 32,000 orders relating to the payment of a lump sum or the transfer of property and approved another 48,000 ancillary relief orders which were made with the consent of the parties.

ENFORCEMENT

One of the problems with the maintenance system was that people just did not pay. Enforcement procedures are available. For example, where the relevant ex-spouse is in work, the other former spouse may ask the county court for an *attachment of earnings order* which requires the employer to pay a proportion of salary or wages to that former spouse. Some 800 such orders were made in 1998.

In addition it is possible to register the maintenance order in the magistrates' courts, which are then made responsible for collecting the maintenance. 1,600 registration orders were made in 1998. Failure to pay is a contempt of court, the ultimate sanction for which may be an order committing the person in contempt to prison. This is a threat that on occasion can be used to stimulate the payments due. However the reality is that enforcement of periodical maintenance payments against an ex-spouse who is not willing to make such payments is not easily achieved.

REFORM

At the time of writing, reform of procedures relating to ancillary relief is in the process of being introduced. From October 1996, twenty-nine courts were involved in a pilot scheme which used new procedures designed to promote early settlement between the parties, to eliminate unnecessary delay, and to keep costs down.[14] As with the broader reforms to the Civil Justice system (see Chapter 8), the key has been active judicial case management, combined with the need for proportionality—ensuring that the costs of the proceedings are proportionate to the assets in dispute. Both sides will be required to make the other party aware of how costs are mounting up, particularly if there is unnecessary delay in reaching a conclusion. The present intention is that the new procedures should be adopted throughout England and Wales from June 2000.

[14] An extreme example of costs not being proportionate to the resources available is found in *Piglowska v. Piglowska* [1999] 2 FLR 763 (HL).

CHILD SUPPORT

One of the most controversial recent structural changes made to the Family Justice system has been the creation of the child support system, operated by the Child Support Agency. It runs its own collection and enforcement service for child maintenance assessments.

The principle behind its establishment in 1993[15] was straightforward. Far too many single parents, mostly women, found it impossible either to obtain a court order for the maintenance of their children, or if they did obtain an order, they were unable to enforce it. A consequence of this was that lone parents were heavily dependent on the provision of social security benefits for the financial resources to bring up their children, rather than being supported by the child's natural but absent parent. Indeed during the preceding decade, while the number of children living in lone parent families increased substantially, the proportion of children receiving maintenance fell. In 1989, 23 per cent of lone parents claiming income support were receiving maintenance, compared to around 50 per cent in 1979. The child support system was intended to reverse this decline, by providing consistent rules for assessing maintenance liability, and a readily accessible means for collecting and enforcing payment that was due. A system for getting the absent parent to pay for their children was introduced in Australia in the 1980s, apparently with great success. Thus, it was argued, a similar scheme could be introduced in the United Kingdom.

From the outset the child support legislation and its implementation has been dogged by controversy. One crucial difference between the British and Australian models was that in the former, for every pound paid by the absent parent, a pound of social security benefit was lost; in Australia, for every dollar of maintenance paid by the absent parent, the parent with care lost only 85 cents of her social security payments. Although the Australian model was less advantageous from a purely public expenditure point of view, it had the supreme psychological advantage that the absent parent felt that (usually) he was, by making the payments, actually improving the quality of life for his child(ren). In the United Kingdom, by contrast, there was no such positive incentive.

The force of these criticisms was to a limited degree acknowledged by the previous government in the Child Support Act 1995. This introduced:

- the *child maintenance bonus*, intended as an incentive to encourage parents with care into work; and
- the *departures* scheme which allows for the normal rules for the assessment of child support liability to be departed from in order to take account of exceptional circumstances not recognized in the formula-based assessment.

[15] Child Support Act 1991.

However, these changes did not go far enough. The outcome has been legislation that has never fully worked as it was intended to do. Indeed, there is evidence that, notwithstanding the efforts in other parts of the Family Justice system to reduce tensions between former partners, the child support system has actually exacerbated the problems existing between them.

The system has also been severely criticized for damaging the new relationships that the absent parent may be trying to establish. The reason for this is that the formula for determining the amount to be paid to the parent with the care of the child led to not insubstantial sums having to be paid, with the result that the level of resource available for the new family was thereby reduced.

There is a substantial literature on the child support scheme.[16] The underlying principle, on the face of it, seems reasonable. Certainly it seems to be accepted and defended by the main political parties. However, its implementation in practice has been a disaster—the antithesis of 'justice'. This is not a part of the English legal system that is currently fit for the task it should be seeking to perform.

NEW REFORM PROPOSALS

Given these difficulties, the present Labour Government has recently introduced a bill to enable further reform of the child support system to be put in place.[17] The government defined the principal problems thus:

- while the CSA has almost 1.5 million children on its books, only around 300,000 gain financially from child support payments. Of these 300,000, only around 100,000 see the benefit of all the maintenance that is due;

- the complexity of the current formula led to long delays in assessing liability. This in turn made it difficult to ensure that child support was paid regularly. Because the assessment process is complex, the CSA had less time to help parents understand what they should pay or to chase up non-payment;

- families living on income support do not gain from the payment of maintenance as their benefit is reduced by an amount equal to the maintenance paid.

The key changes proposed in the White Paper to address these issues were:

- simplification of the way in which child support liability is assessed by replacing the current complex assessment formula with a simple percentage of the non-resident parent's net income;

- the introduction of a child maintenance premium in income support and

---

[16] See for example, Davis, Gwynn, Wikeley, Nick, and Young, Richard (and others), *Child Support in Action* (Oxford: Hart Publishing, 1998).

[17] The Child Support etc. Bill 1999. Proposals were first published in July 1998 in the consultation document *CHILDREN FIRST: A New Approach to Child Support* (Cm 3992). This led to the White Paper *A New Contract for Welfare: Children's Rights and Parents' Responsibilities* (Cm 4349) published on 1 July 1999.

income-based jobseeker's allowance that will enable families receiving these benefits to keep up to £10 a week of the maintenance paid for their children;

- strengthening the sanctions regime by building on existing powers contained in the current scheme, and introducing new measures to improve compliance;

- reforming the CSA's service to its customers by increasing use of the telephone and face-to-face contact, directing a greater proportion of its resources to making sure maintenance is paid on time, and sorting out disputes about liability or payment arrangements as soon as possible and, wherever possible, without the need to refer the dispute to an appeal tribunal.

The provisions in the bill, which replace the existing formula with a simpler system of rates and clarify the responsibilities of parents, cover in particular:

- the processes for applying for child support and the way in which child support liability will be decided;

- the rates used for calculating maintenance liability, based on 15 per cent of the non-resident parent's income for one child, 20 per cent for two, and 25 per cent for three or more;

- what is to count as income;

- clear penalties for parents who deliberately misrepresent their circumstances to the CSA—and for those who refuse to provide the information needed to calculate liability and collect maintenance;

- the variation of the normal rate of maintenance liability to recognize certain exceptional costs and sources of income;

- rights to dispute and appeal decisions on child support liability and the processes by which liability will be kept up-to-date;

- the formation of a complete and comprehensive collection scheme with financial and other penalties for late and non-payment;

- improvements to the provisions for establishing paternity;

- transitional provisions and phasing processes to allow movement from the existing scheme to the new scheme; and

- other matters such as:

    (1) the relationship between court orders for child maintenance and the child support system;

    (2) liability for certain non-resident parents living abroad;

    (3) the introduction of fees for child support services when these reach an acceptable standard; and

    (4) benefit penalties when a parent with care on income support opts out of child support arrangements without good cause.

Given the history of the scheme, there is bound to be scepticism as to whether the problems that have attracted so much criticism will in fact be addressed, particularly as much of the problem stems from the reluctance of absent parents in particular to cooperate with the working of the scheme. However, a more reasonable scheme may make it easier for the government to gain the public support it needs to take effective steps against those who still refuse to cooperate.

DOMESTIC VIOLENCE

Another way in which the Family Justice system has been transformed over the last twenty-five years has been the recognition of the problem of domestic violence and the need for the law and legal procedures to deal with cases swiftly and effectively. There are now two principal items of legislation relevant in this context:

- Family Law Act 1996, Part IV;
- Protection from Harassment Act 1997.

FAMILY LAW ACT 1996, PART IV

This act provides for a single body of remedies in cases of domestic violence which can be sought either in the county court, or the magistrates' court, or (rarely) in the High Court. Two types of order may be made:

- A *non-molestation order* which is an order to prohibit a person from behaving in a particular way towards another or which may seek to prohibit molestation in general; and
- An *occupation order* which can define or regulate the rights of a person to occupy a home (irrespective of his ownership rights in that home).

This body of law is available not only to married couples, but much more widely to cohabiting couples, others who live or have lived in the same household as the person seeking the order (though not tenants, boarders, or lodgers), certain relatives (such as parents, or brothers or sisters), and those who have agreed to marry.

If the court thinks that the respondent has used or has threatened violence against either the applicant or any child of the applicant, then the court must attach a power of arrest to the order, unless satisfied that the applicant or child will be adequately protected without such a power being attached.

In addition, the court may at the same time add an *exclusion requirement* to an *emergency protection order* or *interim care order* made under the Children Act 1989 (see above, pp. 151–2), so that the suspected abuser (rather than the abused child) may be removed from the dwelling.

There is a substantial caseload arising from these provisions. In 1998, over 18,000 applications for non-molestation orders were made, and over 11,000 applications for occupation orders—all but a handful in the county court. In the same year over 19,000 non-molestation orders were made, of which 15,500 had the power of arrest attached. Around 9,000 occupation orders were made, with the power of arrest attached to just under 7,000 of them. There were a further 4,700 cases in which the court did not make a formal order, but instead accepted undertakings as to behaviour from the respondent. In the same year, just over 200 arrest warrants were issued.

PROTECTION FROM HARASSMENT ACT 1997

This act was initially introduced to combat the problem of stalking but it applies more generally to the victims of harassment. Section 3 allows civil proceedings to be taken against anyone pursuing a course of harassment. The remedies available are an injunction—an order to prevent such behaviour in the future—and/or damages. Since September 1998, the courts have had power to make breach of an injunction enforceable by warrant of arrest. To date no information is available on the use of these new provisions.

THE PRACTITIONERS

LAWYERS

Given the fact that so many aspects of family life are regulated by law, in particular the issues noted above relating to children, relationship breakdown, and other financial matters, it is inevitable that legal practitioners should be deeply involved in family law issues. This is indeed a very considerable area for legal specialism, with large numbers of lawyers offering family law services. A considerable part of the legal aid budget (now the Community Legal Services Fund) is devoted to family law issues.

Practitioners have given considerable thought to the proper role of the lawyer in assisting the resolution of family disputes. For example, should they engage in heavily adversarial forms of litigation process designed to advance their client's interest, irrespective of the interests of the other party to the marriage or relationship, and the children? Or should they adopt a more conciliatory approach?

The perception that lawyers often added to the problems of separating couples rather than helping their resolution led, some years ago, to the formation of the Solicitors' Family Law Association. (There is an equivalent for barristers—the Family Law Bar Association.) It set itself the aim of bringing a less hostile atmosphere to the resolution of family disputes.

Recent research suggests that, in general, solicitors have been rather successful at not exacerbating the conflicts between couples. This is not to say that lawyers are above criticism in the area of family disputes. They are criticized for, for example:

- a desultory approach to negotiation;
- large case loads with little activity on each one;
- high costs;
- high levels of pressure to reach final settlements, as cases approach court.

Nevertheless client demand for legal services to assist in the resolution of family disputes has remained high. Surveys of clients' responses to the legal services provided has, in general, been positive.

One of the ways in which practitioners have sought to develop the nature of their work with clients in the family law area has been through schemes of specialist training. For a number of years, the Law Society has run a *Children's Panel*, aimed particularly at solicitors who act for children in public law cases. Admission to the panel involves the lawyers demonstrating appropriate levels of qualifications and experience. Though a step in the right direction, the most recent Annual Report of the Advisory Board on Family Law noted:

- the scheme was not compulsory;
- it did not apply to solicitors who acted for parties other than the children;
- there was no equivalent scheme for the Bar.

However there were clear indications that these gaps were in the process of being closed.

In addition, the Law Society, during 1999, announced that it would establish a Family Law Panel. Also, the Solicitors Family Law Association announced that it was establishing its own Family Law Panel. Indeed, in 1999, it launched its own scheme for the accreditation of those lawyers who sought to join the panel.

Thus those involved in the practice of family law have recognized the particular character of the work they have to undertake, not only dealing with the very considerable complexities of the law, but also the strong emotional context within which such work has to be carried out. As the need for special training of the judiciary has been accepted, the importance of special training for practitioners has also been acknowledged.

MEDIATION AND MEDIATORS

Notwithstanding the efforts of professional lawyers to shape the nature of family law practice to the needs of clients, the view of government has been that there need to be further changes in the ways in which family disputes are resolved, particularly those which are funded by the state. This has led to the view that a preferable way of resolving family disputes should be through *mediation* outside the courts, rather than *litigation* in the courts.

Mediation is in effect a form of negotiation. However, instead of the process taking place just between the parties to the dispute and/or their representatives, mediation involves the intervention of an impartial third party, the mediator. The mediator's function is to attempt to assist the parties to a dispute to reach an agreement that is acceptable to both sides. While the mediator cannot impose any solution on the parties, nevertheless the presence of the mediator can in practice contribute to the pressure to settle disputes.

Mediation services are provided, broadly, by two distinct groups:

- a 'not-for-profit' largely volunteer sector of people who have received special training in the mediation process and are affiliated to specialist organizations that provide mediation services; and

- a 'for-profit' sector, principally lawyers who have received specialist training, and who want to add mediation (and other forms of ADR) to the range of professional services that they are able to offer to clients.

Mediation to resolve family disputes has been used for many years. Experience suggests that it is often successful in bringing the parties to an agreement. There is also evidence that it is liked by those who have gone through the process. Nevertheless, despite the enthusiasm of those who offer mediation services, there is also clear evidence that only a small number of parties to family disputes actually ask for their dispute to be the subject of mediation.

Notwithstanding this relative lack of consumer demand, the previous government decided that it would wish to encourage the use of mediation in the context of family disputes. At least one of the reasons in the government's mind at the time was that use of mediation might well save costs, particularly for those who were using legal aid funding to obtain a divorce or obtain other remedies from a court.

Part III of the Family Law Act 1996 amended the Legal Aid Act 1988 by providing that legal aid money could be used to pay for mediation services. These provisions were to apply in the context of all 'family matters',[18] not just divorce proceedings. The key test in the legislation was whether or not mediation might be suitable in any particular case. Those engaged in mediation were to operate under a code of practice which provided, for example, that mediation would clearly not be suitable if there was any fear of violence; nor, more generally, if either of the parties was not willing to use mediation. The 'teeth' in the new provisions were found in section 29, which provided that before legal aid for representation of a party before a court could be granted, the party to a family dispute who was seeking legal aid (usually the woman) had to attend a 'mediation meeting' to determine whether or not mediation would be suitable. These provisions were introduced in September 1998, and then only in six pilot areas.

The impact of these provisions on costs and outcomes is currently being researched on behalf of the Legal Aid Board. One of the researchers' preliminary findings is that the number of cases deemed not suitable for mediation has risen substantially, doubtless because prior to the introduction of section 29, only volunteers sought to use mediation services. However, relatively few cases got beyond the intake appointment

---

[18] Defined in s. 26(1). Broadly this covers most of the issues considered in this chapter.

stage. In addition, the researchers have found that the bulk of the work is provided by 'not-for-profit' providers, rather than by 'for-profit' providers. The challenge which the researchers have identified is that the statutory goal, of establishing a national network of specialist mediation services, provided by the 'not-for-profit' sector is unlikely to be achieveable cost-effectively, at least while levels of the use of mediation remain so low.

A number of more specific problems have also been identified:

- solicitors remain reluctant to use mediation, and are critical of the delays that are now inherent in the process, particularly in cases where mediation would clearly not be suitable;

- very little can be done at present to engage the second party, particularly if he will not attend the intake appointment. Even if a case is deemed suitable for mediation, subject to the second party being willing to enter the process, mediation cannot go ahead if the second party is not willing to contemplate mediation;

- a lot of resource is expended on the intake appointment in situations where no actual mediation results.

Notwithstanding all these difficulties, the new funding code for the provision of the Community Legal Service (see further below) makes it quite clear that the principles set out in the Family Law Act, Part III are to be retained and carried into the new funding regime. The present government has accepted the view that in many family disputes mediation should be the preferred form of dispute resolution process, though the details of how this principle is translated into practice may need rethinking when the final research report becomes available.

COUPLE COUNSELLING: THE WORK OF RELATE

Relate is a national charity—formerly known as the Marriage Guidance Council. It offers counselling services either to couples or to individuals, whose relationships are in difficulty. Counsellors undergo a lengthy period of training. The primary object of their work is not so much to 'save' marriages (or other long-term relationships) as to assist partners to understand better the nature of the difficulties that have arisen in the relationship. This may, of course, have the effect of enabling couples to rethink their relationship and may lead to the relationship continuing. Equally it may help couples to realize that the relationship is unlikely to succeed, but by assisting understanding of the reasons for the relationship failure, this may lead to less friction after the relationship has ended. This may be of particular benefit in helping the children of a relationship adjust to the consequences of the relationship failure. Relate is not the only agency offering such services, but is perhaps the best known.

At present the provision of counselling services, whether through Relate or otherwise, is patchy; thus the ability of people to take advantage of the service will depend on whether or not a service is available in any given location. In addition, the fees payable for the service vary considerably. Many Relate centres have to charge quite high fees just to cover their overhead costs. This has the effect of preventing the less well-off from using the service. Finally the service will only be used by those who wish to take advantage of it. Many of those who might benefit most from the service will not do so, as they will not see themselves as the sorts of person for whom counselling will be of assistance. The government has recently been considering the extent to which the provision of such services should form part of its family policy (see Box 7.3). In this sense, this service may be seen as a part of the Family Justice system, in the broad sense adopted in this book.

Box 7.3 THE FUNDING OF MARRIAGE SUPPORT

A recent report by Sir Graham Hart[19] notes that marital breakdown and divorce not only cause much damage to couples and their children, but also impose very substantial costs on the taxpayer—estimated at around £5bn a year.

Sir Graham was asked to consider the extent to which support for marriage might be developed and funded. He defined marriage support to include not only support when relationships were going wrong, but also the provision of help and support for people to enable them to enter and maintain long-term and stable relationships. Where marriage support can help to save marriages, there is a direct saving to the taxpayer.

Current provision is through voluntary sector organizations, such as *Relate* and *Marriage Care*. But the availability of services throughout the country is patchy, and many of those seeking divorce never use their services. Those that do often do so very late in the day when difficulties are extreme and the marriage is close to breakdown.

While Sir Graham saw the development of marriage support as the responsibility of the voluntary sector, in partnership with local authorities, relevant statutory bodies, and the universities, he thought this would only occur with increased investment by government in the funding of this provision. In addition, he felt that the Lord Chancellor's Department, as the department with a prime responsibility for family policy, should take a positive role in the promotion of these developments.

Sir Graham argued that it was important to develop service provision by assisting with the costs of running nationally provided services. He also suggested it was necessary to invest in relevant research and development projects to be the basis for yet further development. Although initially large sums of public money were not thought necessary (an increase of only £1m for each of the next three years), this would form the platform for further expansion thereafter. Official response to these proposals is not yet forthcoming, but is likely to be an important addition to institutional developments in the family justice arena.

---

[19] Published by the Lord Chancellor's Department, November 1999.

FUNDING FAMILY LAW CASES

Family law matters have long been subject to special rules under the former Legal Aid scheme. Under the Access to Justice Act 1999, the special rules relevant to the provision of funded legal services in family law matters continue to apply. Under the Community Legal Service *Funding Code*[20] family proceedings are defined to apply to all proceedings which arise out of family relationships, including cases in which the welfare of children is determined.

A new level of service, *approved family help*, is to be created. It will take one of two forms:

- either *help with mediation*, for clients who need legal advice in support of the mediation process;
- or *general family help* to obtain disclosure from the other party to enable negotiations to take place, leading to early settlement of cases where this is possible.

The approach to the funding of mediation in family disputes and the possibility that a client who refuses to use mediation services may be denied further legal aid funding[21] are carried forward into the new *Funding Code*. The requirement to mediate does not, however, apply in domestic violence cases, nor in public law children cases.

General family help is an alternative form of approved family help for those cases which either do not have to be referred to a mediator, or which are unsuitable for a mediator, or where a mediation has broken down. This is designed to cover investigation, disclosure, and negotiation to resolve a dispute as quickly as possible, without recourse to substantive court action.

CHILDREN ACT PROCEEDINGS

Funding remains automatically available for a child in respect of whom an application for a care or supervision order, a child assessment order, an emergency protection order, or the extension or discharge of an emergency protection order has been made. In addition funding will be available for any parent, or person with parental responsibility for such a child. A child against whom a secure accommodation order might be made restricting the child's liberty will also obtain legal services funding. This applies only to first instance proceedings. However, funding for any appeal will be subject to a merits test—assessing the merits of the case. A limited merits test will also operate in the case of adoption proceedings.

In the case of private law children disputes, legal representation may be refused

---

[20] Discussed in more detail, below Chapter 10. See also Maclean, Sarah, *Legal Aid and the Family Justice System: Report of the Case Profiling Study* (London: Legal Aid Board Research Unit, 1998).
[21] Introduced into the Legal Aid Act 1988 by the Family Law Act 1996 s. 29.

unless reasonable attempts to resolve the dispute through negotiation or in other ways without recourse to proceedings have been made. A similar principle applies in cases relating to financial provision and other proceedings, such as contested divorce proceedings or nullity proceedings. Special rules apply to child abduction cases.

CONCLUSION

There is no doubt that family law disputes involve extremely difficult decisions, which have to be handled with particular care—especially where children are involved. The evidence suggests that this is an area both of substantive law and legal practice which has evolved considerably in recent years, and will no doubt continue to do so. It is also an area in which the impact of research on the development of law and practice has been significant.

Looking to the future, many of the issues likely to come onto the agenda for the reform of family law will be very controversial, particularly if there are significant moves away from thinking of the heterosexual, married family as the central unit for the attention of law and policy. The government will face difficult issues about the educational 'message' the adoption of a more liberal legal regime might send to the public at large. Although governments may claim that they are happy for individuals to make their own choices about how they should structure their lives and relationships, a desire to get 'back to basics' is one that successive prime ministers seem to find hard to resist.

8

THE CIVIL AND COMMERCIAL JUSTICE SYSTEMS

INTRODUCTION

In this chapter, mechanisms for the resolution of all those disputes that fall outside the Criminal Justice, Family, and Administrative justice systems are considered. The scope of civil and commercial justice is thus very extensive, embracing a wide range of issues relating to legal obligations and entitlements. It is in the context of the Civil and Commercial Justice systems that many of the relationships between law and society considered in Chapter 2 are seen to operate—particularly those relating to law and the preservation of economic order. The Civil Justice system is where protection of property and other rights may be asserted. Questions of the ownership of title to land, or to intellectual property, or to other forms of personal property are determined within the Civil Justice system. So too are the consequences of breaches of contract, and the committing of acts of negligence.

Much of the conceptual framework of the civil law has been shaped by the common law. The fundamental principles of contract, negligence, trusts, and property, the principles of the law of equity, for example, have all been the creation of the courts. However, in response to considerable social pressures, the common law principles have either been supplemented or even replaced by a great deal of legislation, whereby Parliament has enacted measures designed to protect the weaker party.[1] A great deal of the work of the courts is thus taken up with the application of fundamental common law principles, as moderated by modern protective legislation.

There are constant pressures to add to the scope of civil justice. For example:

- As commercial interests become ever more complex as the economy becomes more global, new needs for the protection of those interests arise.
- New forms of financial instruments have been created to take advantage of the internationalization of banks and other players in the capital markets, which

---

[1] Honoré, Tony, *The quest for security: employees, tenants, wives* (London: Stevens & Sons, 1982); Anderman, Steve *et al.* (eds.), *Law and the Weaker Party: An Anglo-Swedish Comparative Study* (Abingdon: Professional, 1981).

need protection not only within English domestic law but taking European and other legal regimes into account as well.

- New technologies also present major challenges. There is much current debate about the legal implications of the use of the internet for commercial activity on the fundamental principles of the law of contract. How are consumers and indeed suppliers of goods and services through the internet to be protected?

- The legal implications of newly emerging bio-technologies must also be addressed. What can be patented? Which legal system should provide protection of the intellectual and other property rights involved? What are the legal implications of the 'mapping of the human genome' project?

While these issues may not regularly trouble the minds of the district judge dealing with a list of possession cases or other routine matters, they emphasize the point that the civil and commercial branches of the English legal system cannot be divorced from their social and economic context. The legal system will always need to change in response to external social and economic pressures. Apart from any other consideration, if the English legal system does not respond, other legal systems will.

The globalization of economic activity implies increased globalization of legal activity. If those who seek the law's protection cannot find it in England, they will take their work elsewhere.

Notwithstanding these broader considerations, the bulk of the work of the courts is devoted to more mundane matters: dealing with the consequences of people getting into debt (breach of contract) or being the victims of personal injuries (negligence). There are also more specialist areas of activity—for example relating to bankruptcy and the winding-up of companies.

Thus the Civil and Commercial justice system plays a significant role both in economic life, and in the regulation of other social relationships, by seeking to ensure that bargains are kept, other entitlements are protected, and that compensation for the adverse consequences of legally unacceptable behaviour may be awarded to those who have been affected.[2]

LITIGATION AND SOCIETY

One complaint that is often heard is that modern society is now too litigious.[3] It is asserted that people are too willing to rush to court when something has gone wrong. This is an argument that needs thinking about with some care.

It could be argued that, with better education, more people are now able to take advantage of those procedures and facilities that in the past were only open to the rich

---

[2] The importance of these propositions is reinforced when one considers what happens in those countries where the rule of law to regulate social and economic behaviour is not accepted. It is extremely hard to attract investment into a country where there can be no guarantee that contracts will be enforced or property rights upheld.

[3] For current statistical trends in civil litigation see below p. 182.

and powerful. Thus, rather than being a bad thing, an increase in the use of litigation may indicate that ordinary people are no longer willing to accept things without question, as they might have done in the past. On that basis an increase in litigation might not only be expected, but welcomed.

There may come a point where the level of litigation suggests something rather different—a desire to complain and to put blame on others in situations where one should be taking responsibility oneself. This in turn may start to lead to unacceptable levels of resource—both cash and manpower—being expended on taking or defending cases in court, which could be better spent in more socially productive activity.[4] But the view that *any* rise in levels of litigation is automatically a symptom of a society ill at ease with itself, as is sometimes suggested, should not be accepted uncritically.

Indeed there is empirical evidence that one of the key problems which continues to confront the Civil Justice system is that too many people still do not know how to assert their legal entitlements through the legal system, either through ignorance or through fear of the costs that may be involved.[5]

THE PROVISION OF A CIVIL JUSTICE SYSTEM

One question that does get raised is the fundamental one whether the state should provide a system of civil justice at all. Since the disputes arising are, by definition, private disputes between private parties, why should they not make arrangements for resolving those disputes themselves? There are many answers to this challenging and provocative question, which go back to the important constitutional role of the legal system in the overall system of government.[6] Among the answers are:

(1) As discussed in Chapter 3, the common law system requires a mechanism for the development of the principles of the common law. Fundamental legal concepts could not develop without the existence of the courts, and the authority that our constitutional arrangements give to them, and the judges that sit in them. Although the law-making functions of the Parliament and other institutions are now far more predominant than they were 100 years ago, modern statute law is still set in the common law context which has been developed by the senior courts.

(2) The very fact that statute law is now a much more significant source of law means that there is a constitutional need for a body—the court system—to provide independent interpretations of the meaning of statutory provisions. All legislation has social and political objectives. Much modern legislation is designed to reduce imbalances in power, for example between landlords and

---

[4] For example something seems to be wrong if, as was the case in the state of Massachusetts a few years ago, one third of all professionally qualified obstetricians were engaged full-time giving expert testimony in litigation being brought against their professional colleagues.

[5] See Genn, H., *Paths to Justice* (Oxford: Hart Publishing, 1999).

[6] See above, Chapter 2.

tenants, or employers and employees, or manufacturers and consumers. If the courts did not exist, much of this protective legislation—designed to achieve a wide range of policy objectives, including altering the nature of the relationships between parties—would be rendered even less effective than is often the case in any event.

(3) A third reason is more legalistic. Article 6 of the European Convention on Human Rights, incorporated into English law by the Human Rights Act 1998, provides that people should have a right to a fair trial for the determination of civil as well as criminal matters. The provision of a court system is therefore necessary to satisfy this international obligation.

(4) A fourth reason for the continued existence of a Civil Justice system is that there would be a danger that resort to private disputes resolution procedures would, in practice, be likely to benefit more those who could afford to establish them and take advantage of them, than those who could not afford them. At least the rhetoric and ambition of the courts is that all those who appear before them should be treated equally, even if this does not always happen in practice.

THE PROBLEMS WITH THE CIVIL JUSTICE SYSTEM

Notwithstanding all these arguments, there has in recent years been a very wide recognition that the Civil Justice system has not been operating effectively. The main objections were that:

- it cost too much to bring cases to court;
- the system was too slow;
- court procedures were surrounded by unnecessary complexity; and
- even if an issue was resolved by a court, it might be impossible to enforce the decision.

These are not new problems. Over the last 100 years, there have been numerous reviews of and attempts to change the Civil Justice system. And these problems are not unique to England; they can be found in most other countries with well-developed economies and justice systems. However, the last few years have witnessed the latest attempts at reform, which culminated in the introduction, on 26 April 1999, of a new set of principles as well as new procedural rules for the operation of the Civil Justice system.

ACCESS TO JUSTICE:
THE REFORM OF THE CIVIL JUSTICE SYSTEM

The process began in 1994 when Lord Woolf was asked to undertake a review of the Civil Justice system. He produced first an interim and then, in 1996, a final report under the title 'Access to Justice'. He had a vision that those who sought to bring cases to court should be able to do so efficiently, and at a cost proportionate to the amount in dispute. To put it at its most ambitious, Lord Woolf sought to change the culture of litigation by creating a framework within which both professional lawyers and those who wished to take their own cases to court (litigants in person) could do so with their eyes focused on the crucial issues which needed determination by a judge, and by setting aside those matters which were not essential to the determination of the issue. Following a further review of the potential impact of Lord Woolf's proposals by Sir Peter Middleton, the government accepted that a programme of change to the Civil Justice system should be introduced. This decision was supplemented by the enactment of the Civil Procedure Act 1997.

TRACK ALLOCATION AND CASE MANAGEMENT

There are two essential features to the reformed Civil Justice system. First, potential cases are allocated to a 'track', the allocation depending on the size and complexity of the case:

- 'small claims track' for the simpler, low value cases;
- 'fast track' for moderately valued cases (usually £5,000–£15,000);[7] and
- 'multi-track' for the most complex.

Once the track allocation has been made, the progress of the case is to be determined by judges managing the timetable for the case, rather than, as used to happen, the parties (or more usually their lawyers) being largely in control of progress. Both these principles—track allocation, and case management—are directed to tackling delay, and to ensuring that costs do not get out of proportion to the value of what is in dispute.

CIVIL PROCEDURE RULES

Before 1999, procedure in civil litigation was subject to two distinct codes of practice:

- the *Rules of the Supreme Court* for cases dealt with in the High Court; and
- the *County Court Rules* for cases heard in the county court.

---

[7] The limit is £1,000 for personal injury cases and housing cases.

These two bodies of procedural law had broadly the same purpose, but there were myriad differences between them that added to the complexity of proceedings. These two codes have been replaced by a single code of procedural law, the *Civil Procedure Rules 1999*, and are made by the Civil Procedure Rule Committee (see Box 8.1).

Practice directions

In order to keep the structure of the new procedural rules relatively straightforward, a feature of the new scheme is that much of the detailed implementation of the rules is found in supplementary *practice directions*. These have been used before, but not to the same extent as under the new scheme. This has a very practical consequence that both practitioners and other potential users of the Civil Justice system will need to be as aware of the directions and the requirements they impose, as of the rules them-selves. The mix of rules and practice directions, and the frequency with which they are currently being amended, may result in the re-introduction of some of the complexity it was hoped the new system might eliminate.

Pre-action protocols

One of the most significant innovations of the post-Woolf era is that of the *pre-action protocols*. These are in effect guides to good litigation practice, setting standards and timetables for the conduct of cases before court proceedings are started. These are

Box 8.1　CIVIL PROCEDURE RULES AND THE RULE COMMITTEE

The Civil Procedure Rules are, in effect, a special form of secondary legislation. They are made under the authority of section 1 of the Civil Procedure Act 1997. In addition, section 5 of the act provides for the making of practice directions, as part of the rule-making process.

Both the rules and the practice directions are made by the Rule Committee, which is given its legal authority by section 2 of the same act. The Rule Committee is chaired by the Head of Civil Justice, the Vice-Chancellor.

The rules have to be approved by the Lord Chancellor and they are then published as statutory instruments. In addition, the rules are published in a loose-leaf format, now also accompanied by a CD, which enables judges, practitioners and others who need to know the rules and directions to keep fully up-to-date. Keeping up with the changes has been a significant challenge for many practitioners. It may be anticipated that the pace of change will slow as experience with the operation of the new rules increases.

Unlike their predecessors, the rules have been consciously drafted in a more 'plain English' style than had previously been adopted. They also incorporate at the outset a statement of the overriding objectives of the new rules, against which arguments about the meaning of specific rules must be set.

designed to ensure more exchange of information and fuller investigation of claims at an earlier stage so that potential litigants may be able to assess better the merits of a case and to ensure that proper steps are taken to resolve as many of the issues in dispute as possible, prior to the parties getting anywhere near a court room. At present only a limited number of protocols have been issued, relating to personal injury and clinical negligence claims. If introduced more widely, this could do more than anything to achieve the change in litigation culture which Lord Woolf was seeking.

OTHER REFORMS

Many other related reforms have been introduced as well. They include:

Legal language. A great deal of the language of the rules has been changed in an attempt to make it more easily understandable. For example, those who bring cases to court are now referred to as 'claimants' rather than 'plaintiffs'; they swear or affirm 'statements of truth' instead of 'affidavits'; the claimant may seek 'specified damages' instead of 'liquidated damages' or 'unspecified damages' instead of 'unliquidated damages'. The essential features of the case are set out in a 'statement of case' instead of 'pleadings'. There are numerous other examples. In short, the new rules seek to eliminate the Latin phrases and other old terminology which were thought to make legal proceedings more complex than they really needed to be.[8]

Forms. A related development, which continues a process begun some years ago, is that the Lord Chancellor's Department has done a great deal to devise forms which can be used to start and progress potential cases. Again this is designed to make it easier for the ordinary individual to use the courts, and to reduce professional costs by ensuring that particular documents do not always have to be specially drafted by a professional adviser—they simply download the relevant document and fill it in.[9]

Use of experts. Another change introduced by the rules relates to the use of experts. Lord Woolf had wanted to limit the use of experts to one; this was felt to be too draconian a step to take. Nevertheless the Civil Procedure Rules provide that experts have a duty to help the court on matters within their expertise, and this duty overrides any obligation to the person by whom they have been instructed or by whom they are paid. Experts will only give evidence if the court gives permission. Instructions to experts are no longer privileged, and thus their substance must be disclosed in their report.

---

[8] Of course, the law student will still have to be aware of the former terms, as an understanding of reported decisions made before the changes came into effect will depend on that knowledge. But for the future, things should be clearer.

[9] The forms are available on the Court Service website—www.courtservice.gov.uk—and also on CD-ROM.

THE PURPOSE OF THE CIVIL JUSTICE SYSTEM: THE FORUM OF LAST RESORT

It follows from the above that it might be thought that the primary purpose of the Civil Justice system was the resolution of disputes by a judge. While it would be overstating it to say that nothing could be further from the truth, the situation is much more complicated than that. The courts have long been used very much as a last resort in situations where the parties to a dispute cannot themselves resolve their differences without a court hearing. Even before the Woolf reforms were introduced, the 'typical' dispute was resolved by negotiation and settlement, not by any trial in court. For example in 1998–9 over two million cases were started in the county court, but there were only around 12,000 trials plus around 100,000 small claims arbitrations.[10] The 'typical' civil proceeding was thus resolved outside the court room, not in it. The Civil Justice system was much more frequently used *indirectly* as part of the process of resolution, rather than *directly* with a case being tried before a judge.

There were many incentives for parties to settle:

- *Costs.* The cost of litigation increases dramatically as soon as the parties get close to the court room door. It is at this point that the numbers of lawyers involved in a case tend to increase and where barristers are used, their fees are significantly higher when they are appearing in court, than when they are sitting in chambers providing written advice to clients.

- *The costs rules.* These provide that, in the usual case, the loser of the case pays most of the costs of the winner. Given that clear-cut cases should not be coming to court at all, and that therefore there is always some uncertainty as to the outcome of a trial,[11] this rule also helps to 'concentrate the minds' of litigants.

- *Payments into court.* The costs rules were supplemented by other rules which provided that a party who offered to settle a case could pay a sum of money into court. If this sum was not accepted by way of settlement, and the case proceeded to trial, the party who refused the payment into court faced a further potential costs penalty. Even if she won the case, but was awarded by the judge a sum lower than the sum that had been paid into court, despite winning the case, she would still pay the costs of the other side, from the date when the payment into court was made.

The Woolf reforms have retained these incentives to settle (save that for smaller cases dealt with by the small claims and the fast tracks, the level of costs should come down). However, the former system did little to prevent delay. Although incentives to settle

---

[10] With the introduction of the new Civil Procedure Rules, these are now allocated to the small claims track and are known as small claims hearings.

[11] The trial process has been described as *the forensic lottery*; see Ison, Terence G., *The Forensic Lottery: A Critique on Tort Liability as a System of Personal Injury Compensation* (London: Staples Press, 1967).

were present, they did not really bite until a trial date was getting near. And the speed at which a trial date approached was on the whole determined by the parties to the dispute and their advisers. There was considerable scope for delay. By giving the judges clear power to set the timetable for the litigation process,[12] the Woolf reforms are intended to insure that even settlements are reached much more speedily than was formerly the case.

The Woolf reforms have made it explicit that the courts must be the forum of last resort for the resolution of disputes.

ALTERNATIVE DISPUTE RESOLUTION (ADR)

In pursuance of this aim, the Woolf reforms embraced another development that has occurred over recent years—*alternative dispute resolution* (see Box 8.2). Alternative dispute resolution—or, as it is perhaps better labelled, Appropriate Dispute Resolution—is an umbrella term describing a range of practices designed to assist parties to achieve a resolution of their dispute without the necessity of going to court for a full trial in a court room. Many of these techniques have been developed in the USA where they are widely used. Their use in England has been less marked[13] but seems likely to grow, though the extent of that growth is by no means clear.

Box 8.2 FORMS OF ADR

ADR comes in a variety of forms.[14] The principal ones are:

- arbitration;
- conciliation/mediation; and
- early neutral evaluation.

Arbitration is a process whereby the parties to a dispute choose an arbitrator to determine their dispute. It is a private process. The arbitrator is often an expert in the matter which is the subject of the dispute, say a building contract. The parties are usually bound, contractually, to accept the decision of the arbitrator. It is thus, like a court decision, an 'imposed' decision, though unlike the court the whole process takes place in private, out of sight of the general public. Indeed confidentiality is one of arbitration's perceived advantages for many disputants.

---

[12] Each court circuit now has a special *Designated Judge* who acts with the authority of the Vice-Chancellor, the Head of Civil Justice, to ensure that judges are actively managing the case timetables.

[13] For the use of mediation in the Family Justice system, see Chapter 7, p. 161.

[14] For a helpful review, see Genn, Hazel, *Mediation in Action: Resolving Court Disputes without Trial* (London: Calouste Gulbenkian Foundation, 1999).

Conciliation and mediation are two techniques which, for some, are seen as very distinct, but actually form part of a spectrum whereby a third party—conciliator or mediator—who is neutral so far as the parties to the dispute are concerned, attempts to explore the possibilities for the parties reaching an outcome which satisfies both of them. This is sometimes known as 'win-win', to contrast it with a court process which may be characterized as 'win-lose'. This outcome will not necessarily be one which a court would have reached (or would have had power to reach), for example because the particular remedy—for example saying sorry—is not a remedy available in court. It has the advantage that the decision may well be one at which the parties have themselves arrived, albeit with the advice and assistance of the conciliator/mediator. There is also a hybrid form of ADR known as *med-arb*, which combines features of mediation with features of arbitration.

Early neutral evaluation is a process where someone with legal or other relevant expertise is given a preliminary view of the case and is asked to provide a frank appraisal of the likely outcome, should the case go as far as court. This may be used as a stage in attempting to reach a settlement by negotiation, rather than going to a full trial in court.

In the case of small claims, the court system itself has long used a form of ADR, as the district judges who determine these cases do so not in a formal trial but by an informal arbitration, with only the parties to the dispute present, and—usually—lawyers excluded. Although, since the introduction of the small claims track, such cases are now known as small claims hearings, rather than as arbitrations, the same procedural informality will apply.

In addition an ADR scheme has been available in the Commercial Court (see below) since 1993. An ADR scheme is also available in the Court of Appeal. The largest-scale experiment in the use of ADR was in the Central London County Court, started in May 1996. This was the subject of detailed evaluation by Professor Genn.[15]

The common feature of all these experiments is that, to date, their use has been very modest. There is evidence that those who take advantage of ADR in general find it a helpful way of resolving their disputes. But the use of ADR has not become as widespread as in other countries, particularly the USA, and certainly not as widespread as those who provide ADR services would like.

The importance of ADR to the success of the Woolf reforms is also not yet clear. There are those who argue that the procedural changes, combined with changes in the rules on the funding of litigation (see Chapter 10), will result in a substantial increase in the potential use of the courts. This will lead to a need to divert cases from the

---

[15] *Central London County Court Pilot Mediation Scheme: Evaluation Report, Research Series 4/98* (London: Lord Chancellor's Department, 1998).

courts, and thus ADR will become an important means of achieving such diversion. However, if levels of civil litigation commenced in courts continue to fall, which has happened in recent years, these particular pressures may not materialize.

A rather different set of arguments suggests that a consequence of the new procedural rules will be to change the 'litigation culture'; that as the nature of litigation changes so both clients and their professional advisers will want to move away from the adversarial procedures of the litigation process, towards the less confrontational forms of ADR to resolve disputes. However, it is far too early to predict whether this will actually happen. No doubt much will depend on the extent to which lawyers and other ADR providers become entitled to receive payments for this form of dispute resolution, particularly from the Community Legal Services Fund (see below, Chapter 10).

The post-Woolf Civil Justice system does give power to the judge, as part of the case management strategy, to stay a case for up to 28 days to give the parties a chance to use ADR where this seems to be appropriate. The extent to which this power is being used is not currently known. If used widely, this too could be an incentive for much greater use of ADR.

THE FUTURE OF ADR

The LCD currently appears to be a little uncertain as to the importance or otherwise of ADR. In recent months, the Lord Chancellor has made speeches lauding the use of ADR where possible. But officials are moving cautiously. The only initiative to date has been the publication of a discussion paper inviting comments on the potential use of ADR and the part that government should (or should not) play in its development.

There are a number of difficult issues relating to the development of ADR which, at the time of writing are quite unresolved, but which, once resolved, are likely to influence the way in which ADR develops and its relationship to the Civil Justice system as a whole. Among these issues are:

- *Compulsion.* At present no court can *require* the use of ADR.[16] Experience in the USA suggests that use of ADR does not take off until at least an element of compulsion is introduced. But is it right for the courts to require parties to a dispute to pay for something that may not resolve the matter but only add to costs and delay?

- *Standards.* If ADR is to become in some sense compulsory, how are proper standards for those who offer ADR services to be achieved? At present there are many different groups offering ADR services. But there is no common training programme nor any mechanism for complaint where things go wrong (if things go wrong). Those providing ADR services are moving towards the setting of

---

[16] For the position in the Family Justice system, see above, Chapter 7, p. 162.

common standards, but agreements on these have not at present been finalized. It is difficult to see how ADR could be made compulsory without the resolution of these issues.

- *Costs.* Another question relates to the costs of ADR. There is at present no intention on the part of the government to include ADR services within the framework of the Court Service. Nor, save for measures in the Community Legal Service (see Chapter 10) are there any other proposals for the government funding of ADR. But ADR services have to be paid for. If the costs are too high and nevertheless parties are required by the courts to use a process of ADR, may this not add to the cost of dispute resolution—something the Woolf reforms were attempting to reduce?

- *Outcome.* Will the fact that the parties may well be happier at the end of the ADR process than they might have been at the end of a trial compensate them for the expense of using ADR? It may well do. One of the most powerful claims for ADR is *not* that it is cheaper, but that it enables parties to disputes to retain control of the dispute resolution process, which may in turn enable them to move on with their lives more amicably than they might be able to do after a court hearing. But this will not always be the case. Indeed there will always be those who, on principle, will want to litigate and refuse to use any form of ADR.

THE COURT STRUCTURE: PRELIMINARY ISSUES

Having considered the context within which the Civil and Commercial justice systems have developed in recent years, and noted the very considerable changes that have occurred, the structure of the courts will now be considered. Four preliminary issues will be considered.

GENERALIST VS SPECIALIST

One of the claims made for the courts in the Civil Justice system is that they are, and should be, generalist rather than specialist in nature. Certainly, any type of case that does not fall into any other of the jurisdictional categories considered in this book must be disposed of in the civil courts. While the claim that the courts are generalist in nature is still to a large extent true, it is a claim that should be treated with caution. There is now an increasing number of specialist courts that have been created, primarily because of the technicalities of the law and issues to be determined by those courts. This raises the obvious further question whether there should be more specialist courts. In recent years arguments have been made, for example, for the creation of a specialist housing court, and more recently for a specialist environment court. Some of the tribunal systems considered in Chapter 6 have also asserted claims to become specialist courts.

There are many arguments in favour of greater specialization. The judges dealing with the issues should be better informed about the relevant law; thus the quality and consistency of decision-making might be enhanced. Procedures could be better adapted to suit the users of the specialist courts and the types of issues to be dealt with in those courts. For example, special facilities might be available to deal with the particular types of emergency case that might arise out of ordinary court hours. The practitioners who specialize in the areas of law concerned might be able to operate more efficiently by concentrating their resources in more specialized courts. Against, it is argued that judges might become too narrowly focused. As a consequence judges might become bored with the tasks they were required to perform. Judicial manpower in specialist courts could not be used efficiently if the caseloads in those courts were insufficient to keep the relevant judges busy. Given recent trends, however, it seems likely that there will be more rather than less specialization in the years ahead.

COURT FEES

A second preliminary issue that needs to be borne in mind is the decision by government that the Civil Justice system should be—broadly—self-financing.[17] A consequence of this policy decision is that the Court Service sets court fees which claimants have to pay before they can get their cases started and allocated to the appropriate track. This has led to considerable controversy. One of the objections now heard is that when this policy was introduced, in the early 1990s, it took place without any proper Parliamentary announcement or debate.

There are those who argue that, on principle, 'justice' should be regarded as a 'free good', which should not be subject to the principle of self-financing at all. Access to the courts for the determination of legal rights and entitlements is a constitutional right to which there should be no barriers—certainly not financial ones. Against that, others argue that the well heeled, who may be fighting over financial matters worth thousands if not millions of pounds, should make—through the payment of fees—a relatively modest contribution towards the running of the Civil Justice system.

There was a chorus of complaints from judges, lawyers, and consumer groups that the combination of the fee for issuing the claim together with the fee that had to be paid when a case was allocated to a particular track was having a disproportionately adverse impact on those bringing small claims. This was deterring access to justice rather than improving it. The government has therefore recently decided to abolish the £80 allocation fee for defended civil actions worth £1,000 or less.[18] However, it seems unlikely that there will be any other relaxation in the civil justice fees regime; indeed other court fees are being adjusted upwards to cover the cost of this concession.

---

[17] The cost of judicial salaries and pensions is excluded from this principle. This is in contrast to the situation in the Criminal Justice system and, in general, to the non-court parts of the Administrative Justice system, where fees are not paid for bringing cases.

[18] This decision is effective from April 2000.

ENFORCEMENT OF JUDGMENTS

A third issue against which the Civil Justice system needs to be seen is the problem of enforcement of judgments. There can be nothing more frustrating than taking a case to court, winning it, but then finding that it is well-nigh impossible to obtain satisfaction of the judgment. Of course, in situations where the loser has the backing of an insurance company, or (either private individual, company, or other legal body) is extremely resource-rich, this will not usually be a problem. But where the person against whom proceedings are brought is herself of moderate means or is a company without extensive resources, enforcement may be a great problem.

The government has recognized this and, as part of the continuing programme of reform of the Civil Justice system, has undertaken a new review of the procedures available to the courts for the enforcement of judgments. This is, in fact, an exceptionally difficult issue. There would be considerable political opposition to a return to the Dickensian days of throwing debtors into jail.[19] Yet there is no doubt that the inability of the Civil Justice system to ensure that those against whom judgments are made, in particular awards of damages, is seen by users of the system as a serious weakness.

DELIVERING THE COURT SERVICE: LOCAL INITIATIVES AND CENTRALIZED JUSTICE

The courts are managed by the Court Service, an executive agency set up in April 1995. The day-to-day running of the courts is carried out on a regional basis through six *circuits*.[20] Supervision of the judicial work of each circuit is the responsibility of the *Presiding Judges*. These are judges of the High Court appointed—two for each circuit—by the Lord Chief Justice. They operate under a Senior Presiding Judge.

One of the issues which Lord Woolf highlighted when he was preparing his Access to Justice Report was that many courts had developed their own particular procedures for dealing with specific types of matter. This did not imply that the outcomes of cases would differ, but the ways in which the court worked certainly did. Lord Woolf felt that it was important that someone appearing for trial in one town should be dealt with in essentially the same way as in any other. One of his hopes for the reform of the Civil Procedure Rules was that this would encourage greater uniformity of process. Given the not inconsiderable discretion that is given to judges to manage cases it may well be that Lord Woolf's hopes in this respect will not be fully realized.

Indeed there is an argument that a degree of procedural experiment should be encouraged to see whether the work of the courts can be made more efficient. However this should probably be as part of a controlled programme of pilot projects which can be properly evaluated by the Court Service, rather than the result of

---

[19] Even under present law, failure to pay certain taxes—a particular form of debt—can result in the imposition of a prison sentence.

[20] Midland and Oxford, run from Birmingham; North Eastern, from Leeds; Northern, from Manchester; South Eastern, from London; Wales and Chester, from Cardiff; and Western, from Bristol.

individual courts going their own way. It is also important that when new procedures are tested and found helpful, the results of good practice should be spread throughout the court system as a whole, not kept as a 'private custom' in a particular court or circuit. This is only likely to occur if innovations are managed by the Court Service.

THE COUNTY COURT

The court which deals with the largest numbers of civil cases is the county court. Founded in 1846 it was designed to provide a forum for the resolution of what would these days be regarded as relatively modest consumer complaints.[21] Over the years, its jurisdiction has been expanded. Today all civil actions can be started in the county court, save for a small number of cases in which there are special statutory rules which require proceedings to be started in the High Court, (see below).

Thus county courts deal with all contract and tort cases, and all proceedings for the recovery of land, irrespective of value. They deal with certain equity and contested probate actions (for example arising from alleged breaches of trust obligations, or questions about the administration of a will) where the value of the trust fund or the estate does not exceed £30,000, plus any case which the parties agree can be heard in the county court.

Each court is assigned at least one circuit judge[22] and one district judge. Although circuit judges are full-time appointments, most do not spend all their time on civil matters, but also sit as trial judges in criminal cases in the Crown Court. The district judges, however, work full-time on civil issues (including some family justice matters).[23] There are about 550 circuit judges in England and Wales, compared with around 360 district judges. The former sit for a total of around 15,000 days a year on civil matters; the latter for over 48,000 days. District judges thus carry out the bulk of the work in the county court.

WORKLOAD

According to the latest edition of *Judicial Statistics*[24] there are around 230 county courts in England and Wales; and over 2.2 million cases were started in the county court. Despite the expansion in the jurisdiction of the county court, there is a downward trend in the activity levels of the county court—which may challenge the claim that we are becoming an increasingly litigious society. Indeed, the LCD's *Court Service*

---

[21] *Small Claims in the County Court* (London: Lord Chancellor's Department, 1986); Polden, Pat, *History of the County Court* (Cambridge: Cambridge University Press, 1999).

[22] They are assisted by over 1,200 part-time recorders who are in effect potential judges in training.

[23] They may be assisted by deputy district judges who are also judges in training who sit part-time.

[24] *Judicial Statistics, 1998* (Cm 4371) (London: Stationery Office, 1999).

Plan, 1998–2001 predicts that by 2000–01, the number of cases started will have fallen to below 2 million. The number of trials is also predicted to fall by some 50 per cent over a five-year period—from over 18,000 in 1996–7 to a mere 9,400 in 2000–01. The one increasing level of activity is in the area of small claims arbitrations, now small claims hearings, by the district judges, where there is a rising trend, up from around 95,000 in 1996–7 to an estimated 110,000 in 2000–01.

What is not at all clear, at the time of writing, is whether the changes to the Civil Procedure Rules and the new emphasis on Access to Justice, together with new modes of funding litigation will result in a continuing fall in this work, or reverse the trends indicated.

THE HIGH COURT

The High Court consists of three divisions. The Family Division has been considered in Chapter 7. The other two divisions are:

- The Queen's Bench Division; and
- The Chancery Division.

These two divisions handle different types of civil and commercial work.

The courts in these divisions handle both cases arising at first instance (i.e. cases being determined for the first time) and on appeal from courts lower in the hierarchical structure—the county court and a number of administrative tribunals. When sitting as an appeal court and when dealing with analogous matters such as judicial review, the High Court is known as the *Divisional Court*.

THE QUEEN'S BENCH DIVISION

The Queen's Bench Division is headed by the Lord Chief Justice,[25] who is supported by sixty-six full-time High Court Judges.[26] It deals primarily with common law business—actions relating to contract[27] and tort. Torts (civil wrongs) embrace not only negligence and nuisance, but also other wrongs against the person, such as libel, or wrongs against property, such as trespass. Contract cases involve, for example, failure to pay for goods or services, or other alleged breaches of contract. Some fact situations give rise to actions both in tort and contract.

It is central to the philosophy of the post-Woolf era that only the most important cases should be dealt with in the High Court. As a result only personal injury claims

---

[25] Currently Lord Woolf.

[26] They are assisted by part-time deputy High Court judges, and circuit judges sitting as High Court judges. These part-time judges deal with nearly 50% of all trials.

[27] Some questions of contract are referred to the Chancery Division.

with a value of £50,000 or more may be started there. In other cases the claim must be for £15,000 or more. In addition, three specialist jurisdictions come within the scope of the Queen's Bench Division:

- the Admiralty Court;
- the Commercial Court; and
- the Technology and Construction Court (see further below).

Cases to be tried in these courts are required to be started in the High Court, irrespective of financial amount (though in practice they will usually be substantial). There are also a number of other types of proceeding which, by statute, must be started in the High Court.

Jury trial

There is a right to trial by jury in civil proceedings for fraud, libel, slander, malicious prosecution, or false imprisonment. In other cases, a judge may in her discretion allow trial by jury; but this rarely happens. Where there is a jury, the jury will not only decide liability (for example, were the words used libellous or not) but, if they were, will also determine the amount of any damages.

Workload

In 1998, just under 115,000 proceedings were started in the Queen's Bench Division.[28] About 75 per cent were for debt; and a further 8 per cent for personal injury. During the same year, nearly half the cases started in London[29] ended with a judgment being given in default (because the person against whom the action was brought did not defend it). About a quarter of the cases were disposed of following some court intervention, but there were trials in only a tiny minority of cases. Only 480 out of the nearly 3,400 cases disposed of after intervention by the court involved a trial.

In those cases where damages were sought, awards in excess of £10,000 were made in nearly all cases where the claimant won; most personal injury cases resulted in awards in excess of £50,000.

Divisional court

When sitting as a Divisional Court, the Queen's Bench Division deals with judicial review cases,[30] appeals by way of 'case stated',[31] habeas corpus,[32] committal for con-

---

[28] Of these, just over 21,500 were started in London, and just under 93,500 in centres outside London.

[29] Statistics relating to disposal are only available for cases dealt with in London.

[30] Powers of judicial review are exercisable both over inferior courts and tribunals—for example where it is alleged that there has been a breach of proper fair procedure or an incorrect interpretation of the law—and against public bodies or government ministers or others carrying out public acts or duties. Judicial review is considered further in Chapter 6 on Administrative Justice.

[31] A process used, for example, by a Crown Court or a magistrates' court to obtain a ruling on a particular provision of criminal law.

[32] Where unlawful detention is alleged.

tempts of court committed in an inferior court, or appeals and applications under a variety of statutory provisions.[33] The bulk of the work is judicial review. Over 4,500 applications for leave to bring judicial review proceedings were made in 1998, of which nearly 60 per cent were granted. The largest single group of cases—over half the total—relates to matters arising out of decisions relating to immigration law.[34] This area of the High Court's work has been subject to rapid increase. Appeals and applications rose by nearly 13 per cent in 1998. This aspect of the work of the High Court, known as the Crown Office List, has recently been the subject of review by Sir Jeffrey Bowman, which was presented to the Lord Chancellor in March 2000. This has already produced the announcement that the Divisional Court will be renamed the Administrative Court. The government has also issued a new consultation paper on the procedures relating to judicial review, which will eventually lead to some procedural change. It seems clear that part of the motivation for these changes is concern about the additional workload that will be created following the coming into force of the Human Rights Act 1998 in October 2000.[35]

THE CHANCERY DIVISION

The Chancery Division of the High Court comprises the Lord Chancellor (who rarely sits as a Chancery judge in practice), the Vice-Chancellor[36] (the effective head of the Chancery Division), supported by some seventeen other High Court judges.[37]

The principal categories of business dealt with by the division relate to corporate and personal insolvency disputes; disputes relating to business trade and industry; the enforcement of mortgages; intellectual property matters including copyright and patents; disputes relating to trust property; and disputes arising from wills and the administration of deceased people's estates (probate matters). (For uncontested probate matters, see Box 8.3.) The bulk of the work is handled in the Royal Courts of Justice in London, together with eight provincial centres which have High Court Chancery jurisdiction.[38]

In 1998 a total of nearly 37,500 proceedings were started in the Chancery Division; but only 601 cases were disposed of following a trial. The Chancery Division also disposed of 154 appeals in 1998, over half being appeals on bankruptcy matters.

In addition to the general work of the Chancery Division, there are two specialist jurisdictions: the Companies Court and the Patent Court, considered further below.

[33] For example under the Town and Country Planning legislation.

[34] Bridges, Lee, Meszaros, George, and Sunkin, Maurice, *Judicial Review in Perspective* (London: Cavendish, 1995).

[35] The Law Commission also issued a report on this matter in 1995.

[36] The present Vice-Chancellor, Sir Richard Scott, also holds the post of Head of Civil Justice, and has been responsible for much of the detailed work associated with the reform of the Civil Justice system.

[37] They are assisted, as needed, by deputy High Court judges, who are either practitioners approved to act as such by the Lord Chancellor, or retired High Court or Circuit judges. The extent of their use depends on the level of business before the courts.

[38] Birmingham, Bristol, Cardiff, Leeds, Liverpool, Manchester, Newcastle upon Tyne, and Preston.

Box 8.3 UNCONTESTED PROBATE MATTERS: THE FAMILY DIVISION

Although the Chancery Division deals with contested probate matters, uncontested matters are dealt with in the Principal Registry of the *Family* Division of the High Court or any of the eleven district probate registries that exist in England and Wales. Grants of probate are made in cases where there was a will; grants of administration, where there was not. There is a heavy workload involved. Over 250,000 grants were issued in 1998, of which nearly 75 per cent were grants of probate, the remainder grants of administration.

As with other parts of the Civil Justice system, the court is very much the place of last resort for the resolution of disputes.

THE COMMERCIAL JUSTICE SYSTEM

Notwithstanding the reluctance, noted above, of the judiciary to specialize, the fact is that both within the High Court, and the County Court systems, there now exists a range of specialist courts, established to deal with a range of (primarily) commercial and company law matters. These developments reflect the position of London in the global economy, and the need for the courts to provide appropriate levels of expertise in specialist areas. They have spread to provincial centres where there is also significant commercial activity. The specialist courts may be listed as follows.

THE COMPANIES COURT

This court is part of the Chancery Division of the High Court. It deals primarily with the compulsory liquidation of companies and other matters arising under the Insolvency Act 1986 and the Companies Acts. For example, a registered company which seeks to reduce its capital may only do so with the approval of the court. The bulk of this work is done in London, but eight provincial district registries have the same powers. Just over 18,000 cases were started in these courts in 1998.

THE PATENTS COURT

This is another specialist part of the Chancery Division, dealing not only with patents, but other forms of intellectual property including registered designs. It also hears appeals against decisions of the Comptroller General of Patents.

Cases suitable for determination by a county court are heard in a specially designated county court—the Central London County Court. The workload of this court is not high—only 289 matters were dealt with in 1998.

THE ADMIRALTY COURT

This is part of the Queen's Bench Division of the High Court, dealing—as the name suggests—with shipping matters, principally the consequences of collisions at sea and damage to cargoes. As with patents, most cases are dealt with in London, but there is power to refer suitable cases to specially designated county courts. Three hundred and eighty actions were started in 1998; only seventeen trials were actually heard in the court.

THE COMMERCIAL COURT

This is also part of the Queen's Bench Division of the High Court. This deals with a wide range of commercial matters, for example, banking, international credit, and the purchase and sale of commodities. It also deals with shipping matters not handled by the Admiralty Court—contracts relating to ships, carriage of cargo, insurance, as well as the construction and performance of mercantile contracts more generally. The Commercial Court also deals with the practice of arbitration and questions which might arise from arbitrations. Just under 1,500 claims were started in this court in 1998; only twenty-three judgments were made following a trial.

THE TECHNOLOGY AND CONSTRUCTION COURT

This is the new name given in 1998 to the former Official Referees' Court. This is another section of the High Court which sits in London with eight full-time *circuit* judges, presided over by a High Court judge. The court deals primarily with building and engineering disputes, and also computer litigation. It can also deal with other matters such as valuation disputes and landlord and tenant matters involving dilapidations; it also handles questions arising from arbitrations in building and engineering disputes. During 1998, 538 proceedings were started; only sixty-three trials were held in London.

THE RESTRICTIVE PRACTICES COURT

Constituted under the provisions of the Restrictive Practices Court Act 1976, this court deals with a very small number of cases relating to disputes as to whether particular trade agreements are contrary to the public interest. This court is unusual in that the judge sits with specially appointed lay members (unless the case is solely about a matter of law). It is being replaced by new arrangements put in place following the coming into force in April 2000 of the Competition Act 1998.

OTHER COURTS AND OFFICES

In addition to the courts so far identified, there are also a number of other offices which form part of the Supreme Court. These include:

- *The Official Solicitor's Department.* This operates under the authority of section 90 of the Supreme Court Act 1981. Its primary duties are to protect the interests of children and mental patients, i.e. those who do not have full legal capacity to look after their own affairs. This department has a fairly substantial workload, dealing with around 3500 cases in 1998.

- *The Court of Protection.* This is an office of the Supreme Court which exercises judicial functions in respect of the property and financial affairs of persons incapable, by reason of mental disorder, of running their own affairs. The principal legislation conferring power on the court is the Mental Health Act 1983, and the Enduring Powers of Attorney Act 1985. It has a significant workload— around 60,000 orders were made in 1998. Although labelled a court, most of its work is carried out by specially nominated officers. The Law Commission recommended, in 1995, that it should not remain an office of the Supreme Court, but become a proper court of record, with a broader jurisdiction. The government is currently considering this.

- *The Public Trust Office.* This is now an executive agency within the Lord Chancellor's Department. It has wide responsibilities to manage the property and affairs of private individuals. Assets totalling around £3.8bn were under the office's management in 1998.

APPEALS AND THE APPEAL COURTS

We have already noted in passing that many of the courts listed above have power to hear appeals in defined circumstances. Many appeals are satisfactorily disposed of in that context.

However, there is also a number of courts that deal exclusively with appeals. They are particularly important in the English legal system, not just because they have greater authority within the hierarchical court structure, but also because it is through the reported judgments delivered in those courts that the primary source of authority for the development of the common law and the interpretation of statutes is to be found. (See above Chapter 3.) It can be argued that these appeal courts are the only truly 'generalist courts' in that they have the responsibility for dealing with whatever is presented to them by way of appeal.

POLICY ISSUES

In recent years, it has been suggested that there may be too many avenues for appeal; and that the level of court at which an appeal is determined may not always be the right one. To deal with this, important changes of principle have been introduced into the law on appeals by the Access to Justice Act 1999.

Permission to appeal

It was always the case that, in order to bring an appeal in the Court of Appeal it was necessary for the appellant to seek the permission (or—as it used to be called—the leave) of the court to bring the appeal. Section 54 of the Access to Justice Act 1999 permits rules of court to be made that will require permission to appeal to be obtained for all appeals to the county courts, the High Court, or the Court of Appeal (Civil Division). There will be limited exceptions, for example appeals relating to court orders which affect the liberty of the individual. There will be no appeal against a decision either to give or refuse permission. Where permission is refused, there will remain the possibility of making a further application for permission, either in the same or another court.

Second appeals

Once a county court or the High Court has decided a matter on appeal, section 55 of the Access to Justice Act provides that there will be no possibility of a further appeal unless either the appeal would raise an important point of principle or practice, or there is some other compelling reason for the appeal to be heard. All applications for permission to bring a further appeal will be dealt with by the Court of Appeal, irrespective of the court which determined the first appeal. If permission is granted, the Court of Appeal will hear the appeal as well.

Destination of appeals

Section 56 of the Access to Justice Act gives the Lord Chancellor power to vary, by order,[39] the avenues of appeal to and within the county court, the High Court, and the Court of Appeal. The government's intentions currently are that:

(1) for fast track cases heard by a district judge, appeals will lie to a circuit judge;

(2) for fast track cases heard by a circuit judge, appeals will lie to a High Court judge;

(3) in multi-track cases, appeals against interlocutory decisions by a district judge will be to a circuit judge; by a master[40] or circuit judge to a High Court judge; and by a High Court judge to the Court of Appeal;

(4) in multi-track cases, appeals against final orders will be direct to the Court of Appeal, irrespective of the court making the initial decision.

---

[39] The order will be subject to the *affirmative resolution procedure* (see p. 44) and cannot be made without consulting the heads of the divisions of the High Court (see above p. 182).

[40] Masters are judicial officers of the High Court who determine interlocutory matters.

A consequence of these changes is that the Court of Appeal is likely to have a caseload reduced in terms of numbers, but potentially more focused on issues that are relevant to the development of the law.

THE COURTS OF APPEAL

The particular Courts of Appeal to be considered here are:

- the Judicial Committee of the Privy Council;
- the House of Lords;
- the Court of Appeal.

THE JUDICIAL COMMITTEE OF THE PRIVY COUNCIL

This remains the final Court of Appeal for twenty-four British Commonwealth Territories[41] and six independent republics within the Commonwealth.[42] It also acts as a constitutional Supreme Court determining constitutional issues arising from those independent territories that have a written constitution. The Judicial Committee also has jurisdiction over a number of domestic matters,[43] and 'pastoral' matters (which relate to the Church of England). The statutory powers of the committee derive from the Judicial Committee Act of 1833, though the history of the committee can be traced back to medieval times. The judges who sit in the Judicial Committee are (broadly) the same as those who sit in the House of Lords (below), though they are on occasion joined by a senior member of the judiciary from the country whence the appeal has come.

Many find the jurisdiction of the Judicial Committee highly anachronistic—a throw-back to a British imperial past that is long gone. Nevertheless the Judicial Committee has a steady stream of work. Seventy-eight appeals and ninety-five petitions for special permission to appeal[44] were lodged in 1998; and the court sat on 105 days. The issues it deals with are, by definition, of very considerable legal and social importance not just for the country in question, but also for the common law world in general.

---

[41] This group includes both independent territories that retained this right of appeal when they achieved independence—for example, New Zealand and Jamaica; and United Kingdom overseas territories that remain dependent on the United Kingdom, for example, Gibraltar, and the Cayman Islands.

[42] This group includes Mauritius and The Gambia.

[43] Hearing appeals from a number of professional bodies, in particular under the Medical Act 1983 and the Dentists Act 1984. The Judicial Committee has recently been given power to deal with 'devolution issues' arising out of the passing of the Wales Act 1998 and the Scotland Act 1998.

[44] These special petitions relate to appeals in criminal cases where the Judicial Committee will not hear an appeal unless satisfied that the case raises a matter of great general importance or where there appears to be the danger of a grave miscarriage of justice.

THE HOUSE OF LORDS

This is the supreme court of appeal in Great Britain and Northern Ireland, although it cannot hear appeals in Scottish criminal cases. The House of Lords can, with permission, hear appeals from any order or judgment of the Court of Appeal in England, the Court of Session in Scotland, or the Court of Appeal in Northern Ireland.[45] In addition, appeals may be taken, with permission, from the High Court when it has been sitting as a Divisional Court (i.e. as a court of appeal or when dealing with cases such as judicial review). In limited circumstances, an appeal may be brought direct from the High Court or the High Court in Northern Ireland, when sitting as a trial court.[46]

Permission may be granted either by the relevant Court of Appeal or, if that is not forthcoming, by the Appeal Committee of the House of Lords. (If a lower court grants permission, the House of Lords cannot overturn that decision.) In practice, permission is granted by the lower courts rather infrequently.[47] In 1998 the Appeal Committee dealt with some 270 petitions for permission to appeal; less than 25 per cent were allowed. The right of the citizen to 'take her case to the highest court in the land' is in reality a highly contingent right, subject to considerable procedural constraint. The House of Lords is, thus, a judicial resource that is sparingly used.

Appeals themselves are heard by an Appellate Committee of the House of Lords, consisting usually of five Lords of Appeal. Hearings are tightly time controlled, lasting usually only two to three days. In 1998 sixty appeals were determined, forty-five of which came from the Civil Division of the Court of Appeal, and related to a wide variety of quite different issues.[48]

THE COURT OF APPEAL

The Court of Appeal is divided into two divisions: the Criminal and the Civil. The two senior judges are the Lord Chief Justice, who heads the Criminal Division, and the Master of the Rolls, who heads the Civil Division. They are assisted by, currently, thirty-five Lords Justices of Appeal.[49] Both the President of the Family Division and the Vice-Chancellor of the Chancery Division sit in the Court of Appeal for part of their time. By contrast with the House of Lords and the Privy Council, the Court of Appeal has a substantial caseload.

---

[45] Save in the case of Northern Ireland or Scotland, where this is prevented by statute.

[46] This is known as 'leapfrogging' and can occur where it is clear that the law in question needs clarification at the highest level, perhaps because there are inconsistent decisions from the Court of Appeal. The process is rarely utilized.

[47] It is not uncommon for the Criminal Division of the Court of Appeal to certify that a point of law of general public importance is involved in a case, but still to refuse permission to appeal to the House of Lords.

[48] The largest single group was eight cases relating to employment matters: see *Judicial Statistics, 1998*, table 1.5.

[49] Other High Court judges assist, as required and as available, in the Criminal Division.

The Criminal Division

As with the House of Lords, appeals either against sentence or conviction can only be made with the leave (now, the 'permission') of the court. In 1998, 8,649 applications were made, of which under 25 per cent were against conviction. Around 2,500 applications for permission were granted by a single judge. Of the 6,000 or so applications for permission which were refused, just under a third were taken to the full court for determination, of which about a quarter (549) were allowed.

Of the actual appeals heard during 1998, 42 per cent of those against conviction were allowed; and 72 per cent against sentence were allowed. Seventy-three retrials were also ordered.

The Civil Division

The number of appeals coming to the Civil Division rose steadily during the early 1990s; they began to fall in 1996, a trend that has continued since. During 1998, some 1,100 final appeals were set down, and a similar number were disposed of, of which about 850 went to a hearing before the court. Just under half of the appeals were allowed. During the same period about 500 interlocutory appeals—on matters that are related to the proceedings, but not finally determinative of the issues in question—were set down, and a similar number were disposed of. About 40 per cent of the interlocutory appeals were allowed.

Delay and reform

These bare statistics do not reveal the very serious problem of delay that has existed in the Court of Appeal in recent years. Following Lord Woolf's report into the Civil Justice system in general, Sir Jeffrey Bowman was asked to undertake a special review of the Court of Appeal.[50] Proposals for reform were published by the Lord Chancellor in 1998.[51] Legislative change has now followed in the Access to Justice Act 1999, part IV.

The act provides that the present situation, where the majority of appeals have to be heard by three Court of Appeal judges is to be replaced by more flexible arrangements. In future, the Master of the Rolls may, with the concurrence of the Lord Chancellor, give directions as to the minimum number of judges of which a court must consist for specified types of proceedings. Subject to these directions the Master of the Rolls, or another Lord Justice of Appeal designated by him, will be able to determine the number of judges to hear any appeal. The prospect of two- and one-judge courts (as well as three-judge courts) is therefore firmly in prospect.

[50] *Review of the Court of Appeal (Civil Division)—Report to the Lord Chancellor*, September 1997.

[51] *Reform of the Court of Appeal (Civil Division): Proposals for Change to Constitution and Jurisdiction* (London: Lord Chancellor's Department, July 1998). A separate review of appeals in family cases was undertaken by the Family Appeal Review Group, chaired by Thorpe LJ, who reported in 1998, and on which the Lord Chancellor's Department is currently consulting.

COMMENTARY

(1) While the popular rhetoric may suggest that it is the right of every English person to have his or her day in court, it has been seen that in practice access to the courts is surrounded by barriers. There are substantial procedural and financial pressures on litigants to settle their differences outside the courts; and appealing the decision of a court is even more problematic.

(2) Judicial manpower is an expensive resource to be used sparingly. There is a notable tendency for much of the simpler case work to be dealt with by part-time judges; whether this will continue after the coming into effect of the Human Rights Act 1998 is yet to be determined. There are also many contexts in which judges sit in a level of court to which they have not been appointed— circuit judges in the High Court; High Court judges in the Court of Appeal, for example. There is thus considerable flexibility in how the available resource is used, though this begs the question—given the policy on court fees—of whether the public is actually getting the judicial service it thinks it is paying for.

(3) Delay and cost were the principal issues identified as in need of reform by Lord Woolf. Early indications are that the new Civil Procedure Rules are working well, and with increased investment in information technology due to be rolled out in the next couple of years, could be expected to get even better. It is too early to say whether the new efficiency will lead to an increase in the courts' work load, or whether the other mechanisms for diverting cases from the courts will be effective.

(4) The changes to the Court of Appeal, though driven by the need for greater efficiency, will alter the character of that court. It will be important to keep the impact of the changes to its procedures under review.

PART III

THE DELIVERY AND FUNDING OF LEGAL SERVICES

9

DELIVERING LEGAL SERVICES: PRACTITIONERS, ADJUDICATORS, AND JURISTS

INTRODUCTION

Discussions about the delivery of legal services tend to focus on the role of the legal profession, and its two branches: *solicitors* and *barristers*. The approach adopted for this book is broader. In the same way that we have argued that the institutional framework of the English legal system can only be understood by referring to a wide range of institutional provisions, not simply the work of the courts, so too a consideration of the full range of those who offer services about legal rights and entitlements involves consideration of a much greater range of actors. The purpose of this chapter is to provide an introductory account of the principal groups that provide legal services. It considers not only the professionally qualified, but also those that provide legal services without necessarily having legal professional qualifications.

The bulk of the chapter focuses on those who deliver legal services directly or indirectly to clients. The chapter also includes consideration of those who provide legal services by adjudicating disputes, whether as judges or other types of dispute-resolver. Finally the role of the jurists—the legal scholars—is considered. Through their teachings and writings they are (or should be) helping to shape both the law and the behaviour of those who deliver legal services to the public.

A. THE PRACTITIONERS

Three groups are considered in this part of the chapter:

- those professionally qualified as lawyers;
- those in professional groups allied to law; and
- lay legal advisers.

PROFESSIONALLY QUALIFIED LAWYERS:
SOLICITORS AND BARRISTERS

There are currently over 71,000 practising solicitors in England and Wales, plus another 12,000 or so barristers. The majority of these are in private practice, though a substantial minority are employed lawyers working 'in-house' for a wide variety of companies, government departments, and agencies. Both these totals have increased very rapidly over the last quarter of a century. They reflect increased demands for legal services resulting from economic growth, structural changes affecting the commercial world such as globalization and involvement in Europe, and numerous other social changes with greater emphasis on citizens' rights.

These global figures mask two important developments. First, there is a significantly better gender balance of those entering the legal profession than there was twenty-five years ago. For a number of years, more women than men have become solicitors. Second, the ethnic balance of entrants, though far from satisfactory, has improved. While the legal profession may still be a predominantly middle-class one, it is a significantly less white and male than it used to be.

WHAT LAWYERS DO

It is impossible to summarize the enormous variety of work that lawyers undertake. A long list could be presented, but would not be particularly enlightening. Much of the work of the large city firms relates to the commercial activities of their clients, for example the headline-grabbing financial deals or takeover bids that shape economic and commercial life. Others offer services focused on the individual client, for example defending people accused of crime, buying and selling property, dealing with divorces, or the consequences of death.

Although the focus of discussion in this chapter will implicitly relate to lawyers who work in private practice, the work of other significant groups of qualified lawyers should also be noted. Three specific examples may be given:

Lawyers in industry. Considerable numbers of lawyers work for industry, not indirectly through the services provided for companies by those in private practice, but directly through their employment by the firms concerned. Most major companies have legal departments, staffed by professionally qualified lawyers, able to advise them on those legal issues which directly affect the company and its operations, for example matters relating to employment law, or health and safety legislation.

Lawyers in the civil service and local government. There are—broadly—two ways in which those professionally qualified as lawyers may be employed in central or local government. First they may be specifically employed for their technical legal expertise: to draft legislation, or to litigate for the branch of government concerned in proceedings that may be brought against the department in question. Alternatively, there are those with law degrees and other legal qualifications who are not employed as lawyers, but who form part of the general civil service complement of government.

Lawyers in court administration. Lawyers play a very important part in the work of those courts and other dispute-resolution bodies which do not use legally qualified adjudicators, for example justices' clerks in the magistrates' courts.

One of the great attractions of the law is the enormous range of employment opportunities that the law provides for those who wish to practice or work in the legal system. There are also increasing opportunities to work in international agencies of various kinds.

Preliminary issues

When thinking about what lawyers do, two preliminary issues may be noted: the distinction between litigious and non-litigious matters; and the distinction between lawyers' services and legal services.

Litigious and non-litigious matters. It is helpful to bear in mind from the outset a fundamental distinction between litigious and non-litigious matters. A great deal of the work of lawyers is directed to non-litigious work. This includes, for example, the provision of advice, or the drafting of documents, designed to ensure that the affairs of people run smoothly without the need to litigate in a courtroom or any other forum. By contrast, litigious work arises where things have gone wrong, where there are disputes either between individuals, or companies, or between the citizen and the state. The right to be heard in a court and the right to conduct litigation are subject to particular statutory rules (see Box 9.2).

Legal services and lawyers' services. A second distinction worth making at this stage is that between *lawyers' services*, services which must be provided only by professionally qualified lawyers, and *legal services*, which may, though do not have to be, provided by professional lawyers. One of the features of the English legal system is that many people, other than those professionally qualified as lawyers, provide legal services, which are required by members of the public, and which deal with legal issues, for example advice about legal entitlements or the completion of legal transactions. The roles of para-legal staff and lay advisers are discussed later in this chapter. (Some examples are set out in Box 9.1.)

PROFESSIONAL ORGANIZATION

The organization of the practising legal profession in England and Wales is very different to the position in many other countries. There is still an important distinction in professional identity between *solicitors*, who are professionally regulated by the Law Society, and *barristers*, who are regulated by the General Council of the Bar (the Bar Council).

Solicitors in private practice usually come together to form partnerships, though a

Box 9.1 LEGAL SERVICES AND LAWYERS' SERVICES

Some examples of the distinction in practice:

- The first source of legal advice for many people faced with problems about their employment ('Have I been unfairly dismissed by my employer?') will be a *Citizens' Advice Bureau,* or a *Trade Union.* The person they see will be trained to give the appropriate advice; they may indeed recommend that the person should see a qualified lawyer. But the initial *legal service* will not usually come from a lawyer, but from a trained lay adviser.

- Similar points may be made in relation to advice sought by a tenant in dispute with her landlord.

- Many people anxious to obtain advice as to their legal entitlements to social security benefits are more likely to turn to the services of a *welfare rights officer*—again a lay person, albeit specially trained, rather than to a professionally qualified lawyer.

- Those who buy or sell houses may use the services of a *licensed conveyancer* rather than a solicitor to complete their transaction.

Some legal services, in the sense set out above, are provided by other professional groups. The most obvious example is that the bulk of matters relating to individuals' legal liability to pay tax are dealt with, not by lawyers, but by *accountants. Legal services* are not provided exclusively by qualified lawyers.

Lawyers' services may be seen as a special sub-set of the total provision of legal services: they are services which either *have* to be provided by those qualified as lawyers (such as the provision of advocacy services in court—which are restricted to those who have achieved particular professional qualifications); or which as a matter of practice are provided by those qualified as lawyers. For example, it is inconceivable that large corporations would turn to lay advisers—however well trained—for advice on questions relating to a corporate takeover. Such clients want the expertise that professional lawyers hold themselves out as offering, and, should anything go wrong, the comfort of the insurance protection that is a part of professional responsibility.

This distinction, between legal services and lawyers' services, should be borne in mind when reading this chapter.

substantial minority practice on their own as 'sole practitioners'. Barristers in private practice come together in 'chambers' but they are all self-employed within those chambers. Barristers are not currently permitted to form partnerships.[1]

---

[1] The ability of the Bar to sustain the notion that barristers are all self-employed and are not permitted to enter into partnerships is coming under attack. The commercial pressures arising from the increased overheads which chambers must absorb suggest that the case for a more commercial approach to the organization of chambers will need addressing in the near future.

INDEPENDENCE

One of the key attributes claimed for the legal profession is that it should be independent. This is, constitutionally, an extremely important claim, as it involves lawyers asserting their right to give advice independent of the view of the government of the day. It also involves a professional obligation to take on cases which may be regarded as disagreeable or distasteful. The proposition that a person is innocent until proved guilty depends on lawyers being willing to develop and advance arguments on behalf of their clients no matter how unpleasant those clients may be. The 'cab-rank' principle which applies to the Bar, whereby barristers are professionally obliged to take on whatever case comes to them next, is perhaps the clearest example of the operation of this principle.

The assertion of independence also implies that the professions should be left free to regulate themselves in accordance with their own rules of professional conduct, and without interference from government. As will be seen, there has been significant erosion of the freedom from government intervention in the legal profession over recent years. The abolition of restrictive practices, the changes to legal aid, and modes of dealing with complaints about the quality of work will all be noted as examples of government intervention. Each example of government involvement may be justi-fied, particularly in contexts where the legal profession has not been willing to reform itself in ways in which the public interest might seem to demand. However, the question of where the boundaries should be drawn in the involvement of govern-ment in the legal profession is one that needs constant attention, if the role of the legal profession in assisting the individual, often against agencies of the state or other powerful agencies, is not to be compromised.

TRENDS IN LEGAL PRACTICE

In the same way that the institutional framework of the legal profession has under-gone profound change in recent years, so too has the legal profession. A number of trends affecting the profession are noted here.

The blurring of the distinction between solicitors and barristers

First, though the line between 'solicitor' and 'barrister' can still be drawn as a matter of professional identity, the practical implications of the distinction are much less today than they were twenty years ago. Many of the services which used to be the exclusive preserve of one branch of the profession are now open to all. (See Boxes 9.1 and 9.2.)

The blurring of the distinction is largely the result of a sustained attack on the restrictive practices of lawyers which has lasted for over thirty years. (See Box 9.3.) But there has also been a concern that there should be no unnecessary restrictions on the tasks which people might perform within the legal system. The most important change, in this context, has been the adoption by statute of the principle that the

Box 9.2 LAWYERS' SERVICES: RIGHTS OF AUDIENCE AND RIGHTS TO CONDUCT LITIGATION

Two of the most important rights asserted by professionally qualified lawyers are to undertake advocacy in the courts, and to prepare cases for court. Before 1990, these were regulated by the professional rules of conduct of the Bar Council and the Law Society. Under the provisions of the Courts and Legal Services Act 1990, the government began to put these rights on a statutory footing. Instead of the professional bodies simply prescribing rules relating to advocacy and litigation, as they had done in the past, the act now permitted authorized bodies (the Bar Council, the Law Society, and the Institute of Legal Executives) to set the rules. The act also provided a statutory process of approval for the adoption of new or altered rules. This turned out to be extremely cumbersome; some applications for approval took years to complete the prescribed procedures.

Under the Access to Justice Act 1999, the government has intervened further. The act makes the following provision:

- All barristers and solicitors are to have the right of audience before every court in all proceedings.[2]

- Crown Prosecutors and other employed advocates (whether solicitors or barristers) will have the same rights of audience as if they were in private practice.[3]

- Advocates and litigators employed by the Legal Services Commission, or by bodies established by the Legal Services Commission will be enabled to provide services directly to the public, without the need to receive instructions through a solicitor or other person acting for the client.[4]

- Where a person has been granted the right of audience by one professional body (e.g. the Bar Council), she is entitled to retain that right if she becomes a solicitor, and thus a member of the Law Society.[5]

- Barristers employed by firms of solicitors are also enabled to act on the same basis as solicitors.[6]

- The General Council of the Bar and the Institute of Legal Executives are given power to grant their members the right to conduct litigation.[7]

[2] Section 36; this is not an unqualified right; those wishing to exercise it must obey the rules of conduct of the professional bodies and meet prescribed training requirements.

[3] Section 37. The campaign fought by the CPS to obtain rights of advocacy under the Act of 1990 was a source of very great frustration.

[4] Section 38.

[5] Section 39.

[6] Section 44; the Bar Council rules that treat barristers employed by solicitors as 'non-practising' and thus able to offer only a limited range of services are disapplied.

[7] Section 40; they are under no obligation to do so.

- Procedures for authorizing (and in extreme cases revoking authorizations) new bodies to grant rights of audience and rights to conduct litigation, and for approving alterations to or the adoption of new regulations or rules of conduct have been streamlined.[8]
- The overriding duties of advocates and litigators to the court to act with independence in the interests of justice, and to comply with their professional bodies' rules of conduct is put on a statutory footing.[9] All authorized advocates and litigators must refuse to do anything required, either by a client or an employer, that is not in the interests of justice (for example the suppression of evidence).

The implications of these changes for the regulation of the legal profession are clear; while it would be going too far to assert that the legal profession is now being directly regulated by government, it is quite clear that the government is—whether the legal professions like it or not—acting in 'partnership' with the professional bodies.

highest judicial offices should be open to solicitors, just as much as to barristers (who formerly had the monopoly in these appointments).[10]

Some of the changes have resulted from the professional bodies deciding to change their rules. Others, particularly in the last decade, have been the result of intervention by government.

Fusion? The obvious question that all these developments pose is whether the time is not approaching when the two branches of the legal profession should now fuse into a single profession, as happens in most other countries in the world. Should the long-standing distinction between solicitors and barristers continue to be defended? This is an issue that has been debated on many occasions, though surprisingly not seriously in the last few years, despite the developments which have occurred and which are sketched out above. The arguments asserted by the Bar for its independence, both in delivering advocacy and other forms of legal advice, are actually very powerful, more powerful than some of the advocates for fusion allow. But in other countries with

---

[8] Section 41 and Sched. 5. There are other professional groups, e.g. patents agents, who might wish to achieve 'authorized body' status. The Lord Chancellor's Advisory Committee of Legal Education and Conduct is replaced, from April 2000, by a new Legal Services Consultative Panel: section 35.

[9] Section 42. This was thought to be necessary to guarantee the ability of the individual lawyer to act independently.

[10] At the time of writing, the appointment of Mr Lawrence Collins, QC, a very distinguished commercial solicitor to the High Court, had just been announced. The possibility of distinguished jurists being appointed to the highest levels of the judiciary is still not formally recognized. The appointment of Dame Brenda Hale (who prior to her appointment as a Law Commissioner had had a distinguished academic career at the University of Manchester) first to the High Court Bench and then to the Court of Appeal is, perhaps, the start of a development in the direction of acknowledging the contribution legal scholars might make to the judiciary. This certainly happens in the European Courts, and in courts in the USA.

Box 9.3 THE ATTACK ON RESTRICTIVE PRACTICES

The attack on the restrictive practices of the legal profession began with a study by the Monopolies Commission which was published in 1968. In his evidence to the commission, Michael Zander provided a devastating critique of various professional practices, which he argued were not in the public interest.[11] Many others joined the attack. For example, during the early 1970s, Austen Mitchell, MP, led a sustained attack on the conveyancing monopoly then enjoyed by solicitors.[12]

A Royal Commission on Legal Services, under the chairmanship of Lord Benson, was established in 1976 and reported in 1979.[13] It came to the conclusion that, while a large number of detailed changes to professional practice needed to be made, many of the practices of the legal professions were in the public interest.

Further pressure to change developed, however, when the Thatcher Government came to power in 1980. Mrs. Thatcher was determined to make the British economy generally much more competitive. The legal profession became caught up in a general attack on monopolistic power.[14]

The first, and probably the most symbolically significant, alteration in the restrictive practices which had been adopted by the legal profession occurred in 1987 when the conveyancing monopoly was broken. Until that date, only solicitors were entitled to charge for the work required to convey the title in real estate from a vendor to a purchaser. Following enactment of the Administration of Justice Act 1985, Part II, a system of licensed conveyancers, regulated by the Council for Licensed Conveyancers, was established. The first licences under the scheme were granted in 1987. In addition, the practice of using fixed-scale fees for conveyancing was stopped. There is no doubt that many solicitors had benefited very substantially from the original arrangements, though there is also evidence that there was at least some indirect social benefit, in that many solicitors used the profit from their conveyancing work to subsidize other less profitable activity in their practices.

The loss of the conveyancing monopoly was not the only change to hit the solicitors' branch of the profession. There were many other significant changes. In particular, rules on advertising were significantly relaxed so that, within the boundaries set by the Law Society's Guide to Professional Behaviour, firms of solicitors were entitled to advertise their services. While advertising in the UK may not have the flamboyance of lawyers' advertisements in the USA, nevertheless this development was a significant break with past tradition. All significant legal practices, both solicitors' and barristers', now engage in a wide range of promotional 'practice development' activity.

---

[11] Zander, Michael, *Lawyers and the Public Interest: A Study of Restrictive Practices* (London: published for the London School of Economics and Political Science by Weidenfeld & Nicolson, 1968).

[12] An attack joined by at least some members of the profession themselves: see, Joseph, M., *The Conveyancing Fraud* (Harmondsworth: Penguin, 1975).

[13] Cmnd 7648 (London: HMSO, 1979).

[14] There is a tendency for each professional grouping to feel that it is being 'picked on' and is being uniquely subject to pressure to change. In fact nearly all professional groups have been subject to these pressures.

fused professions, the independence of the advocate is still strongly asserted. It seems that other ways could be found to protect professional independence. It is inconceivable that at some point in the not too distant future this issue should not again become the subject of public debate.

Growth and globalization

A second trend to be noted is the growth in the size of law firms, and the increasingly global perspective they adopt to practice. These have resulted from the context within which lawyers practice, which cannot be divorced from other changes in the economy at large. The last twenty years have seen a major shift from an economy based on manufacturing to one based on services. Increased globalization of the world economy has led to a growth in the need for lawyers able to advise corporations about all the national contexts within which they are required to operate. There has been a globalization in the provision of legal services which has accompanied the globalization of the economy.[15] British lawyers have responded in a variety of ways:

- Many of the large law firms in the City of London have gone through substantial programmes of merger and expansion.[16]
- Significant groupings of leading firms in provincial commercial centres—for example Leeds, Birmingham, Bristol—have also developed, either through mergers and takeovers, or the creation of networks of legal practices.
- Many of these firms have established presences in other key centres of economic activity, in Europe, the Middle East, the Far East, and the Americas.
- There are beginning to emerge mergers of English law firms with firms in other countries (for example Germany and the US) to create new forms of international partnership.
- There has been a significant increase in the presence of overseas law firms, and in particular US law firms, in London which have added to the competitive pressures on British-based firms.
- There have been moves towards the creation of professional groupings that cut across traditional disciplinary boundaries—in particular, lawyers and accountants. The issue of the establishment of multi-disciplinary partnerships—which has been around for many years—has fast risen up the policy agendas of the professional bodies.

There is every likelihood of further developments of these kinds in the years ahead.

Specialization and niche practices

A third trend to be noted has been the increasing development of specialist/niche

---

15 Halliday, Terence C. and Karpik, Lucien, *Lawyers and the Rise of Political Liberalism* (Oxford: Clarendon Press, 1997); Dezelay, Yves and Garth, Bryant, *Dealing in Virtue: International Commercial Arbitration and the Construction of a Transnational Legal Order* (Chicago: University of Chicago Press, 1996).

16 Galanter, Marc and Pulay, Thomas, *Tournament of Lawyers: The Transformation of the Big Law Firm* (Chicago: University of Chicago Press, 1991).

practices. In part this is a response to the trend towards 'mega-lawyering' noted in the previous section. Increasingly, small firms of solicitors and sets of barristers chambers have come to specialize in particular areas—family law, criminal law, employment law, and housing law to give some examples. These developments have been supported in part by the legal professional bodies themselves. For example, the Law Society has established a number of specialist panels which practitioners may join, including the Childrens Panel, the Mental Health Panel and the Medical Negligence Panel.

In addition, members of the profession themselves have taken the lead in establishing an increasing number of specialist groups, many of which cross over traditional solicitor/barrister boundaries. There are now well over forty such groups. They act in a variety of ways:

- They may be able to act collaboratively (within the competitive market) to promote the specialist services that they offer (thereby seeking to exclude non-specialists from their work).

- Some, such as the Solicitors' Family Law Association have promoted new modes of legal practice, designed to provide a different form of lawyering for their clients—in the context of family law, a less confrontational approach designed to assist those whose relationships have broken down.[17]

- Others, such as the Patent Lawyers' Association, have developed specialist programmes of advanced legal education and training designed to give their members special expertise and thus, it is hoped, competitive edge in the legal services market place.

- The specialist lawyer groups have also developed a very important influence in government. They are able to offer advice on how particular areas of legal practice might be affected by proposed policy changes, in ways in which the general professional bodies such as the Law Society or Bar Council may be unable to achieve.

Legal services to the poor

A fourth noteworthy trend in the shape of the legal profession has been a complete transformation in the operation of the legal aid scheme. The details of the new scheme are considered in Chapter 10. Here the principal point to note is that, whereas ten years ago in effect any firm of solicitors who wished to do legal aid work could do so, now only those firms with a 'franchise' approved by and a contract to provide services from the Legal Services Commission (replacing the Legal Aid Board) will be able to undertake publicly funded legal aid work. Many practitioners who used to do modest amounts of legal aid work as part of a portfolio of general legal services provided to mainly private clients are affected by these changes.

The likelihood of this happening has been obvious for some time, as successive governments have sought to control legal aid expenditure and obtain better value for

[17] See Chapter 7.

money for the legal services they finance. Those who understood how policy in relation to the funding of legal services was likely to develop have been able to take advantage of the new mechanisms for the delivery of funded legal services and offer a service that makes a profit—albeit perhaps not a huge one. Those that resisted these developments or refused to see them coming have suffered severely and may well go to the wall.

High street practice

A consequence of these last two developments is that the general 'high streets practices', found in the high streets of towns, suburban areas, and other locations, which have in the past tended to provide a general service to private client customers, have come under increasing pressure and face considerable uncertainty. The ability to make a living from a mixed practice of some criminal work, some property work such as conveyancing or probate, a little bit of family and divorce work, and some personal injuries work, which even ten years ago was quite common, is now increasingly difficult. Many of the remaining sole practitioners and small firms fall into this category. The future of the generalist high street practice is under considerable threat, unless those who remain in this sector of the legal services market are prepared to rethink their commercial strategies.

Other trends

A graduate profession. A significant change over the last quarter of a century is that the legal profession has become a largely graduate profession. The old days when professional qualifications could be obtained simply by a process of apprenticeship in a solicitor's office or a barrister's chambers (and the passing of some not very demanding professional exams) are now long gone. Despite this, many of the graduates who enter the legal profession come with degrees other than law. They obtain their legal qualifications through conversion courses undertaken following the obtaining of a first degree in other disciplines. This has been the subject of fierce argument between the legal professional bodies and the jurists, the latter asserting that only the grounding of a good law degree gives potential entrants to the legal profession a real understanding of how law is made and the fundamentals of legal principles.

Information technology. Second, and in common with every one else, the legal professions have been affected by the development of new information technologies. To date this has not perhaps delivered all the reductions in the use of paper that might have been anticipated, though it has undoubtedly transformed practice management. But as legal information from government, the legal publishers, and other sources goes electronic, and as court procedures become increasingly technology-driven, the impact of IT on legal practice is bound to intensify.[18] The nature of practice and the services provided by lawyers will change enormously in the next decade.

---

[18] See, for example, the LCD consultation paper *Civil Justice Resolving and Avoiding Disputes in the Information Age* (September 1998).

Pay and conditions. Third, the expectations of those entering the profession about the pay and conditions they should receive has also changed considerably in the last quarter century. A real problem in this context is that the financial rewards for those in some parts of legal practice, particularly the corporate sector, are hugely different from those in many specialist or niche areas, particularly those offering services to the less well-off groups in society. Much of the problem is the result of a type of 'macho' legal journalism which has developed over the last ten to fifteen years, but which arguably is not wholly in the interest of the legal profession. (See Box 9.4.)

Box 9.4 LEGAL JOURNALISM

One consequence of this changed context of legal practice, in particular the relaxation of restrictions on advertising, is that a significant branch of journalism has developed, devoted to the telling of stories about individuals and firms in the law and their doings. All the main broadsheet newspapers have a weekly law section, much of which is concerned with what is in effect legal gossip. In addition there are specialist papers for the profession which focus in particular on the activities of law firms and sets of chambers. The 'free' paper, the *Lawyer*—which appears weekly—is supplemented by the expensive and glossy *Legal Business* which focuses in particular on firms operating in the city and overseas.

One consequence of this new journalism is that public information about lawyers is to a large extent dominated by the stories which the PR departments of the large firms are able to place in this press. Stories about the impact and importance of the small high street firms find little place beside dramatic tales of takeovers, mergers, and other commercial/corporate activity. This creates at least three distortions:

- those thinking of entering the law as a profession are denied the opportunity to consider the full range of legal careers open to them;
- they come to assume that the only type of lawyering worth undertaking is that which pays enormous salaries; and
- the public assume that all lawyers act—and most significantly are paid—in ways suggested by the stories that appear in this press.

Much of the public hostility towards lawyers is, it may be surmised, the result of assumptions that legal services are very expensive and thus only affordable by the very rich. A more balanced picture would indicate that there are still many lawyers providing valuable services to the public for extremely modest fees.

REGULATION OF THE PROFESSIONS: COMPLAINTS AND ETHICAL STANDARDS

Another of the major developments that has taken place over the last fifteen years has been the enormous change in the way in which the legal professions are regulated. There is a wide range of issues that might be discussed under this heading. Two specific issues—dealing with complaints, and setting ethical standards—will be addressed here.

HANDLING COMPLAINTS AND ENSURING QUALITY CONTROL

Until the 1980s the hallmark of any profession was that those who made up the profession were regarded as the best qualified to run the profession, to set standards of practice, and to remove miscreants from their ranks. One of the challenges that has confronted the legal professions over the last fifteen to twenty years is how they should respond to the pressures to deliver a standard of service demanded by an increasingly critical client base. The professional bodies have taken steps designed to ensure that lawyers keep up to date with developments in law and in practice management. For example, both the Law Society and, more recently, the Bar Council have introduced rules requiring practitioners to undergo regular amounts of *Continuing Professional Development*. This might seem to be the least that could be expected of a 'learned profession'.

In addition, in the specific context of the provision of legal aid services (now the Community Legal Service), great attention to quality issues[19] has been paid by respectively the Legal Aid Board, now the Legal Services Commission—arguably doing the work that the professional bodies had failed to do.

In relation to the handling of complaints, both the Law Society (for solicitors) and the Bar Council (for barristers) still to a degree retain the ability to run their professional affairs. But, in common with other professional groups, the former position has been replaced by much greater public and political scepticism. There is now a widespread feeling that professional groups cannot, despite their protestations to the contrary, be fully trusted to run their affairs in the public interest. The legal profession has not been immune from this change in attitude. The arguments of the professional bodies have been regarded by politicians and others outside the law as 'trade union' arguments, designed to advance the private interests of the members of the profession, rather than the broader public interest. Unfair though that charge is in part, it was undeniably the case that too often in the 1970s the legal professional bodies were seen to be defending the frankly indefensible.

The arrival of the Thatcher Government, with a commitment to do away with

---

[19] See further Chapter 10.

restrictive practices that would undermine the competitive economy, led to a series of changes some of which have been considered above, the effects of which are still being worked through. But the argument has not come only from the political right. A recent Fabian Society paper suggested that 'Self-regulation is [now] an out-dated concept and has no place in modern Britain'.[20]

At the same time, there has been a considerable increase in the influence of consumer groups, arguing that the services provided to consumers (which include the provision of legal services to clients) must be to a standard expected by the consumers, not as determined by the providers.

The situation before 1990 was—very broadly—that while the courts were able to deal with the most serious cases of professional negligence, and while the professional bodies were able to control other forms of *gross* misconduct, the more mundane complaints—rudeness, slowness in responding to letters, general inefficiency—were not capable of being dealt with seriously. Yet these were precisely the sorts of issue which the ordinary client, who felt she was not getting good value for the money she was being asked to pay, wanted to complain about. Both the Law Society and the Bar Council took steps to try to address these concerns.

The Law Society started the process in the mid-1980s following the long drawn-out and very unsatisfactory handling of a complaint against one of its Council members, Mr Glanville Davies. In 1985, the society commissioned Coopers and Lybrand to review the society's disciplinary procedures. The consultants recommended that all these procedures be transferred to a new independent agency. The Law Society did not accept this recommendation, but it did in 1986 establish the Solicitors' Complaints Bureau (SCB), relaunched[21] as the Office for the Supervision of Solicitors (OSS) in 1996. The Society's disciplinary powers were delegated to the SCB/OSS. Although established by the Law Society, the SCB/OSS is physically quite separate from the other activities of the Law Society, with premises in Leamington Spa.

In 1991, the Law Society also made a number of changes to its Practice Rules, most notably the introduction of Practice Rule 15, requiring all solicitors to operate a complaints handling procedure designed to ensure that clients know who to approach in the event of a problem with the service with which they have been provided. Part of the reason for the introduction of this rule was to encourage firms to resolve complaints internally, and thus, it was hoped, reduce the pressure on the SCB.

The Bar was slower off the mark. A proposal in 1994 from its Standards Review Body[22] to set up a Barrister's Complaints Bureau did not meet with the approval of the membership of the Bar. Instead the post of Lay Complaints Commissioner was agreed.[23] In addition, the Bar Council in 1995 developed new Practice Management

---

[20] Arora, A. and Andrew, F., *The Rule of Lawyers* (London: Fabian Society, 1998).

[21] Following considerable criticism from both within the profession and outside. See, for example, *The Solicitors Complaints Bureau: A Consumer View* (National Consumer Council, 1994).

[22] Chaired by Lord Alexander of Weedon, QC, former Chairman of the Bar.

[23] The first holder of this post was Sir Michael Scott, appointed in 1997.

Standards,[24] which are not mandatory, but rather guidelines to good practice, and to which the Bar's Code of Conduct requires barristers to have regard. These Practice Management Standards stated that barristers' chambers should have a written code of procedure for dealing with complaints. In 1997, changes were made to the Bar's Code of Conduct. Among other things, this recognized for the first time the concept of 'inadequate professional service',[25] against which the Complaints Commissioner can determine complaints from barristers' clients. This goes at least some way to addressing the gap between what clients typically wanted to complain about, and the rather narrow concepts of 'negligence' and 'gross misconduct' mentioned above.

Recent research into these developments,[26] and in particular into the rules relating to the local office/chambers resolution of disputes suggest that at present the response from practitioners remains somewhat underwhelming. Heads of chambers, for example, still assert that the 'market' will deal with the incompetent—they will not get briefed and thus go to the wall. They are not convinced that taking complaints seriously is either professionally important or commercially desirable.[27] There remains considerable pressure for the creation of a more 'independent' complaints handling procedure.[28]

Statutory developments: Courts and Legal Services Act 1990 and Access to Justice Act 1999

The changes by the professional bodies have been accompanied by significant statutory developments. The Courts and Legal Services Act 1990 established the office of Legal Services Ombudsman and established the Advisory Committee on Legal Education and Conduct. The Access to Justice Act 1999 has extended the power of the ombudsman; abolished the Advisory Committee and replaced it with a Consultative Panel; and made provision for the appointment of a Legal Services Complaints Commissioner.

Legal Services Ombudsman. The office of Legal Services Ombudsman was established by section 21 of the Courts and Legal Services Act 1990. The post-holder cannot be professionally qualified as a lawyer and is independent of the legal profession. She oversees the handling of complaints against solicitors, barristers, and licensed conveyancers. However, complainants cannot come direct to her. They must first utilize the procedures of the Law Society's OSS, the General Council of the Bar, or the Council

[24] One way in which chambers can attest that they fall within the principles implied by the Practice Management Standards is by acquisition of the new 'Barmark', a British Standards Institution accreditation.

[25] 'Conduct . . . or performance of professional services . . . which falls significantly short of that which is to be expected of a barrister in all the circumstances.'

[26] Christensen, Christa and others, *Report of an Investigation into the Operation of Complaint Handling Mechanisms Operated by Barristers' Chambers* (Bristol: University of the West of England, 2000).

[27] In the case of the Bar, which is still in theory based on the principle of the barrister being self-employed, there may be some difficulties in taking a 'corporate' approach to complaints handling. Senior clerks, however, seem much more aware of the commercial importance of chambers presenting a corporate image and learning corporate lessons from individual lapses in standards, than barristers themselves.

[28] The government's power to establish a *Legal Services Complaints Commissioner* is considered below, p. 210.

for Licensed Conveyancers. Because of this filtering process, the numbers of complaints reaching the Legal Services Ombudsman is relatively modest—around 1,500 a year compared with over 27,000 cases taken to the professions. The Legal Services Ombudsman does, however, use her annual report not just to comment on individual cases, but to advise the professions more generally on their complaints handling procedures. One of the pressures on the professions is undoubtedly the Legal Services Ombudsman, who has over the years made trenchant criticisms of the profession's procedures.

In particular, the Legal Services Ombudsman has argued that the professions' procedures must deliver results without undue delay; must be credible to complainants; and must provide effective redress where this is appropriate. Given that, in the case of the Law Society, there is one complaint with the OSS for every three solicitors,[29] the challenge to the professions is clearly significant.

The Access to Justice Act 1999 has extended the powers of the Legal Services Ombudsman, to enable her to make binding orders that a professional body or individual practitioner pays compensation or costs to a complainant. At present, she can only make recommendations.

Advisory Committee on Legal Education and Conduct. The function of the advisory committee was to give the Lord Chancellor advice on applications from groups seeking rights to conduct litigation or rights of audience (as was envisaged by the Courts and Legal Services Act 1990). In addition it was to give general advice on the training and education needed for modern legal practice. The procedures of the Advisory Committee turned out to be very slow in practice, causing frustration both to the legal profession and to those who wished to see new groups authorized to have rights of audience and rights to conduct litigation. Under the Access to Justice Act, the rules on these rights have been changed. (*See Box 9.2 above.*) At the same time, the Advisory Committee is to be abolished and replaced by a new Legal Services Consultative Panel which it is hoped will be able to operate more informally and more speedily.

Legal Services Complaints Commissioner. The Act of 1999 has given the Lord Chancellor the power to establish a Legal Services Complaints Commissioner, to take over the handling of complaints against the legal profession, if the systems in place within the legal profession continue to operate as unsatisfactorily as they currently appear to do. The present intention of government is not to put these provisions into effect; but this restraint is contingent upon the professions being able to demonstrate that they have their own houses in order.

THE PROMOTION OF ETHICAL STANDARDS

The second issue to be considered is the role of the legal professions in the promotion

---

[29] This does not, of course, mean that a third of all solicitors are complained against; there are many solicitors with more than one complaint against them. But it demonstrates the size of the task facing both the OSS and the Law Society to improve public confidence in the performance of solicitors.

of ethical standards amongst practitioners. This is an issue that has received considerable attention in recent years, not only in relation to the work of lawyers, but in all areas of professional activity. Here is not the place to enter a detailed consideration of the need for the legal profession to adopt an ethical approach to its work, nor of the role of the professional bodies in promoting that work. It may be suggested, however, that much contemporary hostility towards lawyers is fuelled by the feeling that in general lawyers are a rather amoral group.[30]

It is perhaps the case that, until relatively recently, the provision of legal services by lawyers was seen by members of the legal profession themselves as a public service, to which, in some rather mysterious way, commercial pressures somehow did not apply. The adoption of an ethical approach was, on this view, inherent in the provision of the service.

Whether or not there was ever any real justification for this belief, there can be no doubt that in the modern world the provision of legal services is quite clearly a business. If lawyers cannot make a profit at the end of the year, they go bust. Legal practice must be subject to the disciplines of financial control, quality control, and efficiency that characterize all business activity. The concern with ethical standards may have arisen from a perception that concentrating exclusively on the financial and commercial imperatives of legal practice may encourage lawyers to forget the ethical principles which should also underpin their work.

The professional bodies seek to provide guidance on professional conduct which is designed to provide some ethical framework for professional activity. Understanding these principles is a key feature in professional legal education, not least because failure to follow the guidance can result, in the worst cases, in loss of the right to practise as a barrister or solicitor.

The question of whether the codes of practice go far enough in incorporating an ethical dimension to legal practice is beyond the scope of this work, though the works cited in the suggestions for further reading take the issue further.

There are, perhaps, two particular respects in which the legal profession is able at least in part to demonstrate its ethical commitment: *pro bono* work; and test case litigation.

Pro bono work. There has long been a tradition that lawyers offer free legal services to the poor; before there was any legal aid, there was a history of such provision in London and other major conurbations. In recent years, there has been a renewed emphasis on *pro bono* work. Perhaps because the large commercial firms in the City of London and other commercial centres have been so obviously financially successful, there has been a renewed interest in the provision of free legal services by their staff in citizens' advice bureaux and other agencies. This may seem to many as little more than a token gesture. But given the precarious funding position that many such agencies are in, it is likely that this activity does make a significant contribution to local legal service delivery.

---

[30] Anti-lawyer jokes certainly reflect this.

Test case litigation. Test case litigation, or as it is sometimes called 'cause lawyering', is also often associated with lawyers being willing to take up broad general issues, particularly on behalf of more disadvantaged groups in the community. Historically, test case litigation in the United Kingdom has not had the same impact as, for example, in the USA, where legal provisions or policies were able to be tested for their constitutionality against the provisions of the US Constitution. However, with ever greater involvement in Europe, both through the European Union and, in relation to human rights, through the Council of Europe, many challenges to English law have been mounted, in some cases with dramatic success. The coming into effect of the Human Rights Act in October 2000 will undoubtedly generate a considerable additional amount of test case legislation, as provisions of English law are tested for their compatibility with the European Convention.

PROFESSIONAL GROUPS ALLIED
TO THE LEGAL PROFESSION

Following the lengthy discussion of the legal profession, consideration of the professional groups allied to the legal profession will be briefer. There are two groups which will be considered here: legal executives; and other specialist groups.

LEGAL EXECUTIVES

Many of the staff employed in solicitors' offices are not formally qualified as solicitors, but nonetheless provide a great many legal services to the public. These are known collectively as 'legal executives'. Many of these are members and fellows of their own professional representative body, the *Institute of Legal Executives* (ILEX). ILEX organizes its own training programmes and examinations which must be passed before a legal executive can call him- or herself a Fellow of the Institute. The Institute has its own code of professional conduct, analogous to that of the Law Society.

Legal executives play a central role in many legal practices, often being more expert in their areas of expertise that their fully professionally qualified colleagues. Legal executives who are fellows of ILEX are able, by taking additional courses and sitting additional examinations, to qualify as solicitors, and a number do so each year.

OTHER SPECIALIST GROUPS

In addition to the legal executives, there are also a number of other more specialist groups providing particular kinds of legal and law-related services whose existence may be noted. These include:

- licensed conveyancers (noted in passing above) whose activities are regulated by the Council of Licensed Conveyancers;
- patent agents;
- insolvency practitioners; and
- tax advisers: this last group is not subject to the same forms of regulation as the other groups mentioned.[31]

LAY ADVISERS AND OTHER PROVIDERS OF LEGAL SERVICES

LAY ADVISERS/ADVOCATES

In addition to the formally qualified, there are substantial numbers of persons who have not obtained legal qualifications, but who nevertheless deliver legal services. These include: the lay advisers who work in advice agencies, such as the citizens' advice bureaux; welfare rights workers, often employed in local-authority sponsored welfare-rights offices; housing-aid workers working in housing advice centres; and many other lay advice workers working in a vast range of social, environmental, and other agencies.

LAW CENTRES

One particular context in which the professionally qualified lawyer and the lay adviser come together is the law centre. The law centre movement started in the 1970s with the specific objective of targeting legal services to those who lived in deprived areas, principally towns and cities. Historically they have had a somewhat hand-to-mouth existence. Some have been funded by local authorities; others by private charities; one or two by central government. The rules of the new funding code which underpins the Community Legal Service provide that those agencies that satisfy standards set by the Legal Services Commission will be able to obtain public funding for defined categories of work. (See Chapter 10.)

MEMBERS' SERVICES

A number of membership organizations also provide legal services to their members. These services may either be general, or related to the matters which arise from membership. Examples at the more general end of provision are the legal services

---

[31] See Green, Sue and Leach, Kathy, *Tax Advice in the UK: Why Things Go Wrong and the Implications for the Tax Adviser's Profession* (London: Chartered Institute of Taxation, 1997).

provided as the result of membership of trade unions or other professional groups (for example the Medical Defence Union); more specific legal services are provided to members of, for example, the Automobile Association or the Royal Automobile Club.

SPECIALIST AGENCIES

In addition to the foregoing, a number of pressure groups also provide legal services. One motivation for this is to find appropriate test cases that might be brought to test the boundaries of statutory provisions. Examples include the Citizens' Rights Office, which is attached to the Child Poverty Action Group; the Public Law Project; Liberty (formerly the National Council for Civil Liberties); and a number of environmental groups, such as Greenpeace. These agencies have been particularly successful in expanding the range of groups entitled to make representations to the courts in judicial review cases.

B. THE ADJUDICATORS: THE JUDICIARY, OMBUDSMEN, AND OTHER DISPUTE RESOLVERS

Much has been written about judges in the English legal system. As with other topics in this book, however, most accounts have focused on a rather narrow body of the judiciary, namely those who sit in the High Court, Court of Appeal, and the House of Lords. There can be no doubting the influence of the judges who sit in these higher courts in shaping English law. But the chances of any one individual member of the public appearing before one of these judges is remote in the extreme. Far more likely is an encounter with a district judge, a lay magistrate, a tribunal chairman, a circuit judge, or one of the army of other dispute-resolvers/complaints-handlers that now exist. It is these adjudicators who are, in practice, the 'face' of the judiciary, as seen by the public at large.

DEFINITION

For the purpose of this book, adjudicators are all those who are empowered by law[32] to determine disputes that have been brought to them for adjudication. This definition includes all the senior judicial figures who sit in the High Court and other courts just mentioned, as well as:

(1) *Circuit judges* who determine civil cases in the county court, and criminal cases in the Crown Court;

---

[32] Thus this definition excludes those who determine disputes under purely private contractual arrangements; for example, internal employment dispute resolution procedures or student disciplinary procedures.

(2) *District judges*, who determine civil cases, including small claims hearings, in the county court;

(3) *Recorders*, who are, in effect, circuit judges in training;

(4) *Magistrates*, both lay and stipendiary,[33] who determine the vast majority of criminal cases which dealt with in magistrates' courts;

(5) *Arbitrators*, who determine a wide range of disputes referred to them under specially agreed arbitration agreements. Arbitrators are particularly used to resolve commercial disputes, both national and international;

(6) *Tribunal members and chairmen* who deal with specific issues arising in defined legislative contexts: for example, disputes about entitlement to social security benefit, which go to Social Security Appeal Tribunals; or disputes about immigration status, which go to Immigration Adjudicators;

(7) *Ombudsmen*, as they appear in their various guises; and

(8) *Mediators, conciliators, complaints handlers*, and others who offer alternative forms of appropriate dispute resolution (ADR).

COMMENTARY

These groups have all been encountered in different contexts earlier in the book. Here a number of general points about those who perform adjudicatory functions in the legal system may be made:

- They are not all professionally qualified as lawyers. Some have other professional qualifications, such as accountants, surveyors, or doctors. But many have no specific professional qualification at all. In the same way that many legal services are provided by persons other than professionally qualified lawyers, so too are many adjudication services provided by those without legal qualifications.

- Many academic lawyers are embraced by this broader definition. The notion that somehow those with an academic background have no capacity to determine disputes in a fair and proper manner is simply not borne out by the evidence.

- Their total numbers are considerably larger than traditional definitions of the judiciary suggest.

- Many adjudication appointments are full time, but many more are part-time positions.[34]

- Only the very highest judiciary hold office 'on good behaviour'—a concept designed to enhance the fundamental independence of the judiciary. Most other

---

[33] About to be renamed *District Judges (Magistrates' Courts)*; see above Box 5.6.

[34] The impact of the coming into effect of the Human Rights Act 1998 on the making of part-time judicial appointments has been noted above at p. 78.

groups, particularly the part-timers, hold office on terms which can result in their being required to step down before an official retirement age.

- Only a limited number are able to take advantage of the attractive (free) pensions that are provided by government to full-time members of the judiciary.

- Many judges sit in more than one jurisdiction. For example a full-time social security tribunal chairman may sit as a part-time circuit judge, thereby enabling him or her to acquire wider judicial experience.

- Many judges now start to sit in their early forties, some even in their thirties.

- There are many more women holding judicial office than is often appreciated, though the numbers at the highest levels are still too low. The numbers from the ethnic minorities are significantly less impressive.

- Most judicial appointments now receive at least some training for the job, though the amount of training decreases with the seniority of the post.[35]

- There is still only a limited amount of monitoring of judicial performance. Such monitoring as does take place is limited to the performance by part-timers, and is often undertaken by those in full-time office. While too heavy monitoring could compromise judicial independence, certain factors, for example the ability to be civil to those appearing before them, or to deliver written decisions within agreed timescales, would not seem impossible targets for assessment.

- Most appointments to adjudicatory positions are now filled only after open competition, following public advertisements in the press.[36]

- There is a huge variety of procedural variation as between each of the adjudicative systems. The formal courts operate within a very detailed procedural framework, with a large number of rules of practice supplemented by yet more practice directions and protocols. Many other bodies have only the barest procedural outline prescribed by law, and instead operate with considerable discretion as to procedural matters.

- Not all tribunals operate on the basis that their 'typical' adjudication will involve a formal hearing of the parties. Many reach determinations on the basis of information presented in written form alone.

- While it is usual for tribunals that hold hearings to sit in public, in the sense that members of the public are entitled to attend hearings should they so wish, many do not, particularly where sensitive personal, or financial information is being discussed.

- The dress of the judiciary is also much more varied than is often realized. The highly formalized process of the High Court, with impressive uniforms, oak

---

[35] For the development of the work of the Judicial Studies Board, see above Chapter 4.

[36] For further discussion about the procedures relating to judicial appointments and criticisms thereof, see above Chapter 4.

panelling, and advocates in wigs and gowns—the image of the television or film drama—is in fact a statistical rarity. The vast majority of adjudicative tribunals operate with none of these formal trappings.

- There is a huge variety of locations for adjudicative bodies. Many take place in court buildings or other specially furnished accommodation. But there are many examples of adjudicative bodies sitting in local authority accommodation, or in hotel accommodation, or even on occasion in people's homes.

If one takes this broader view of the judiciary, therefore, it will be seen that there is considerably more variety and flexibility of approach to adjudication than is often realized. Different procedures and practices have been developed to meet the specific needs of particular bodies.

NUMBERS

It is actually not possible to give a complete picture of the total number of people holding various kinds of adjudicative office. The annual *Judicial Statistics* list numbers of judges who take cases in the formal court system. In addition to the four chief judicial officeholders—the Lord Chief Justice of England, the Master of the Rolls, the President of the Family Division, and the Vice-Chancellor—the number of judicial officeholders at the start of 1999 were as follows:

Full-time Appointments	
Lords of Appeal (House of Lords)	13
Lords Justices of Appeal (Court of Appeal)	35
High Court judges	99
Circuit judges	553
District judges	362
District judges (criminal)	93
Total	1,155

Part-time Appointments	
Recorders	849
Assistant recorder	400
Acting district judges (criminal)	104
Deputy district judges	370
Total	1,723

Justices of the peace	c.30,000

Information about numbers of officeholders in other dispute resolution contexts is harder to establish as the figures are not always easily available, but it may be estimated that there are around 20,000 part-time tribunal chairmen and members.

THE LITERATURE ON THE JUDICIARY

With a few exceptions, books about the judiciary have, in many cases, not been in any strict sense socially scientific. Drawing inferences about how judges think and thus come to decisions simply from the skewed sample of their work represented by reported decisions in the law reports, is a wholly inadequate basis for serious analysis about how judges approach the judicial task.[37] Further, it is all too easy to assume that because someone is white, male, middle-aged, and probably public school and Oxbridge educated, he (or she) brings attitudes to their judicial work which affect the ways in which they work. Such links are not provable without the detailed empirical work that has only rarely been undertaken on the judiciary.[38]

There has, of course, been a problem in that researchers who have sought access to the judiciary in order to conduct research into them have often found such access difficult to obtain. The stereotype of judges as white, male, of middle to late age, and from the (upper) middle class, may, broadly though by no means exclusively apply to the higher judiciary. It is far less accurate as a descriptor of the totality of judges/ adjudicators in the vast array of fora that determine the disputes brought to them by ordinary members of the public.

JUDICIAL INDEPENDENCE

The key claim made for adjudicators of all kinds is that they must not only be, but be seen to be, independent. Judicial independence relates centrally to the constitutional function of judges in interpreting and applying law outside the constraints of internal government departmental policies. Adjudicators not perceived as independent will be fatally compromised in the eyes of the public, particularly by those in relation to whom the adjudicator is reaching a decision. One of the strong claims for adjudicators in the English legal system is that, with rare exceptions, they both appear to act and do act independently. This is not to say that they may not bring their own views of the world into play when reaching decisions or determining facts. But claims of corruption of those who hold judicial office—the worst case that could be imagined for compromising judicial independence—are not heard.

Slightly less dramatic attacks on judicial independence may be made in cases where it is suggested that there may be judicial bias, in the sense that a judge may have some direct personal interest in the outcome of a particular case. This issue has recently

---

[37] Griffith, J. A. G., *The Politics of the Judiciary*, 5th edn. (London: Fontana, 1997); cf. Hodder-Williams, Richard, *Judges and Politics in the Contemporary Age* (London: Bowerdean, 1996).

[38] Cf. Alan Paterson, *The Law Lords* (London: Macmillan, 1982).

been the subject of much public discussion following the revelation that Lord Hoff-man, one of the members of the House of Lords who sat in judgment in the case involving General Pinochet (the former dictator of Chile), was a member of Amnesty International, one of the parties in the proceedings involving the general.[39] The issue having been raised, the House of Lords decided that the decision in which Lord Hoffman had taken part could not be allowed to stand, and the matter was—in an unprecedented move—set aside for determination by another Appeal Committee from the House of Lords.

Shortly thereafter a number of other cases were heard by the Court of Appeal which, though not as dramatic as that involving Pinochet, raised similar issues for consideration. In reviewing the position, the Court of Appeal laid down the following propositions.[40] In general, membership of professional, political, or other organiza-tions would not give grounds for an allegation of bias. Neither would racial or ethnic origin, class, extra judicial activities, sexual orientation, or previous judicial references to parties or witnesses, even if forthright. However personal acquaintance with or antagonism against any individual involved in a case, especially if their credibility might be an issue, would give rise to a real danger of bias. The independent status of barristers when sitting judicially absolved them from responsibility for the interests of other members of chambers. Solicitors, however, maintained responsibility for acts of their partners and owed a duty to their firm's clients, even if they had not acted for them personally.

C. THE JURISTS

Law claims to be a 'learned profession'. If that is so, then a third group, delivering a rather different kind of legal service, and not usually given adequate recognition, should be noted, namely the law teachers and jurists. Law teachers in the university law departments and in other locations where legal education is provided have a variety of functions.

First, law teachers provide basic training in law and legal principles, which provides new generations of lawyers with the fundamental intellectual tools to enable them to become lawyers. The leading university law schools also offer, through their law degrees, a traditional liberal university education, giving students the capacity to think critically about law and its impact on society.

Secondly, law teachers deliver a wide range of professionally focused courses which transform the recent graduate from the preliminary academic stage to a person with the skills required to enter the world of practice. Some of these courses are offered

---

[39] *R. v. Bow Street Metropolitan Stipendiary Magistrates, ex parte Pinochet Ugarte* [1999] 2 WLR 272.
[40] See *Locabail (UK) v. Bayfield* [2000] 1 All ER 65.

within university law departments, but other providers, including the College of Law[41] and other private companies, play a significant part in this market as well.

Thirdly, the law schools together with the private providers offer much of the further education and advanced training in new developments in the law which are needed by legal practitioners to enable them to keep abreast of developments in the law, and to break into new areas of law.

Finally, those law teachers who work in the research universities assist in the development of law and the legal system through the research they undertake, the books and articles they write, and the advice they give to governments and other agencies. The scope of legal scholarship has expanded enormously in recent years, again reflecting the growing complexity of the law, not only domestic law but also law coming from Europe and elsewhere. The impact of this legal scholarship on practitioners is hard to gauge. Certainly the old rule that only dead authors could be cited in court has long been abandoned. Advocates now often refer to academic articles in their submissions, and in many reported cases, the judgments adopt (or reject) the analyses of legal scholars. But this is the tip of the iceberg. Many practitioners developing a legal argument, or simply struggling to understand a particular legal doctrine, will turn to the text book writers for assistance. The importance of the work of the jurists in helping to shape legal argument should not be underestimated. This work is also central to the work of the law reform agencies, particularly the Law Commission.

A number of areas of practice which have developed in recent years have been the result of a combination of the work of legal scholars who helped to shape the areas and the practitioners who took them into practice. Among examples that may be cited is the development of administrative law which has arisen from analysis of the principles of judicial review; many important developments in the area of family law is another; the law of restitution, a third. A number of more specialist areas including private and public international law, housing law and social welfare law have similarly been shaped by important academic contributions.

Notwithstanding these observations, there has been a surprising reluctance on behalf of the jurists to get involved in the scholarly analysis of legal practice and procedure. Thus, while endless books and articles are published offering systematic expositions and analyses of substantive law, it has been left to a very small number of legal scholars to focus on the questions of practice and procedure, which are in fact the lifeblood of most legal practice, an understanding of which is essential to understanding law and the legal system.

In addition, alongside what is sometimes described as 'black-letter' legal research, focusing on the detailed analysis of legal doctrine, there has emerged over the last twenty-five years an increasingly rich body of 'socio-legal' scholarship, in which the law is analysed in an interdisciplinary context, employing insights and methodologies from other social sciences, such as economics, social psychology, politics, and sociology. Much of this research is empirical in nature, and much has involved research

---

[41] An institution operated in close association with the Law Society.

into the practice of law. A number of areas of government legal policy have been significantly affected by the outcomes of socio-legal research.

The university law schools have played a very significant part in opening up access to the legal profession to people from a wider range of backgrounds (a trend noted at the outset of this chapter). Though the extent to which people from different *class* backgrounds have been able to take advantage of these developments may not be as dramatic as is sometimes thought, there is no doubting that the pattern of recruitment to universities in general and to law schools in particular has changed. This has been of particular benefit to women.

Further the fact that the legal profession is now largely a graduate profession has greatly helped to change the nature of the relationship between the legal academic and the legal practitioner. The mutual disdain which all too often characterized the relationship twenty-five years ago has been replaced by much greater mutual understanding and respect.

10

THE FUNDING OF LEGAL SERVICES

INTRODUCTION

The final issue to be considered in this book is how legal services provided to the public are to be paid for. It is essential for the overall effectiveness of the English legal system that services required by the public are actually available to them. This chapter will not devote attention to the funding of legal services for the corporate sector or for wealthy individuals. For present purposes it is assumed that they can afford the services they require. This chapter concentrates on the funding regimes for the delivery of legal services to the less well-off. The discussion is in two unequal sections: the first, and longer, looks at the changing shape of *publicly* funded legal services; the second considers new arrangements to assist the development of *private* funding for legal services.

PUBLICLY FUNDED LEGAL SERVICES

THE DEATH OF LEGAL AID

When the Welfare State emerged in legislative form after the end of World War II, one of the measures introduced by the then Labour Government was the Legal Aid Act 1949. There are many accounts of the history of this fundamentally important development, so the story will not be repeated here. Initially the scope of the legal aid scheme was limited to *civil legal aid*—the provision of legal representation in proceedings taken in the civil courts. It subsequently developed to embrace:

- *criminal legal aid*—funding representation in criminal cases, and eventually including a scheme for the provision of legal advice in police stations;
- a *'green form scheme'* designed to permit the provision by lawyers of legal advice and assistance on any matter of English law; and
- *'assistance by way of representation'* (ABWOR) which permitted, in a limited number of circumstances, the lawyer to extend the assistance offered to the provision of some representation.

Despite these developments, policy on legal aid has been the subject of fierce debate and criticism over the last twenty-five to thirty years.

- Despite its potentially wide coverage, in practice civil legal aid was used primarily to fund litigation on matrimonial matters, and on personal injuries/accidents. Though important, other areas of social law, for example housing, or social welfare provision, were in practice largely ignored by legal aid practitioners.

- The provision of legal aid was subject to means-testing—it only went to those falling below certain income and capital limits.[1] When the first Legal Aid Act was passed it was estimated that nearly 70 per cent of the population were potentially entitled to legal aid. However, as the costs of legal aid increased, one of the mechanisms used by government to restrain levels of public spending was to make the means-tests meaner; thus the percentage of the population covered was severely reduced.

- New forms of legal service delivery—in particular through law centres, which began to develop in the late 1960s—were excluded from funding by the legal aid schemes, save where such centres took on individual cases which qualified for legal aid.

- There were many fora in which legal aid was just not available at all. In particular, there was no legal aid for proceedings before the majority of the tribunals established to deal with disputes between the citizen and the state, arising out of the social provision of the welfare state.[2]

- From the government's point of there seemed to be no way to control public expenditure, since it was a service that was 'demand-led'—the government was committed to paying for all those cases in which the individual established an entitlement to legal aid.

- There were also worries about the quality of some of the work undertaken. Any legal practice could offer to do legal aid work, irrespective of the level of expertise on the issue in question in the firm. This might have the perverse effect of driving legal aid expenditure up, as it could take longer for such a firm to deal with a matter than a firm that had expertise in the area.

Successive governments have been trying to reform the legal aid scheme in a way that would deliver a wider range of services to the public, without public expenditure on legal aid reaching unacceptable levels.[3]

The first change to the administration of the legal aid scheme followed the enactment of the Legal Aid Act 1988. Administration of the scheme was removed from the

---

[1] The criminal legal aid scheme was also subject to means-testing, though the rules were not applied in practice with the rigour that applied in relation to civil law matters.

[2] See further Chapter 6. There were exceptions; legal aid was available for proceedings before the Lands Tribunal, and (later) Mental Health Review Tribunals.

[3] Levels of public expenditure on legal aid have increased markedly in recent years, rising from £1.093bn in 1992–3 to £1.622bn in 1998–9—a 48% increase in expenditure at a time when total inflation was only 16%.

Law Society and transferred to a new government agency—the Legal Aid Board. The board tried to address the problem of providing a quality service by establishing a scheme for 'franchising' legal aid services, under which firms of solicitors could only obtain a franchise if they passed a special quality audit process. Under the scheme, solicitors have, since 1994, been able to obtain a franchise in one or more of up to ten franchise categories.[4] Some 2,900 firms of solicitors obtained at least one of the available franchises. In addition, the Legal Aid Board began a series of pilots to test the viability of franchises being awarded to agencies other than solicitors' firms, such as advice agencies, who might provide legal advice and assistance to the same standards as solicitors' firms.

In 1997, the Legal Aid Board extended the principle by beginning to enter into contracts with franchised firms for the provision of defined categories of legal services. This had the advantage that firms with contracts were able to deliver legal services with reduced bureaucracy. Instead of having to submit claims for each item of legally aided work, they were able to deliver their services within the framework of the contract. A number of legal aid services had to be offered on the basis of a fixed fee, rather than the traditional method of charging by the hour.

However, these measures were still felt to be inadequate to address the paradox of ever-rising costs, without any significant expansion in the range of services that could be funded by the legal aid scheme.[5]

THE REFORM OF LEGAL SERVICES: A NEW DEAL

The Access to Justice Act 1999, which came into effect in 2000, abolishes the legal aid scheme and introduces in its place a new body—the Legal Services Commission— charged with running two new services: the *Community Legal Service* (CLS) and the *Criminal Defence Service* (CDS).

COMMUNITY LEGAL SERVICE

Introduction

Many people obtain advice on legal problems, not by going to see a solicitor in her office, but by visiting one of over 1,500 citizens' advice bureaux, law centres, and other independent advice agencies which it is estimated exist in England and Wales. These services often have lawyers or other professionally qualified staff attached to them. Around 6,000 people with a variety of qualifications work in these agencies, supported by nearly 30,000 unpaid volunteers. They deal with over ten million

---

[4] These include: criminal, family, personal injury, housing, and social welfare. New franchise categories have been developed: for example a clinical negligence franchise was developed in February 1999.

[5] Although costs rose by 48% in a 6-year period, the numbers of people assisted rose by only 7%. Indeed expenditure on civil and family legal aid rose by 42% while the numbers of people assisted fell by 30%.

inquiries each year and receive around £250m from a wide variety of sources of public funding, from both central and local government.

The services that these agencies offer have, however, developed very haphazardly, often in response to specific local initiatives. Coverage throughout England and Wales is therefore patchy. In some areas, there is no effective service at all. In others there may be a number of agencies offering very much the same service. Here there is over-provision and a consequent waste of scarce resources—both cash and manpower.

The *Legal Services Commission* will be responsible for building on the services that already exist to develop, in effect, a national legal service, funded by the Community Legal Service Fund, in partnership with other funders, such as local authorities and central government.

In undertaking its planning the Legal Services Commission will be aided by *regional legal services committees* which were established prior to the creation of the commission[6] to assist in identifying current provision and to help shape the provision of new legal services to the community. It is intended that in each local authority area there will be a *Community Legal Service Partnership*, which will provide a forum for the local authority, the Legal Services Commission, and others jointly to plan and coordinate the funding of local advice and other legal services, to try to ensure that service delivery matches local needs. Funding for the Community Legal Service is under the terms of a *funding code* which sets out the detailed framework within which legal services will be delivered.

It is a key part of the Community Legal Service scheme that legal services will be delivered on the basis of contracts made between the Legal Services Commission and the supplier of legal services. Building on the franchising and contracting initiatives launched by the Legal Aid Board, *only* suppliers with franchises will be able to obtain contracts for publicly funded legal services.

Further, it is a key feature of the new scheme, and in many respects the most controversial, that the funds available to the Legal Services Commission will be cash-limited each year, rather than—as happened under the legal aid scheme—being 'demand led'.

Priorities

In shaping the detail of the scheme, the Legal Services Commission is required to take into account certain priorities for funding legal services, which are set for it by the Lord Chancellor.[7] These priorities include:

- proceedings under the Children Act 1989 for which legal aid was formerly available without either a means or a merits test;[8]

---

[6] They were set up in October 1997 in each of the thirteen legal aid areas—administrative areas into which the country is divided for the purpose of running the legal aid schemes.

[7] Access to Justice Act, 1999, s. 6(1).

[8] See below p. 228.

- civil proceedings where the life or liberty of the client is at risk;[9]
- housing and other social welfare cases that enable people to avoid or to climb out of social exclusion;
- domestic violence cases;
- cases concerning the welfare of children;
- cases alleging serious wrongdoing, breaches of human rights, or abuse of position or power by a public body or servant.

Exclusions

Only services for individuals may be funded under the scheme. Services for firms or other types of non-individual legal persona cannot be provided. In addition, certain types of legal service are excluded from the scheme altogether. These include:

- services relating to allegations of *negligently*[10] caused injury or death, though not allegations of clinical negligence. (The reason for this is that it is assumed that such cases will be very suitable for conditional fee agreements; see below);
- cases relating to injuries caused by negligence, even where the legal claim is not cast in terms of the law of negligence (e.g. tripping cases, where the local authority is alleged to be in breach of a statutory duty to maintain the highway);
- other areas excluded because they have been judged not to have sufficient priority to justify public funding. These include allegations of negligent damage to property;[11] conveyancing; boundary disputes; matters of trust law or the making of wills; and matters arising from company or partnership law or the running of a business;[12]
- also excluded is representation in cases involving defamation and malicious falsehood.

Notwithstanding the general exclusions, help relating to making a will may be available to a person over 70, or a disabled person, or a parent or guardian of such a person who wishes to provide for that person; and in certain cases involving those under the age of 16.

More generally, funding of matters otherwise excluded may be possible:

- Where the matter is only incidental to an issue for which funding is permitted; or where the issue is brought into the proceedings by someone who is not being assisted by the scheme.
- Where there are two distinct claims, one of which is an excluded matter, but

---

[9] This was the principle that led to the recent extension of legal aid to hearings before the Immigration Appeal Tribunal.

[10] The exclusion does not extend to cases of injury arising from an alleged assault or deliberate abuse.

[11] Housing disrepair cases brought by a tenant against a landlord are not excluded, as the property is not owned by the claimant.

[12] The government's view is that these risks should be covered by insurance.

where is it impossible or impracticable to deal with them separately, and the commission thinks they cannot be funded by a conditional fee arrangement or in some other way.

- Issues relating to boundaries, trusts, or company or partnership law which arise in funded housing proceedings or funded family disputes or proceedings may be funded even though they are more than incidental to the principal proceedings.

- So too may conveyancing services where they arise in the course of other funded proceedings, or to give effect to a court order or agreement to settle.

- Furthermore, and notwithstanding the general exclusion of personal injury negligence claims, both *investigative support* and *litigation support* (for definition of these terms, see below) may be made available in such cases if the costs of the claim are exceptionally high (and thus likely to deter insurers or those offering conditional fee arrangements).

- Cases which involve a wider public interest may also exceptionally, even though they would otherwise fall in the excluded categories.

- The broad exclusion of funding services for representation before coroners' courts and tribunals is retained.[13] However, the Lord Chancellor has stated he might on occasion fund exceptional cases before tribunals or the coroner's court where strict criteria were met.[14]

The government has stated that as alternative funding sources develop, such as conditional fee arrangements and legal expenses insurance, then categories of work currently publicly funded may be removed from the scope of the Community Legal Service. Other work, such as some legal representation before tribunals, may then be brought within the scope of the scheme. The political difficulties of achieving this goal should not, however, be underestimated.

Objectives of the Community Legal Service

Under the terms of the 1999 Act, the Community Legal Service has five broad objectives. These are the provision of:[15]

(1) General information about the law and legal system (for example the provision of leaflets in a supermarket or the creation of legal web-sites);

(2) Help by giving advice about how the law applies in particular circumstances (for example the provision of initial advice at a Community Advice Centre or Citizens' Advice Bureau);

(3) Help in preventing, settling, or otherwise resolving disputes about legal rights

---

[13] Funded legal representation before the Lands Tribunal and the Commons Commissioners, which was possible under the legal aid scheme, is withdrawn by the 1999 Act.

[14] His department is undertaking a review of tribunal procedures to ensure compliance with obligations under the European Convention on Human Rights.

[15] Access to Justice Act 1999, s. 4 (2).

and duties (for example the provision of more detailed assistance, such as telephone calls, letter writing, or even some representation by a solicitor);

(4) Help in enforcing decisions by which such disputes are resolved; and

(5) Help in relation to legal proceedings not relating to disputes.

The scheme will fund the provision of services by lawyers (as did the existing legal aid scheme) but will also extend to certain services provided by non-lawyers. To ensure quality, service providers will have to obtain a 'quality mark' relevant to the type and level of service they are offering.[16]

Service levels

The services provided will fall into seven levels:

- legal help (which replaces the former 'green form' advice and assistance scheme);
- help at court;
- approved family help (either general family help or help with mediation);[17]
- legal representation (either investigative help[18] or full representation);
- support funding (either investigative support or litigation support);[19]
- family mediation;
- such other services as are authorized by the Lord Chancellor.

Means test

As with legal aid, clients entitled to funded services will have to demonstrate that they are financially eligible—in other words they are subject to a means test.[20] Where applicants fall below a lower threshold, they pay nothing. If they fall between a lower financial threshold and a higher one, the provision of a funded service will be subject to the funded client making a financial contribution towards the cost.[21] In addition, where the proceedings are designed to obtain an award of damages or other financial provision, any award of damages is made subject to a 'charge' in favour of the Community Legal Service Fund.

Merits test

The general approach to the funding of cases is that funding should be available where

---

[16] *The Community Legal Service: Quality Mark Consultation Paper* (London: Legal Aid Board, 1999).

[17] This is considered in Chapter 7 on the Family Justice system.

[18] This will be available where the size of the claim is likely to exceed £5,000. This will be provided where the strength of a case needs to be assessed; it may lead to full representation.

[19] This is a new form of funding designed to allow a mix of private and public funding in personal injury cases.

[20] The provision of information and the provision of services to proceedings under the Children Act 1989 are outside this rule. For funding in family cases, see above Chapter 7, p. 165.

[21] Legal help, help at court, and family mediation are not subject to the making of a contribution.

a reasonable private paying client would be prepared to fund the case. Thus account must be taken of whether the proceedings would be cost-effective;[22] and there must be an assessment of the prospects of success.[23] Cost–benefit ratios are to be determined by relating the likely costs to the percentage prospect of success.[24] Funding will be refused in cases where a conditional fee agreement should be obtained. There are special rules for cases against public bodies that raise human rights issues. Where a court has given permission for a judicial review case to proceed to a hearing, there will be a presumption that legal services funding will be granted, so long as the client is within the financial threshold.

Very expensive cases

To prevent a large proportion of the Community Legal Services Fund being expended on a relatively small number of very expensive cases, a Special Cases Unit will control the costs of such cases. Cases likely to exceed £25,000 in costs will be referred to the unit. Special arrangements will also continue to be made in relation to multi-party actions, where a large number of claimants are claiming loss from a single event or cause.

Alternative dispute resolution

ADR may be funded where these may be more effective than court proceedings. However, where a complaints procedure or ombudsman scheme is available which might be appropriate to resolve the problem in question, funding will not be considered until these have been exhausted.

COMMENT

Unlike the legal aid scheme which the Community Legal Service is replacing, the new scheme will, as noted above, no longer be 'demand-led' but will be subject to cash limits. The imposition of cash limits has generated considerable controversy. It is argued, in particular, that the need to provide criminal defence services will result in the Community Legal Service being starved of essential resources.

However, as with all public spending, there is a need for financial discipline. Further, the existence of cash limits will not *necessarily* mean that the services needed by the public cannot be delivered. Clearly there are dangers if, for example, a case arising towards the end of the year arises at a time when the cash available for the delivery of the service has run out. (Very similar problems arise in the National Health Service,

---

[22] In framing the Funding Code's provisions on these matters, the Legal Services Commission is required to take into account the *statutory factors*, which are set out in s. 8(2) of the Act.

[23] This criterion will not apply to many housing cases, or cases with a wider public interest. The Legal Services Commission will be advised on the public interest by a Public Interest Advisory Panel.

[24] For example, where prospects of success are 80% or better, the likely damages must exceed the likely costs; where the prospects of success are 60%–80%, the likely damages must exceed likely costs by 2:1; where prospects of success are 50%–60%, likely damages must exceed likely costs by 4:1.

where service deliverers have to manage the resources they have available, notwith-standing the vagaries of demands for clinical services.) Much of the success or other-wise of the new scheme will depend on the level at which those limits are set, and the effectiveness of the use of available resources, to deliver cost-effective legal services. It cannot be assumed *a priori* that the new scheme will not work.

The basic concept of the Community Legal Service (CLS) is not new. The case for the creation of a National Legal Service or a Community Legal Service has been made by many pressure groups and other social activists on numerous occasions over many years. Such plans have not, however, been taken up by the political parties in the past. One of the principal opponents of the idea has been the practising legal profession, fearful that a National Legal Service would 'nationalize' the provision of legal services and destroy the independence of the legal profession.

The importance of the latest developments, however, is that the government has at last accepted that there will never be a truly national provision of legal services—particularly for the less well-off members of the community—funded simply from fees paid, whether by the state or by individuals, to professionally qualified lawyers. It is also accepted that the provision of such services as there are should be much better structured than they have been hitherto.

It is, by definition, impossible at this point to determine whether the new arrange-ments will be more satisfactory than those they are replacing. However a number of comments may be made.

(1) Most of the research on legal services argues that the provision of good quality information and advice at an early stage can save costs later on. The emphasis in the new scheme on these early stages would seem in principle to be correct.

(2) The recognition of non-lawyer agencies as falling within the scope of the Community Legal Service, and able to receive funding is also an important development. There is much evidence to suggest that in important areas, levels of expertise on—for example—welfare rights is actually much higher amongst those without a professional legal qualification.

(3) It is far from clear that the legal profession at large, and particularly those firms of solicitors that do just a little bit of legal aid have fully realized the impact of the changes that are being brought into effect. While those who are already geared up to legal aid service delivery, as a result of the franchising scheme, should be able to adapt to the new regime easily and efficiently, others who have not yet acquired a franchise will fall outside the scope of the scheme.

(4) The main unknown is whether the new CLS will be able to offer the geo-graphical coverage and, thus access to legal advice and assistance, that the network of solicitors was—at least in theory—able to offer under the old scheme.[25]

---

[25] Blacksell, Mark, Economides, Kim, and Watkins, Charles, *Justice outside the City: Access to Legal Services in Rural Britain* (Harlow: Longman Scientific & Technical, 1991).

(5) The ability of the CLS to fund the provision of electronic and telephone services may, however, alleviate problems of physical access, though there will no doubt be concerns that the primary client groups for the CLS may not have the same access to these as other groups in the population.

As with all cash-limited public services there will always be argument about the extent to which further funding should or should not be made available. There will never be public acknowledgement that the service is adequately funded. However, the CLS offers an imaginative framework for the delivery of legal services which goes a considerable way to addressing many of the criticisms that have been raised over the last twenty-five years in relation to legal aid. Whether this optimistic assessment will survive the experience of the CLS, only time will tell.

CRIMINAL DEFENDER SERVICE (CDS)

The CDS is the other legal service introduced by the Access to Justice Act 1999. It will replace and build on the criminal legal aid scheme, which is also abolished by the Act. The Legal Services Commission will have power to secure the provision of legal advice, assistance, and representation for those suspected of committing a criminal offence and thus under investigations, or actually facing criminal proceedings[26] in court. There will be two ways in which these services will be provided:

- Through contracts with lawyers in private practice; or
- Through salaried defenders employed either by the commission or by not-for-profit organizations established for the purpose.[27]

A key difference from the Community Legal Service is that the Criminal Defence Service will remain a 'demand-led', rather than a cash-limited, service.[28]

Since only those firms of solicitors that have a legal aid franchise in the area of criminal law will be able to secure a contract from the Legal Services Commission, the new arrangements mean that the absolute freedom of the suspect or defendant to choose his or her own lawyer will be reduced.[29] The government hopes that, unless there are exceptional circumstances, there will always be more than one provider available to those who have been accused of offences from whom a choice can be made.

---

[26] 'Criminal proceedings' are defined to include not only criminal trials, appeals, and sentencing hearings, but also extradition hearings, binding-over proceedings, appeals on behalf of a convicted person who has died, and proceedings for contempt in the face of any court: Access to Justice Act 1999, s. 12. The Lord Chancellor will have power to add to this list and intends to do so to cover Parole Board reviews of discretionary life sentences.

[27] Such salaried providers will be subject to a code of conduct to be published by the commission and approved by Parliament: Access to Justice Act 1999, s. 16.

[28] Access to Justice Act 1999, s. 18.

[29] In the case of very specialized types of case, such as fraud, the freedom of choice may be restricted further to those with recognized experience in such cases.

A further important feature of the new arrangements is that the decision to fund representation in a criminal case will in future—and unlike the position with the criminal legal aid scheme—not be subject to the carrying out of a means-test. There were two problems with the means-testing of criminal legal aid:

- First, it was wasteful of money. The means-testing process cost the legal aid scheme almost as much as the money raised from individual defendants as a result of the means-testing exercise.

Instead, under the CDS there will be a power for the judge, at the end of the trial, to order that a convicted person pay some or all of his costs. The commission will have a power to investigate the means of individual defendants in order to assist the court in reaching that decision.

- Secondly, it added to delay, in that a trial could not proceed until the issue of representation had been sorted out.

These new arrangements were also matters on which there was considerable controversy as the Access to Justice Bill went through Parliament. Among the issues raised were:

(1) The new regime means that the better-off, who do not rely on publicly funded legal aid, will still have complete freedom of choice over who should represent them. Thus, it was argued, there will be an unacceptable distinction between what the better-off and the less well-off are able to receive by way of legal assistance. However, there is an opposing argument, that those providing legal services, paid for out of public funds, should be able to demonstrate basic levels of professional competence—which acquiring a franchise is designed to achieve—so that there will be some guarantee that public money is not wasted on the incompetent or inexperienced. Given the substantial number of firms that have legal aid contracts in criminal law, the criticisms of the new position may be said to have been overstated, at least in terms of their likely practical outcome. There is no doubt, however, that a point of principle was breached.

(2) There is some evidence from the USA[30] that public defender schemes do not work as well at they should in defending the interests of the accused or suspect. There were therefore considerable worries that if the predominant form of provision in England were to become the public defender system, this would lead to a less competent mode of delivering criminal legal services. This could well become a problem were the publicly funded service to become the sole mode of delivering this form of legal service. However, this is certainly not going to be the situation in the short term. So long as there is a large degree of

---

[30] McConville, Michael and Mirsky, Chester L., 'Criminal Defence of the Poor in New York City', (1986–7) 15 *New York University Review of Law and Social Change*, 581–964.

competition from the private sector, professional competition should ensure that adequate standards are maintained.

Certainly the new arrangements should be more streamlined than the former often highly fragmented provision in which a person might get advice in the police station under one funding scheme; advice in the solicitor's office or in prison under another; and representation in court under yet a third. It is intended that, when fully operational, the new criminal law contracts will provide for a single service from arrest until completion of the case.

The new arrangements will not come into effect at once but will be phased in from April 2001.

PRIVATE FUNDING MECHANISMS

The changes to the legal aid scheme should not be seen in isolation. Other mechanisms to promote the private funding of legal proceedings have also been considered in recent years.

CONDITIONAL FEE AGREEMENTS

Conditional fee agreements (CFAs) are defined in section 58 of the Courts and Legal Services Act 1990, as amended by section 27(1) of the Access to Justice Act 1999. A conditional fee agreement is '*an agreement . . . which provides for . . . fees and expenses, or any part of them, to be payable only in specified circumstances*'. The importance of CFAs in the funding of litigation has been significantly increased, as a result of the enactment of the Access to Justice Act 1999, since it is now a principle that public funding of litigation through the Community Legal Services should not be provided in cases where alternative funding (including CFAs) is available.[31]

Traditionally CFAs, also known as '*no win no fee*', have allowed solicitors to agree to take a case on the understanding that, if the case is lost, they will not charge their clients for all or any of the work undertaken. The client also agrees that if the case is successful, the solicitor can charge a *success fee* on top of the normal fees, to compensate for the risk the solicitor has run of not being paid all or some of her fees. The success fee is calculated as a percentage of the normal fees and the level at which the success fee is set reflects the risk involved. Regulations provide that the 'uplift' of the success fee should be no more than 100 per cent of the normal fee. The Law Society has advised[32] solicitors that, in any event, the uplift should not exceed 25 per cent of any damages recovered, where that figure would be less than the figure

---

[31] See the *statutory factors* in the Act, s. 8(2). This criterion does not apply in all cases, e.g. housing cases.

[32] In addition to providing guidance on the use of CFAs, the Law Society also produced a model CFA. Both have recently undergone review by the Law Society.

agreed in the CFA.[33] (It is not actually a requirement of a CFA that a success fee must be charged, but it usually will be.)

The *no fee* element relates to the solicitor's fees alone and does not cover the ancillary expenses of the case, such as expert reports, and may not cover counsel's fees. However, the solicitor may agree to fund these costs as part of the agreement or may arrange insurance cover of these fees for his client. Alternatively, a CFA can be entered into between a solicitor and counsel or, in very limited circumstances, between client and counsel.

After the event legal expense insurance (LEI) policies (see further below) are now also available which provide cover for the solicitor's fee and/or for the opponent's costs should the case be unsuccessful. The premiums paid for insurance cover are determined by the provider and are dependent on a number of factors, including the strength of the case, the likely measure of damages involved in the case, and the legal representative's experience of undertaking such cases. Premiums may range from £100 to many millions depending on the case insured.

Scope of CFAs

The definition of CFAs in section 58 of that Act excludes criminal and most family proceedings, and is limited to agreements specified by order by the Lord Chancellor, which comply with requirements also prescribed by the Lord Chancellor in regulations.

The first order came into force on 5 July 1995.[34] This limited conditional fee agreements to: personal injury cases, insolvency cases, and cases before the European Court of Human Rights. From that date it was lawful, in those limited categories of case, for a legal representative to enter into an agreement with his client whereby costs would be recoverable from the client only in certain circumstances. The regulations also specified the information which a conditional fee agreement must contain and which must be brought to the client's attention.

In July 1998 the range of proceedings was extended (as far as possible under the 1990 Act) to *all civil proceedings*, other than family cases. This has resulted in an increasing use of conditional fee agreements. The evidence, such as it is, also points to the increasing use of CFAs in areas such as defamation, for which legal aid has never been available. It is likely that many cases, subject to CFAs, would not have been brought but for the existence of conditional fees. To date there have been very few complaints about the way in which CFAs have operated, but it is not clear whether this is because there are no problems, or whether there are problems which have yet to come to public attention.

---

[33] Despite this linkage with damages, it should be stressed that CFAs are related only to the professional fees charged, *not* to damages. Any arrangements to recover a percentage of damages recovered—contingency fees—are not lawful in England and Wales.

[34] The Conditional Fees Regulations 1995.

OTHER SPECULATIVE AGREEMENTS

While the extension of conditional fee agreements to all civil business has provided access to justice for individuals who may not have otherwise litigated, the definition of a conditional fee agreement is limited, and does not encompass all situations where a legal representative agrees to act for his client at different rates to that which he will seek to recover from his client's opponent.

Two recent decisions in the Court of Appeal tested the way in which alternative agreements for funding cases are viewed: *Thai Trading Co. (A Firm) v. Taylor* [1998] 3 All ER 65 and *Bevan Ashford v. Geoff Yeandle (Contractors) Ltd* [1998] 3 All ER 238. In the former, the Court of Appeal held that there were no longer any public policy grounds to prevent legal representatives agreeing to work for less than their normal fees in the event that they were unsuccessful, provided they did not seek to recover more than their normal fees if they were successful. In *Bevan Ashford*, the Vice Chancellor held that where a person funds the use of an alternative remedy to court proceedings by means of a speculative agreement, in a class of proceedings where conditional fee agreements are lawful in the courts, and that all the relevant provisions relating to the form and content of the agreement as prescribed by the relevant regulations were complied with, then there were no public policy grounds for holding the agreement unlawful. On the contrary, it would be of benefit for clients to have access to these agreements to enable them to use alternative dispute mechanisms.

THE IMPACT OF THE ACCESS TO JUSTICE ACT 1999

The Access to Justice Act received Royal Assent on 27 July 1999. Sections 27 to 31 relate to conditional fee agreements and insurance premiums.

- Section 27 replaces section 58 of the Courts and Legal Services Act 1990 and provides a clearer definition of *conditional fee agreements*. It incorporates the decisions in *Thai Trading* and *Bevan Ashford* (above) by providing that *all* agreements to work for less than normal fees are made subject to the new section 58 of the Courts and Legal Services Act. This is designed to ensure greater certainty and means that such agreements can be properly regulated, for example by requiring solicitors to give relevant information to potential clients.[35] It also makes the winning party's success fee potentially recoverable from the other side. Section 27 also amends section 58 of the Courts and Legal Services Act to allow cases to be brought under section 82 of the Environmental Protection Act using a CFA, even although these are technically criminal cases.[36]

- Section 28 introduces a new concept, the *litigation funding agreement*. This allows a party to be funded by a third party (rather than the solicitor), for

[35] Details about CFAs are set out in regulations.

[36] These cases concern orders requiring persons to stop a statutory nuisance, e.g. the failure of a landlord to ensure that a house that has been let is not prejudicial to health.

example, a trade union, or other prescribed group. In these cases the funder pays the solicitor's normal fees. However, where the case is won, the funder is entitled to be paid the success fee by the losing side, and is able to retain that element of the fee to cover losses on cases which are not won.

- Section 29 enables the costs of the winning party's 'after the event' insurance premium to be recoverable from the other side.[37]

- Section 31 is an enabling provision giving the Lord Chancellor power to amend the common law principle of indemnity—that the loser pays the costs of the winning party—which underlies costs. Any amendment of the indemnity principle will, however, be effected through Rules of Court, on which consultation has recently taken place.

Enforceability

A CFA which complies with these requirements shall not be unenforceable by reason of its being a CFA, unless it relates to criminal proceedings, family proceedings, or proceedings which have not been specified. Where the CFA relates to such categories of proceeding, or otherwise does not comply with the requirements in the regulations, the act explicitly provides that the agreement is unenforceable. The success fee is enforceable only where the agreement complies with the prescribed requirements; relates to specified proceedings; and the percentage increase does not exceed that set out in the order specifying the proceedings.

LEGAL EXPENSES INSURANCE

By comparison with many other countries, notably Germany, the development of commercially provided legal expenses insurance has been extremely slow in England. This is probably due to the fact that, by comparison with most other countries, legal aid in England has been relatively generously funded.

Legal expenses insurance comes in a variety of guises:

- Stand alone

- Add-on

- After the event

Stand alone policies are those which are sold principally by specialist legal expense insurance providers for those who wish to obtain general cover against the possibility that at some point they may have to incur legal expenses. Although legal expense insurance has been available in the United Kingdom for many years, take-up has not been widespread.

---

[37] Section 30 allows a body, such as a trade union, that funds litigation on behalf of its members out of its own resources, who do not therefore take out separate insurance, to include in their costs an amount equivalent to the insurance premium that would have been recoverable were an insurance policy in place.

Add-on policies are those where, as an additional benefit to other cover, for example household contents insurance, or travel insurance, or motor insurance, related legal expenses may be covered. It is thought that many people who have these forms of insurance cover do not actually realize this. It is part of the 'small print' of insurance contracts which they do not read.

After the event insurance is a newer form of policy devised in the context of the new rules relating to conditional fee arrangements, as discussed above. These are bought when the purchaser is contemplating taking legal proceedings, but before the outcome of the case has been determined, and cover the solicitor's fees in cases where the case is lost. The latest rules relating to CFAs allow the costs of premiums to be recovered from the losing party by the winner.

One of the problems with the current provision of LEI is that it is suspected that many people to not realize that they may have such insurance as an add-on to another insurance policy, or do not know about the possibilities of purchasing after the event insurance. The Funding Sub-Committee of the Civil Justice Council is currently exploring means to improve awareness of these categories of insurance, and their potential effect on Access to Justice.

CONCLUSION

Access to Justice is essential if the claim to have an efficient legal system is to be sustained. Debate on legal aid was, in the past, dominated to a large extent by the legal profession. The legal aid scheme was largely designed and developed by the Law Society. While there should be no doubt that those who undertook this work were determined to create a scheme that did deliver a needed service to the public, it is also the case that the legal profession were in many ways also principal beneficiaries of it. The injection of £1.6bn into law firms—the amount of public expenditure on legal aid—is not a trivial sum. It was obvious that the rate of growth of public expenditure in this area—despite rhetorical claims that 'justice is without price'—could not be sustained.

Put another way, if policy makers had started the legal aid scheme from scratch with a budget of £1.6bn, would they have devised the legal aid scheme that eventually developed? Those who accept that the answer to this question must be 'no' must then think what the shape of any alternative might be. The Access to Justice Act 1999 has provided the opportunity for a new scheme by creating a new statutory framework. The new state-funded scheme will inevitably build upon its historical legacy. It may not achieve all that those who have put it in place claim that it will achieve. There is every chance that the CLS will prove to be more fit for its purpose than the civil legal aid scheme it has replaced; the jury is still out on the CDS. The potential relationship between public funding and the new incentives to encourage the private funding of litigation are less clear, though lawyers do have considerable ability to turn new opportunities for earning a living to their advantage. In so doing, there is a least a reasonable prospect that the individual will have greater access to justice.

CONCLUSION

11

IS THE ENGLISH LEGAL SYSTEM FIT FOR ITS PURPOSE?

INTRODUCTION

At the start of this book, the question was posed whether the English legal system is currently fit to meet the demands placed upon it. In subsequent pages, a wide range of issues has been considered. What are law's functions? How is law made? What are the contexts in which it is practised? Who are the different actors in the legal system? How are legal services funded? A number of specific issues about the fitness of the legal system to achieve its apparent purposes have been raised in context above.[1]

In this final chapter I return to that initial question, to raise for further consideration matters not specifically considered earlier, or which raise important and interesting issues. The purpose of the chapter is not to provide definitive answers to these questions, but to offer some views for readers to reflect on which may provoke their own thinking about law and the legal system.

There can be little doubt that law plays a variety of key roles, not necessarily consistent with each other, in the organization of our modern society. Countries where the rule of law seems to be less well established than in the United Kingdom may be seen to be at something of a disadvantage. However, the world is going through a period of rapid and considerable change. Is the English legal system able adequately to respond to this changing world?

IMAGES OF LAW

Chapter 1 suggested that those without direct experience of lawyers or of going to court might come to the study of law with pre-conceptions about the law and the legal system that were at best limited, at worst seriously distorted. In subsequent chapters it has been demonstrated that there is much more to law than criminal justice; that

---

[1] Just by way of example, note the comments on the Child Support system above, at Chapter 7, p. 158.

those providing legal services are far more varied than the 'fat-cat' lawyers sometimes portrayed in the press; that both the institutions of the legal system and those who deliver legal services are undergoing profound change; that problems of inefficiency and delay, particularly in the litigation process, are being increasingly acknowledged and are beginning to be addressed.

Institutional innovation is driven in large part by the present government's modernization agenda, but the needs of an increasingly global economy also contribute to the pressure for institutional change. The leaders of the bodies that represent the legal profession may, on occasion, appear too resistant to change as they seek to defend the interests of those practitioners who may fear an uncertain future, and lack the willingness to embrace change. But very many individual practitioners and firms of lawyers have demonstrated considerable dynamism and imagination in shaping their practices to respond to clients' needs.

There are many other indicators that suggest that negative images of law and the legal system are unfair. There is still a great desire on the part both of professionally qualified lawyers and other lay legal advisers to deliver legal services to all sections of the public, not just the well heeled and powerful. Standards of education and training of lawyers and other advisers have increased greatly in recent years. The judiciary are essentially free of corruption.

But to stop at this point would risk the complacent conclusion that the English legal system *is* the best in the world, requiring at most only modest further adjustment. The fact is that there are many other issues on which one can be more critical. It is important that those coming to the legal system for the first time think about those features which are open to criticism. The future development of robust legal institutions lies at least in part in the hands of those now entering the legal system.

One key issue is the treatment of legal issues in the mass media. Apart from the drama of the big trial or a scandal involving a miscarriage of justice, discussion about law in the mass media is not well rounded. With notable exceptions such as the BBC radio programme, *Law In Action*, or the weekly law pages in the broadsheet newspapers, together with a number of consumer programmes which touch on aspects of the law, there is little public discussion about law-making, the practice of law, or the impact of law on the citizen. Unlike other aspects of our intellectual life, such as history, or science, or medicine, law is not regularly the subject of mainstream media programming.

Yet the centrality of law to different social orders suggests that the present media neglect of law and legal issues is unsatisfactory. Of course, programme-makers may feel that law is too complex and difficult a subject to make it attractive for mass programming. But such an approach simply contributes to the mystique of law, and enhances the power of the lawyer in society, at a time when, arguably, opportunities for greater general understanding of and access to law should be growing.

Part of the reason why public discussion of legal issues is so limited may be that those who operate within the legal system themselves have shown only limited interest in presenting their work to a wider audience. Certainly, much professional legal activity is conducted on the basis of secrecy and confidentiality, which may result in a lack of individual enthusiasm to enter the public eye. Furthermore, there are still those in the legal profession who think that it goes against the professional grain to seek publicity for their work. However, a consequence of such attitudes may equally be that the law and its practitioners only hit the headlines when things have gone wrong. These days considerable effort is expended on placing stories in the media which forms part of the public relations activity of promoting the work of individual legal firms or practices.

Lawyers and other practitioners should be even more willing than they have been hitherto to shape a more educational public information agenda, and to work with the media to develop opportunities for a more rounded understanding of law and the legal system in all our lives. While the difficulties of making a wider range of programmes about law may be substantial, nevertheless the challenge for the years ahead remains to provide a new, more informed, treatment of legal issues in the mass media, which would play an important part in the shaping of public perceptions about the legal system and those who work in it, which could contribute to making the legal system function more effectively.

One particular idea that arises in this context which does need careful thought is whether more trials should be televised. This happens a great deal in the USA; there was a notable recent experiment in the United Kingdom, when a number of trials in Scotland were shown in edited form on television. While such a step might give the appearance of greater openness of the legal system to the public, it should be remembered that in many ways televising trials merely serves to exacerbate current images of law—that the typical legal process is a criminal one, and one in which there is a lengthy trial of the case for and against the accused. There is little discussion about televising cases in the administrative justice, family justice or civil justice arenas; nor programmes dealing with the vast majority of cases that are resolved without a full-scale trial.

In addition to the treatment of law in the media, other issues also need consideration. First, there are still important questions to be resolved about the patterns of recruitment to the legal profession. Although there are now considerably greater opportunities for women to become lawyers than was the case some years ago, they do not yet appear to be achieving their full potential to rise to the most senior positions in the legal world. In addition, the improvement in the opportunities for women to enter law does has not appear to have been matched by comparable increases in the opportunities for those coming from working-class backgrounds, nor for those from ethnic-minority backgrounds. Given the importance of equality of treatment and even-handedness in the delivery of legal services, it is important that those running the profession and the institutions of the law take these issues of recruitment and advancement seriously.

Secondly, are current modes of dress really appropriate in the twenty-first century? As noted in Chapter 9, a large number of actors in the legal system do not put on any kind of ritual clothing before they undertake the services required of them by the public. The question still arises, however, whether the use of wigs and gowns in the higher courts is necessary. Some believe that the use of such costumes is intimidating and creates a distant relationship between the lawyer or judge and those who appear in court. For this very reason others argue that such a sense of distance is necessary. It may be particularly desirable for some categories of judge, especially those in the criminal courts, to wear distinguishing garb to provide an added sense of authority to those who appear before them. But the question remains: is the present system of wigs and robes still essential? If not, how should it be altered?

LAW'S FUNCTIONS

A wide range of issues about the social functions of law were considered in Chapter 2. In relation to many of these, readers will have their own views, not all of which can be canvassed in an introductory work. The tension between the use of law to control and regulate behaviour and the use of law to protect people by giving them rights and entitlements was particularly emphasized.

The issue that arises out of that discussion which perhaps bears most fundamentally on the question whether the English legal system is fit for its purpose is whether there is now too ready a recourse to the use of law to try to deal with the issues facing modern society. There are occasions on which politicians and others pay lip-service to the proposition that law should not be used to regulate human activity more than absolutely necessary. But there are few incentives not to make law. Politicians' and civil servants' reputations are based on the laws they create, not those that they prevent. And the reputation of practitioners is enhanced by their pushing at the boundaries of law, as they try to establish new areas of legal liability, not by their seeking to limit the scope of law. The coming into effect of the Human Rights Act will dramatically add to these pressures. Certainly the amount and complexity of the law that emerges from government and the courts is constantly increasing.

In this context, the proposition that ordinary citizens can in any real sense be assumed to know the law that governs their lives is just not sustainable. While it may not be realistic to complain that there is too much law, the implications for law-makers and others involved in the working of the legal system in providing better information about law are clear. The current lack of investment in the provision of useful information about the law and its procedures must be seen as a weakness in the current institutional arrangements of the legal system. As with the challenge of providing better general information about law through the mass media, there is also a considerable challenge to be faced, particularly within government, about the use of new information and communication technologies to make information about citizens' rights available to a much wider public than is presently the case. This is an area of activity in which it may be anticipated that there will be rapid progress in the years ahead, particular as increased use of the internet develops. Indeed a number of initiatives have been started in this field, but they have not yet progressed very far.

LAW-MAKING—LEGITIMACY AND AUTHORITY

The primary law-making bodies today are the legislative institutions of the European Union and the United Kingdom. Both claim to derive legitimacy for the exercise of legislative powers from political theories of democracy. However, the extent to which ordinary people understand the nature of such assertions of legitimacy must be open to doubt. The processes of the British Parliament and the institutions of the European Union are poorly understood. There is great ignorance about the links between institutional assertions of legitimacy and the democratic will of the people. Even less clear is the relationship between majority opinion and the protection of minorities—a key issue in modern pluralist societies.

There is evidence that this is an issue that is beginning to be taken seriously. Many of the institutional and constitutional reforms both in the United Kingdom and in Europe are influenced by an increasing acknowledgement that voter apathy is not a satisfactory basis on which to claim legitimacy for the exercise of law-making power. At some point, unless more is done to encourage people to understand that, for example, elections are important, there will be a danger that those theoretically governed on the basis of consent may come to deny the legitimacy of their governors to govern. Consideration, by the present British government, of introducing instruction on 'citizenship' into the school curriculum is perhaps some indication of its recognition of the potential importance of this issue.

A likely trend in the next decade is much greater effort by government institutions to explain what they are doing, and to encourage input into the law-making process. Many of the recent procedural innovations to the law-making machinery in the United Kingdom—considered in Chapter 3—reflect this need. Questions remain, though: Do these changes go far enough? Should recent procedural changes in both the British and European Parliaments be taken further? Should there be further changes to the electoral system? To what extent is there a 'democratic deficit'? If there is such a deficit, what measures are needed to reduce it? Should there be greater opportunities for lobbyists and other groups to influence the shape and content of legislation?

At the same time, the law-making functions of the judges are about to come under intense scrutiny with the coming into force of the Human Rights Act 1998. There is already sharp debate between those who have argued for the legislation and the powers this gives to the judges to determine the compatibility of government policy with Human Rights principles and those who see this as usurping the essentially political functions of Parliament and the executive to deliver its political agenda.

There can be little doubt that, at least initially, the act will generate a great deal of innovative litigation, the outcome of which cannot currently be predicted. While, no doubt, most governments would claim that they operate within both the spirit and letter of the European Convention on Human Rights, a moment's reflection indicates clearly that in difficult cases, there is potential for considerable tension to develop between the legislative and executive branches of government and the judicial branch. If a significant political/legislative objective is declared incompatible with the European Convention on Human Rights by the courts, whether in the United Kingdom or in Strasbourg, this may at best result in embarrassment for the government, at worst considerable frustration. There is a powerful argument that adherence to human rights standards by government should be a political responsibility, not a judicial one.

Experience in the USA, where the Supreme Court has long asserted a power to review legislation in the context of the US Constitution and the Bill of Rights, may suggest that the impact of the courts, though significant when it is felt, may be limited. Thus the British judges may only seek to limit the freedom of governments to legislate in the very last resort. Experience in other countries—for example, Canada—suggests that such a view may be too sanguine. Whichever way the British judiciary goes, it seems inevitable that the constitutional role of the judiciary will become the focus of sharp debate in the years ahead.

This specific issue leads to the broader question of whether the time has come for the creation of a written constitution, which seeks to provide specific legitimacy for the different branches of government, and the systems of checks and balances that should operate to preserve the rule of law and prevent abuse of power. At present, this would seem to be an unlikely development, but is an issue which, following the present round of significant constitutional change, is unlikely wholly to disappear.

Notwithstanding all the procedural changes to the law-making process, there remain many practical questions about the law-making process which still need addressing. For example, where there is agreement that a particular rule of law needs changing, the problem of Parliamentary time means that this cannot easily be achieved. A substantial number of Law Commission reports remain unimplemented. And in situations where the common law lacks clarity or certainty, the ability of the judiciary to develop legal principle is dependant on the right case being brought before them. Should special procedures, either in Parliament or before the courts, be made more readily available where the state of the law is clearly unsatisfactory?

A different issue relates to styles of legislative drafting. One of the reasons why legislation, in particular, is so hard to understand, is that legislative draftsmen seek to define everything in legislation—whether primary, secondary, or tertiary—with a very high degree of linguistic precision. This leads to very considerable complexity. In turn this raises the question whether a more 'plain English' approach to the drafting of statutes might be appropriate. Certainly, the new Civil Procedure Rules were drafted on the basis that they should be easier to read and understand. And there are lawyers who have signed up to the Plain English Campaign's initiative for clearer drafting of legal documents. The question of the extent to which such initiatives should spread more widely into legislative drafting practice is being considered. A particular difficulty is to know whether new drafting practices would lead to more or less legislative uncertainty. It is likely that, to be fully effective, any new legislative drafting practices would have to be supported by the senior judiciary.

JUSTICE AND EFFICIENCY

The chapters in Part 2 of the book reveal a number of common themes. Most prominent is the considerable pressure in all justice systems to deal with cases as expeditiously and as economically as possible. These are perfectly proper aims, but nevertheless raise the question of the extent to which the shaping of the legal system should be driven by demands for efficiency and value for money, as opposed to other demands, such as the need for the justice system to be just. While unnecessary delay and expense must be deplored, it should still be asked whether current trends to dispose of cases rapidly, or even to divert them completely from courts and other dispute-resolution fora, will always operate in the interests of justice.

These issues cannot be addressed by vague assertions that 'justice has no price'. Justice quite clearly does have a price, which has to be paid for either by the citizen or by the state (whose resources come from the taxpayer). However, at the same time important principles relating to the need for the fairness of trial processes must be borne in mind. There must be some doubt, especially in the context of criminal justice, whether the apparently increasing focus on a 'crime control' model of criminal justice can be compatible with a 'due process' model. In turn, this may beg serious questions as to whether the system will be compliant with the human rights standards set down in the European Convention on Human Rights, and which have already been the subject of adverse rulings by the Strasbourg Court.

Another set of issues relates to avenues of appeal. In the context of the Criminal Justice system, for example, at least some of the recent serious cases of miscarriages of justice seem to be been exacerbated, at least in part, by the rather restrictive bases on which the Court of Criminal Appeal may determine criminal appeals. The creation of the Criminal Cases Review Commission was designed in part to assist. Will this be enough to prevent further serious miscarriages of justice? What other mechanisms are needed to ensure not only that the innocent are not convicted and sentenced, but also that those who have committed offences are brought to trial?

In relation to administrative justice and civil justice, the question was raised whether there were too many avenues of appeal and complaint for the individual to pursue. Changes to appeal routes in the Civil Justice system will have the effect of reducing the numbers of appeals that can be brought in that context. Should there not also be a review of the administrative justice system to examine whether the balance of interest between the citizen and the state has been correctly drawn? The recently announced review of the tribunal system may be a first step in this process.

A fundamental issue that affects the whole of the institutional framework of the English legal system is whether all citizens, and particularly members of ethnic minorities, feel that they are dealt with fairly. The aftermath of the Stephen Lawrence case is currently being digested by policy-makers. It is highly significant that, just as the writing of this book was nearing completion, the LCD should announce that the next round of its research activity should focus particularly on the experience of those from the minority groups in all parts of the legal system, not just the Criminal Justice system. Clearly, if the legal system is revealed as being unable to deliver equal treatment to all those who come into contact with it, as is now often asserted, this will be a concern of the utmost importance which will have to be dealt with as a matter of considerable urgency.

One pressure for change not considered in the main text is a set of ideas currently being developed within the policy-making bodies in Europe which might lead towards the development of a more Europe-wide court system. There could be some merit in these ideas. If the EU is able to encourage greater movement of its citizens around the different countries of Europe, should it not also facilitate the ability of those citizens to enforce their rights in the country of their choice? However, for many the very idea of such integration would be anathema, to be resisted at all costs. This is not an idea that is currently well developed, has certainly not been widely discussed, and will not be pursued further here. But it is an issue to which attention needs to be drawn. Were such moves to be seriously contemplated, the major distinctions between the British common law approach to law and the continental European civil law approach would be likely to prove a major hurdle to the integration of judicial systems. It is in this context that the suggestion of the need for closer legal integration between the common law countries of Europe, principally the United Kingdom and Ireland, might gain more significance.

PROFESSIONAL ORGANIZATION

Chapter 9 considered a number of questions relating to professional organization. It considered the increasing part played by government in seeking to regulate standards of professional activity. It was suggested that this could prove a worrying trend, for although there is no current suggestion that government will seek to limit the proper independence of the professionally qualified lawyer to take up controversial or unpopular cases, this does not mean that this could not happen at some future time if the trend towards greater government intervention accelerates.

There are a number of issues relating to professional regulation that are not currently well handled by the lawyers' professional bodies. In particular, there is an unsatisfactory muddling of the regulatory functions of the professional bodies—designed to ensure their members deliver services to proper professional standards—

with the professions' 'trade union' functions—designed to ensure that the interests of professional lawyers are as fully protected as possible. Unlike the medical profession, where the former function is performed by bodies such as the General Medical Council and the latter by the British Medical Association, the Law Society and Bar Council perform both functions. Perhaps the time has come for a similar division of responsibility in the context of the practising legal profession. This may be the only way to stave off yet further government involvement in the regulation of the legal profession.

Related to this is another more subtle question about the effectiveness of the professional bodies, and in particular the Law Society, to perform its trade union functions. Many now argue that the interests of those who practise in the large global law firms in the City of London are so far removed from the interests of the sole practitioner in a rural area that it is absurd to suggest that they should be represented by the same professional body. Indeed the recent announcement of the creation of a new grouping to represent the City of London firms might indicate that the role of the Law Society, as it currently exists, is about to change, perhaps in a radical way. Certainly one of the issues that will continue to need discussion in the year ahead is what the basic notion of 'the professional lawyer' should be, and how the identity of that professional person should best be sustained without fragmentation into a vast array of sub-specialisms.

THE FUNDING OF LEGAL SERVICES

The final issue addressed in the book is whether the new arrangements for the funding of legal services will—in some general sense—'work'. The new arrangements for the state-funded community legal service and criminal defence services, and the related arrangements for alternative ways for funding other forms of litigation are too recent for any conclusion to be reached. I anticipate that those critics who are most hostile to the new arrangements, who predict a complete breakdown in the provision of quality legal services to the public, will be confounded.

However, the changes are likely to have a big impact on the legal profession, particularly small firms or sole practitioners in small towns or rural areas, where it is hard to see their being able to generate the levels of business needed to stay financially afloat. It is likely that there will have to be the same sorts of mergers and consolidations to increase business efficiency that has already taken place at the more commercial end of the legal professional market.

More generally, whether all the promises offered by government for the effectiveness and impact of the new structure will be delivered must also be open to doubt. What will be needed is agreement on a reasonable level of government expenditure on the delivery of legal services, accompanied by an acceptance by legal practitioners that they must justify the £1.6 billion of public money that is paid to them. At the same time, it does seem inevitable that the line between legal services and lawyers' services will continue to get even more blurred, with more legal services being delivered by those without formal professional legal qualifications.

CONCLUSION

Much of the English legal system is pretty fit for purpose. But there is always room for change and improvement. It will never be a perfect system. Those coming new to law should seek to support what is good, but not seek to defend the indefensible. I hope the discussion in these pages will encourage the thought, reflection, and indeed action needed to bring about necessary change, while preventing undesirable change.

SUGGESTIONS FOR FURTHER READING

The scope of this book is very extensive. A complete bibliography would be as long again. Here a number of suggestions for further reading are offered as starting points for the student who wishes to go beyond the introduction to the subject provided in the main text.

CHAPTER 1: 'KNOWLEDGE', THEMES, AND STRUCTURE

BAILEY, S. H. and GUNN, M. J., *The Modern English Legal System*, 3rd edn. (London: Sweet & Maxwell, 1996).

BANKOWSKI, ZANON and MUNGHAM, GEOFF, *Images of Law* (London: Routledge & Kegan Paul, 1976).

COWNIE, FIONA and BRADNEY, ANTHONY, *English Legal System in Context* (London: Butterworths, 1996).

GENN, HAZEL, *Paths to Justice* (Oxford: Hart Publishing, 1999).

GRIGG-SPALL, IAN and IRELAND, PADDY, *The Critical Lawyer's Handbook* (London: Pluto Press, 1992).

HARRIS, PHIL, *An Introduction to Law*, 5th edn. (London: Butterworths, 1997).

JUSTICE, *Miscarriages of Justice: A Report by Justice*, Chairman of Committee, Sir George Waller (London: Justice, 1989).

PODGORECKI, ADAM et al., *Knowledge and Opinion about Law* (London: Martin Robertson, 1973).

WARD, RICHARD, *Walker and Walker's English Legal System*, 8th edn. (London: Butterworths, 1998).

WHITE, ROBIN C. A., *The English Legal System in Action: The Administration of Justice* (Oxford: Oxford University Press, 1999).

ZANDER, MICHAEL, *A Matter of Justice: The Legal System in Ferment*, rev. edn. (Oxford: Oxford University Press, 1989).

ZANDER, MICHAEL, *Cases And Materials on the English Legal System*, 7th edn. (London: Butterworths, 1996).

http://library.ukc.ac.uk/library/netinfo/intnsubg/lawlinks.htm

CHAPTER 2: LAW AND SOCIETY: THE PURPOSES AND FUNCTIONS OF LAW

ABEL-SMITH, BRIAN, and STEVENS, ROBERT, *In Search of Justice: Society and the Legal System* (London: Allen Lane, 1968).

ALLOTT, ANTONY, *The Limits of Law* (London: Butterworths, 1980).

ANDERMAN, STEVE et al. (eds.), *Law and the Weaker Party: An Anglo-Swedish Comparative Study* (Abingdon: Professional, 1981).

BARKHUYSEN, T., VAN EMMERIK, M. L., VAN KEMPEN, PIET HEIN (eds.), *The Execution of Strasbourg and Geneva Human Rights Decisions in the National Legal Order* (The Hague and London: Martinus Nijhoff, c.1999).

BLOM-COOPER, LOUIS and DREWRY, GAVIN, (eds.), *Law and Morality: A Reader* (London: Duckworth, 1976).

BRAKE, MICHAEL and HALE, CHRIS, *Public Order and Private Lives: The Politics of Law and Order* (London: Routledge, 1992).

COTTERRELL, ROGER, *The Sociology of Law: An Introduction*, 2nd edn. (London: Butterworths, 1992).

DELUPIS, INGRID, *The International Legal Order* (Aldershot: Dartmouth, c.1994).

DE SMITH, S. A., *The New Commonwealth and its Constitutions* (London: Stevens, 1964).

DICKSON, BRICE, (ed.) *Human Rights and the European Convention: The Effects of the Convention on the United Kingdom and Ireland* (London: Sweet & Maxwell, 1997).

DRZEMCZEWSKI, ANDREW Z., *European Human Rights Convention in Domestic Law: A Comparative Study* (Oxford: Clarendon Press, 1997).

DYZENHAUS, DAVID (ed.), *Recrafting the Rule Of Law: The Limits of Legal Order* (Oxford: Hart Publishing, 1999).

FREEMAN, M. D. A., *The Legal Structure* (London: Longman, 1974).

HONORÉ, TONY, *The Quest for Security: Employees, Tenants, Wives* (London: Stevens and Sons, 1982).

JACOBS, FRANCIS G., and WHITE, R.C.A., *The European Convention on Human Rights*, 2nd edn. (Oxford: Oxford University Press, 1996).

LEE, SIMON, *Law and Morals* (Oxford: Oxford University Press, 1986).

McDOUGAL, MYRES, S., LASSWELL, HAROLD D., and CHEN, LUNG-CHU, *Human Rights and World Public Order: The Basic Policies of an International Law of Human Dignity* (New Haven, Connecticut: Yale University Press, 1980).

REINER, ROBERT and CROSS, MALCOLM, (eds.), *Beyond Law and Order: Criminal Justice Policy and Politics into the 1990s* (Basingstoke: Macmillan, 1991).

ROBERTS, SIMON, *Order and Dispute: An Introduction to Legal Anthropology* (Harmondsworth: Penguin, 1979).

SCHACHTER, OSCAR and JOYNER, CHRISTOPHER C. (eds.), *United Nations Legal Order* (Cambridge: Grotius, 1995).

SHAPIRO, IAN, (ed.), *The Rule of Law* (New York: New York University Press, 1994).

TOWNSEND, PETER, *Poverty in the United Kingdom: A Survey of Household Resources and Standards of Living* (Harmondsworth: Penguin, 1979).

VAN WYK, DAWID et al., *Rights and Constitutionalism: The New South African Legal Order* (Kenwyn: Juta, 1994).

http://www.icj-cij.org/

CHAPTER 3: LAW-MAKING:
AUTHORITY AND PROCESS

BIRCH, A. H., *Representative and Responsible Government: An Essay on the British Constitution* (Ann Arbor, Mich.: U.M.I., 1989).

BRAZIER, RODNEY, *Ministers of the Crown* (Oxford: Clarendon Press, 1997).

BRAZIER, RODNEY, *Constitutional Practice: The Foundations of British Government* (Oxford: Oxford University Press, 1999).

COSGROVE, RICHARD A., *The Rule of Law: Albert Venn Dicey, Victorian Jurist* (Chapel Hill, NC: University of North Carolina Press, c.1980).

DREWRY, GAVIN, *Law, Justice and Politics*, (London: Longman, 1975).

FINE, BOB, *Democracy and the Rule of Law: Liberal Ideals and Marxist Critiques* (London: Pluto Press, 1984).

HARDEN, IAN and LEWIS, NORMAN, *The Noble Lie: The British Constitution and* the Rule of Law (London: Hutchinson, 1986).

HARTLEY, T. C., The Foundations of European Community Law: An Introduction to the Constitutional and Administrative Law of the European Community, 4th edn. (Oxford: Oxford University Press, 1998).

HARTLEY, T. C., Constitutional Problems of the European Union (Oxford: Hart Publishing, 1999).

HOLLAND, JAMES A., and WEBB, JULIAN S., Learning Legal Rules: A Student's Guide to Legal Method and Reasoning, 4th edn. (London: Blackstone Press, 1999).

JACOB, JOSEPH M., The Republican Crown: Lawyers and the Making of the State in 20th Century Britain (Aldershot: Gower, 1996).

JOWELL, JEFFREY and OLIVER, DAWN (eds.), The Changing Constitution, 3rd edn. (Oxford: Oxford University Press, 1994).

MARSHALL, GEOFFREY (ed.), Ministerial Responsibility (Oxford: Oxford University Press, 1989).

NORTON, PHILIP, The Constitution in Flux (Oxford: Blackwell, 1982).

PUBLIC SERVICE COMMITTEE Ministerial Accountability and Responsibility: Second Report, H.C.313 (London: HMSO, 1996).

TWINING, WILLIAM and MIERS, DAVID, How to do Things with Rules: A Primer of Interpretation, 4th edn. (London: Butterworths, 1999).

VILE, M. J. C., Constitutionalism and the Separation of Powers, 2nd edn. (Indianapolis: Liberty Fund, c.1998).

ZANDER, MICHAEL, The Law-making Process, 5th edn. (London: Butterworths, 1999).

http://www.parliament.uk/
http://europa.eu.int/
http://www.hmso.gov.uk/acts.htm
http://www.courtservice.gov.uk/judgmentsdb_intro.htm
http://www.lawreports.co.uk/
http://www.the-stationery-office.co.uk/
http://www.echr.coe.int
http://www.coe.fr/index.asp

CHAPTER 4: SHAPING THE INSTITUTIONAL FRAMEWORK: THE ROLE OF GOVERNMENT

ABEL-SMITH, BRIAN and STEVENS, ROBERT, In Search of Justice: Society and the Legal System (London: Allen Lane, 1968).

ANDREW, SIR ROBERT, Review of Government Legal Services (London: HMSO, 1989).

BEAN, DAVID (ed.), Law Reform for All (London: Blackstone, 1996).

HEUSTON, R. F. V., Lives of the Lord Chancellors, 1885–1940 (Oxford: Clarendon Press, 1964).

LORD CHANCELLOR'S DEPARTMENT, Modernising Justice: The Government's Plans for Reforming Legal Services and the Courts, Cmnd 4155 (London: Stationery Office, 1998).

POLDEN, PATRICK, Guide to the Records of the Lord Chancellor's Department (London: HMSO, 1988).

STEVENS, ROBERT, The Independence of the Judiciary: The View from the Lord Chancellor's Office (Oxford: Clarendon Press, 1993).

THOMAS, CHERYL and MALLESON, KATE, Judicial Appointments Commissions: The European and North American Experience and the Possible Implications for the United Kingdom: Discussion Papers (London: Lord Chancellor's Department, 1997).

http://www.courtservice.gov.uk/cs_home.htm
http://www.open.gov.uk/lcd/
http://www.open.gov.uk/lcd/research/introfr.htm

http://www.gtnet.gov.uk/lawcomm/
  homepage.htm
http://www.gtnet.gov.uk/lawcomm/misc/
  lurhmpge.htm

http://www.homeoffice.gov.uk/
http://www.criminal-courts-review.org.uk/
http://www.jsboard.co.uk/index.htm

CHAPTER 5: THE CRIMINAL JUSTICE SYSTEM

ASHWORTH, ANDREW, *Sentencing and Criminal Justice*, 2nd edn. (London: Butterworths, 1995).

ASHWORTH, ANDREW, *The Criminal Process: An Evaluative Study* (Oxford: Clarendon Press, 1998).

BALDWIN, JOHN and McCONVILLE, MICHAEL, *Negotiated Justice: Pressures to Plead Guilty* (London: Martin Robertson, 1977).

BALDWIN, JOHN and McCONVILLE, MICHAEL, *Jury Trials* (Oxford: Clarendon Press, 1979).

BARCLAY, GORDON and TAVARES, CYNTHIA (eds.), *DIGEST 4—Information on the Criminal Justice System* (London: Home Office, 1999).

COLVIN, MADELEINE, *Negotiated Justice: A Closer Look at the Implications of Plea Bargains* (London: Justice, 1993).

CORNISH, W. R., *The Jury* (Harmondsworth: Penguin, 1971).

GIBSON, BRYAN, *Introduction to the Magistrates' Court*, 2nd edn. (Winchester: Waterside Press, 1995).

HOME OFFICE, *The Victim's Charter: A Statement of Service Standards for Victims of Crime* (London: Home Office, 1996).

HOOD, ROGER, in collaboration with CORDOVIL, GRAÇA, *Race and Sentencing: A Study in the Crown Court: A Report for the Commission for Racial Equality* (Oxford: Clarendon Press, 1992).

JUSTICE, Committee on the Role of the Victim in Criminal Justice, *Victims in Criminal Justice* (London: Justice, 1998).

KEANE, ADRIAN, *The Modern Law of Evidence*, 4th edn. (London: Butterworths, 1996).

LEVI, MICHAEL and PITHOUSE, ANDREW, *Victims of White Collar Crime: The Social and Media Construction of Business Fraud* (Oxford: Clarendon Press, 1997).

McCABE, SARAH and PURVES, ROBERT, *The Jury at Work: A Study of a Series of Jury Trials in which the Defendant was Acquitted* (Oxford: Blackwell for the Oxford University Penal Research Unit, 1972).

McCABE, SARAH and PURVES, ROBERT, *The Shadow Jury at Work: An Account of a Series of Deliberations and Verdicts where 'Shadow' Juries were Present during Actual Trials* (Oxford: Blackwell for the Oxford University Penal Research Unit, 1974).

McCONVILLE, MIKE and BRIDGES, LEE (eds.), *Criminal Justice in Crisis* (Aldershot: Edward Elgar, c.1994).

MACPHERSON OF CLUNY, SIR WILLIAM, *The Stephen Lawrence Inquiry Report*, Cmnd 4262 (London: Stationery Office, 1999).

MAGUIRE, MIKE, MORGAN, ROD and REINER, ROBERT, *The Oxford Handbook of Criminology*, 2nd edn. (Oxford: Clarendon Press, 1997).

ROBERTSHAW, PAUL, *Jury and Judge: The Crown Court in Action* (Aldershot: Dartmouth, 1995).

ROCK, PAUL, *Helping Victims of Crime: The Home Office and the Rise of Victim Support in England and Wales* (Oxford: Clarendon, 1990).

ROYAL COMMISSION ON CRIMINAL PROCEDURE (Chairman, Sir Cyril Phillips),

Report, Cmnd 8092 (London: HMSO, 1981).

ROYAL COMMISSION ON CRIMINAL JUSTICE (Chairman, Viscount Runciman), *Report*, Cmnd 2263 (London: HMSO, 1993).

SANDERS, ANDREW and YOUNG, RICHARD, *Criminal Justice*, 1st edn. (London: Butterworths, 1994) (2nd edn. forthcoming).

SKYRME, SIR THOMAS, *The Changing Image of the Magistracy* (London: Macmillan, 1979).

TAPPER, COLIN, *Cross and Tapper on Evidence* (London: Butterworths, 1999).

TWINING, WILLIAM and STEIN, ALEX (eds.), *Evidence and Proof* (Aldershot: Dartmouth, 1992).

WRIGHT, MARTIN, *Justice for Victims and Offenders: A Restorative Response to Crime* (Winchester: Waterside Press, 1996).

ZANDER, MICHAEL and HENDERSON, PAUL, *Crown Court Study*, Royal Commission on Criminal Justice Research Study No. 19 (London: HMSO, 1993).

ZUCKERMAN, A. A. S., *The Principles of Criminal Evidence* (Oxford: Clarendon Press, 1989).

http://www.criminal-justice-system.gov.uk/
http://www.open.gov.uk/mcsi
http://www.sfo.gov.uk/
http://www.homeoffice.gov.uk/viccont.htm
http://www.cps.gov.uk/

CHAPTER 6: THE ADMINISTRATIVE JUSTICE SYSTEM

BRIDGES, LEE, MESZAROS, GEORGE, and SUNKIN, MAURICE, *Judicial Review in Perspective* (London: Cavendish, 1995).

GENN, HAZEL and GENN, YVETTE, *The Effectiveness of Representation at Tribunals: Report to the Lord Chancellor* (London: Queen Mary College, London, Faculty of Laws, 1989).

HARLOW, CAROL and RAWLINGS, RICHARD, *Law and Administration*, 2nd edn. (London: Butterworths, 1997).

HARRIS, M. and PARTINGTON, M. (eds.), *Administrative Justice in the 21st Century* (Oxford: Hart Publishing, 1999).

JORDAN, GRANT, *The British Administrative System, Principles vs. Practice* (London: Routledge, 1994).

LEWIS, NORMAN and BIRKINSHAW, PATRICK, *When Citizens Complain: Reforming Justice and Administration* (Buckingham: Open University Press, 1993).

NATIONAL CONSUMER COUNCIL, *A to Z of Ombudsmen: A Guide to Ombudsmen Schemes in Britain and Ireland* (London: NCC, 1997).

RICHARDSON, G. and GENN, H. (eds.), *Administrative Law and Government Action* (Oxford: Clarendon Press, 1994).

SMITH, RUSSELL G., *Medical Discipline: The Professional Conduct Jurisdiction of the General Medical Council, 1858–1990* (Oxford: Oxford University Press, 1994).

WOODHOUSE, DIANA, *In Pursuit of Good Administration: Ministers, Civil Servants, and Judges* (Oxford: Clarendon Press, 1997).

WOOLF, LORD and JOWELL, JEFFREY (asst. ed. LE SUEUR, A. P.), *Judicial Review of Administrative Action*, 5th edn. (London: Sweet and Maxwell, 1995).

http://www.euro-ombudsman.eu.int/
http://www.ombudsman.org.uk/
http://www.open.gov.uk/lgo/
http://www.intervid.co.uk/bioa/
http://www.servicefirst.gov.uk/
http://www.appeals-service.gov.uk/
http://www.irssf.gov.uk/
http://www.courtservice.gov.uk/tribunals/court02.htm
http://www.employmentappeals.gov.uk/
http://www.customs.co.uk/tribunal.html
http://www.tribunals.review.org.uk/

CHAPTER 7: THE FAMILY JUSTICE SYSTEM

BRIDGE, CAROLINE, *The Legal Regulation of Family Relations* (Manchester: University of Manchester, Faculty of Law, 1992).

BROPHY, JULIA and SMART, CAROL, *Women-in-law: Explorations in Law, Family and Sexuality* (London: Routledge & Kegan Paul, 1985).

CRETNEY, S. M. and MASSON, J. M., *Principles of Family Law*, 6th edn. (London: Sweet & Maxwell, 1997).

CRETNEY, STEPHEN, *Law, Law Reform and the Family* (Oxford: Clarendon Press, 1998).

DAVIES, GWYNN, *Partisans and Mediators: The Resolution of Divorce Disputes* (Oxford: Clarendon Press, 1998).

DAVIS, GWYNN, CRETNEY, STEPHEN, and COLLINS, JEAN, *Simple Quarrels: Negotiations and Adjudication in Divorce* (Oxford: Clarendon Press, 1994).

DEWAR, JOHN, *Law and the Family*, 2nd edn. (London: Butterworths, 1992).

DINGWALL, ROBERT and EEKELAAR, JOHN, *Divorce Mediation and the Legal Process* (Oxford: Clarendon Press, 1988).

EEKELAAR, JOHN, *Family Law and Social Policy* (London: Weidenfeld & Nicolson, 1984).

EEKELAAR, JOHN and MACLEAN, MAVIS (eds.), *Family Law* (Oxford: Oxford University Press, 1994).

FISHER, THELMA, *National Family Mediation Guide to Separation and Divorce: The Complete Handbook for Managing a Fair and Amicable Divorce* (London: Vermilion, 1997).

FREEMAN, MICHAEL D. A. (ed.), *The State, the Law, and the Family: Critical Perspectives* (London: Tavistock Publications, 1984).

HAYES, MARY and WILLIAMS, CATHERINE, *Family Law: Principles, Policy and Practice* (London: Butterworths, 1999).

LAW COMMISSION, *Family Law: The Ground for Divorce* (London: HMSO, 1990).

MACLEAN, SARAH, *Legal Aid and the Family Justice System: Report of the Case Profiling Study* (London: Legal Aid Board Research Unit, 1998).

MURCH, MERVYN and HOOPER, DOUGLAS, *The Family Justice System* (Bristol: Family Law, 1992).

O'DONOVAN, KATHERINE, *Family Law Matters* (London: Pluto, 1993).

PARKINSON, LISA, *Family Mediation* (London: Sweet & Maxwell, 1997).

ROBERTS, MARIAN, *Mediation in Family Disputes: Principles of Practice*, 2nd edn. (Aldershot: Ashgate Publishing, 1997).

http://www.open.gov.uk/lcd/lcdseafr.htm
http://www.sfla.co.uk/index.html

CHAPTER 8: THE CIVIL AND COMMERCIAL JUSTICE SYSTEMS

ABEL, RICHARD L., *The Politics of Informal Justice*, 2 vols. (London and New York: Academic Press, 1982).

BALDWIN, JOHN, *Small Claims in the County Court* (Oxford: Clarendon Press, 1996).

BALDWIN, JOHN, *Monitoring the Rise of the Small Claims Limit: Litigants' Experiences of Different Forms of Adjudication* (London: Lord Chancellor's Department, 1997).

BLOM-COOPER, LOUIS and DREWRY, GAVIN, *Final Appeal: A Study of the House of Lords*

in its Judicial Capacity (Oxford: Clarendon Press, 1972).

BROWN, HENRY and MARRIOTT, ARTHUR,
ADR Principles and Practice, 2nd edn.
(London: Sweet & Maxwell, 1999).

COLMAN, SIR ANTHONY, *The Practice and
Procedure of the Commercial Court* (London: Lloyds of London Press, 1995).

GENN, HAZEL, *Mediation in Action—
Resolving Court Disputes Without Trial*
(London: Calouste Gulbenkian Founda-
tion, 1999).

JACOB, SIR JACK I. H., *The Fabric of English
Civil Justice* (London: Stevens, 1987).

NATIONAL CONSUMER COUNCIL, *Ordinary
Justice: Legal Services and the Courts in
England and Wales* (London: HMSO,
1989).

POLDEN, PATRICK, *A History of the County
Court, 1846–1971* (Cambridge: Cambridge University Press, 1999).

ROBERTS, SIMON and PALMER, MICHAEL,
Dispute Processes: Text and Materials
(London: Butterworths, 1998).

WOOLF, LORD, *Access to Justice: Final Report
to the Lord Chancellor on the Civil Justice
System in England and Wales* (London:
HMSO, 1996).

ZUCKERMAN, A. A. S. and CRANSTON, ROSS
(eds.), *Reform of Civil Procedure: Essays on
'Access to Justice'* (Oxford: Clarendon
Press, 1995).

ZUCKERMAN, A. A. S., *Civil Justice in Crisis—
Comparative Perspectives of Civil Procedure*
(Oxford: Oxford University Press, 1999).

http://www.open.gov.uk/lcd/
http://www.open.gov.uk/civjustice/index.htm
http://www.cedr.co.uk/

CHAPTER 9: DELIVERING LEGAL SERVICES: PRACTITIONERS, ADJUDICATORS, AND JURISTS

ABEL, RICHARD L., *The Legal Profession in
England and Wales* (Oxford: Basil Blackwell, 1988).

ABEL-SMITH, BRIAN and STEVENS, ROBERT,
with the assistance of BROOKE, ROSALIND,
*Lawyers and the Courts: A Sociological
Study of the English Legal System 1750–
1965* (London: Heinemann, 1967).

ABEL-SMITH, BRIAN, ZANDER, MICHAEL,
and BROOKE, ROSALIND, *Legal Problems
and the Citizen: A Study in Three London
Boroughs* (London: Heinemann Educational, 1973).

BALDWIN, ROBERT, *Regulating Legal Services*
(London: Lord Chancellor's Department,
1997).

BLACKSELL, MARK, ECONOMIDES, KIM, and
WATKINS, CHARLES, *Justice Outside the
City: Access to Legal Services in Rural Brit-
ain* (Harlow: Longman Scientific and
Technical, 1991).

COMMITTEE ON LEGAL EDUCATION, *Report*,
Cmnd 4595 (London: HMSO, 1971).

DEVLIN, BARON PATRICK, *The Judge*
(Oxford: Oxford University Press, 1979).

DWORKIN, RONALD, *Political Judges and the
Rule of Law* (Oxford: Oxford University
Press, 1980).

ECONOMIDES, KIM (ed.), *Ethical Challenges
to Legal Education and Conduct* (Oxford:
Hart Publishing, 1998).

GENN, HAZEL, *Hard Bargaining: Out of
Court Settlement in Personal Injury
Actions* (Oxford: Clarendon Press, 1987).

GRIFFITH, J. A. G., *The Politics of the
Judiciary*, 5th edn. (London: Fontana,
1997).

HODDER-WILLIAMS, RICHARD, *Judges and
Politics in the Contemporary Age* (London:
Bowerdean, 1996).

JUSTICE, *The Judiciary: The Report of a
Justice Sub-committee* (Chairman of

Sub-committee, Peter Webster) (London: Stevens, 1972).

JUSTICE, *The Judiciary in England and Wales: A Report by Justice* (Chairman of Committee, Robert Stevens) (London: Justice, 1992).

LEE, SIMON, *Judging Judges* (London: Faber, 1989).

LEWIS, P. S. C., *Assumptions about Lawyers in Policy Statements: A Survey of Relevant Research* (London: Lord Chancellor's Department, 2000).

NATIONAL CONSUMER COUNCIL, *Information and Advice Services in the United Kingdom: Report to the Minister of State for Consumer Affairs* (London: National Consumer Council, 1983).

NICOLSON, DONALD and WEBB, JULIAN, *Professional Legal Ethics: Critical Interrogations* (Oxford: Oxford University Press, 1999).

PANNICK, DAVID, *Judges* (Oxford: Oxford University Press, 1987).

PATERSON, ALAN, *The Law Lords* (London: Macmillan, 1982).

SARAT, AUSTIN and SCHEINGOLD, STUART, *Cause Lawyering and Professional Responsibilities* (New York: Oxford University Press, 1998).

SHETREET, SHIMON, *Judges on Trial: A Study of the Appointment and Accountability of the English Judiciary* (Amsterdam and Oxford: North-Holland, 1976).

STEVENS, ROBERT, *Law and Politics: The House of Lords as a Judicial Body, 1800–1976* (London: Weidenfeld & Nicolson, 1979).

STEVENS, ROBERT, *Law School: Legal Education in America from the 1850s to the 1980s* (Chapel Hill, NC: University of North Carolina Press, c.1983).

TWINING, WILLIAM, *Blackstone's Tower: The English Law School* (London: Stevens & Son/Sweet & Maxwell, 1994).

WILSON, GEOFFREY P. (ed.), *Frontiers of Legal Scholarship: Twenty-five Years of Warwick Law School* (Chichester and New York: Wiley, 1995).

ZANDER, MICHAEL, *Lawyers and the Public Interest: A Study of Restrictive Practices* (London: published for the London School of Economics and Political Science by Weidenfeld & Nicolson, 1968).

http://www.lawsociety.org.uk/Index.asp
http://www.barcouncil.org.uk/
http://www.law.warwick.ac.uk/ncle/

CHAPTER 10: THE FUNDING OF LEGAL SERVICES

DAVIS, GWYNN, DONKOR, KWABENA, and MORGAN, ROD, *Ethnic Minorities' Legal Needs and Perceptions of Legal Services: Report of a Pilot Investigation for the Law* (London: The Law Society, 1993).

KEMPSON, ELAINE, *Legal Advice and Assistance* (London: Policy Studies Institute, 1989).

LEGAL ACTION GROUP, *A Strategy for Justice: Publicly Funded Legal Services in the 1990s* (London: Legal Action Group, 1992).

LORD CHANCELLOR'S ADVISORY COMMITTEE ON LEGAL EDUCATION AND CONDUCT: *Setting Standards for Community Legal Services* (London: Lord Chancellor's Department, 1999).

LORD CHANCELLOR'S DEPARTMENT, *Striking the Balance: The Future of Legal Aid in England and Wales* (London: HMSO, 1996).

MIDDLETON, SIR PETER, *Review of Civil Justice and Legal Aid: A Report to the Lord Chancellor's Department, 1997* (London: HMSO, 1997).

REGAN, FRANCIS et al., *The Transformation of Legal Aid: Comparative and Historical Studies* (Oxford: Clarendon Press, 1999).

ROBERTSHAW, PAUL, *Rethinking Legal Need: The Case of Criminal Justice* (Aldershot: Dartmouth, 1991).

SMITH, ROGER (ed.), *Shaping the Future: New Directions for Legal Services* (London: Legal Action Group, 1995).

STEELE, JANE and SEARGEANT, JOHN, *Access to Legal Services: The Contribution of Alternative Approaches* (London: Policy Studies Institute, 1999).

THOMAS, PHILIP A. (ed.), *Law in the Bal-ance: Legal Services in the 1980s* (Oxford: M. Robertson, 1982).

ZANDER, MICHAEL, *Legal Services for the Community* (London: Temple Smith, 1978).

http://www.open.gov.uk/lcd/
http://www.legalservices.gov.uk/
http://www.lag.org.uk/
http://www.nacab.org.uk/
http://www.justask.org.uk/

TABLE OF REFERENCES

INDEX